D1621224

THE SECOND QUEBEC CONFERENCE REVISITED

The Franklin and Eleanor Roosevelt Institute Series on Diplomatic and Economic History

General Editors: Arthur M. Schlesinger, Jr., William vanden Heuvel, and Douglas Brinkley

FDR AND HIS CONTEMPORARIES
FOREIGN PERCEPTIONS OF AN AMERICAN PRESIDENT
Edited by Cornelis A. van Minnen and John F. Sears

NATO: THE FOUNDING OF THE ATLANTIC ALLIANCE AND THE INTEGRATION OF EUROPE
Edited by Francis H. Heller and John R. Gillingham

AMERICA UNBOUND
WORLD WAR II AND THE MAKING OF A SUPERPOWER
Edited by Warren F. Kimball

THE ORIGINS OF U.S. NUCLEAR STRATEGY, 1945-1953
Samuel R. Williamson, Jr. and Steven L. Rearden

AMERICAN DIPLOMATS IN THE NETHERLANDS, 1815-50
Cornelis A. van Minnen

EISENHOWER, KENNEDY, AND THE UNITED STATES OF EUROPE
Pascaline Winand

ALLIES AT WAR
THE SOVIET, AMERICAN, AND BRITISH EXPERIENCE, 1939-1945
Edited by David Reynolds, Warren F. Kimball, and A. O. Chubarian

THE ATLANTIC CHARTER
Edited by Douglas Brinkley and David R. Facey-Crowther

PEARL HARBOR REVISITED
Edited by Robert W. Love, Jr.

FDR AND THE HOLOCAUST
Edited by Verne W. Newton

THE UNITED STATES AND THE INTEGRATION OF EUROPE
LEGACIES OF THE POSTWAR ERA
Edited by Francis H. Heller and John R. Gillingham

ADENAUER AND KENNEDY
A STUDY IN GERMAN-AMERICAN RELATIONS
Frank A. Mayer

THEODORE ROOSEVELT AND THE BRITISH EMPIRE
A STUDY IN PRESIDENTIAL STATECRAFT
William N. Tilchin

TARIFFS, TRADE AND EUROPEAN INTEGRATION, 1947-1957
FROM STUDY GROUP TO COMMON MARKET
Wendy Asbeek Brusse

SUMNER WELLES
FDR'S GLOBAL STRATEGIST
A Biography by Benjamin Welles

THE NEW DEAL AND PUBLIC POLICY
Edited by Byron W. Daynes, William D. Pederson, and Michael P. Riccards

WORLD WAR II IN EUROPE
Edited by Charles F. Brower

FDR AND THE U.S. NAVY
Edward J. Marolda

THE SECOND QUEBEC CONFERENCE REVISITED
Edited by David B. Woolner

THE SECOND QUEBEC CONFERENCE REVISITED

WAGING WAR, FORMULATING PEACE: CANADA, GREAT BRITAIN, AND THE UNITED STATES IN 1944-1945

EDITED BY
DAVID B. WOOLNER

ST. MARTIN'S PRESS
NEW YORK

ISBN 0-312-21555-X

Library of Congress Cataloging-in-Publication Data

The second Quebec Conference revisited / edited by David B. Woolner.
    p. cm.
    Includes bibliographical references and index.
    ISBN 0-312-21555-X
    1. Quebec Conference (2nd : 1944) 2. World War, 1939-1945-
-Congresses. 3. World War, 1939-1945--Canada. I. Woolner, David
B., 1955- .
    d734.Q4 1944zb
    940.53'141--dc21   98-38004
                                                            CIP

Design by Acme Art, Inc.

First edition: November, 1998
10 9 8 7 6 5 4 3 2 1

CONTENTS

PART I: STRATEGY AND HIGH POLICY
AT THE SECOND QUEBEC CONFERENCE

PART II: CANADA'S ROLE IN THE LATTER STAGES
OF WORLD WAR II

Acknowledgments

A major international event such as the fiftieth anniversary commemoration of the Second Quebec Conference that took place in Quebec City in October 1994 would not have been possible without the assistance of many individuals and a number of key institutions. The inspiration for the conference came from Verne Newton, the director of the FDR Library, whose constant enthusiasm and encouragement helped propel this project forward in the limited time that was available. I am also grateful to William J. vanden Heuvel, Frederica Goodman, and John F. Sears of the Franklin and Eleanor Roosevelt Institute for their tireless efforts in organizing the conference and commemorations from the New York side of the border. I would also like to thank Arthur Schlesinger, Jr., and John Kenneth Galbraith for providing us with their special perspectives on this momentous period in history.

For the organization of the Canadian side of this event, thanks must first go to Ginette Lamontagne, the director of Government Relations at McGill University, whose expertise and enthusiasm proved singularly important. Ronal Bourgeois, the director of Heritage Policy and Research at the Department of Canadian Heritage, also deserves special recognition for his sage advice and unswerving support. Professors Carman Miller and John Zucchi of the McGill Department of History provided invaluable assistance in organizing the academic portion of the conference, and Professor Norman Hillmer of Carleton University furnished patient counsel. I am most grateful to McGill University's Chancellor, Gretta Chambers; the Principal, Dr. Bernard Shapiro; and the Chairman of the Board of Governors, Richard Pound, for their support and participation.

The organization of the events in Quebec City would not have been possible without the assistance of Laval University and its Institut québécois des hautes études internationales. For this I thank Michel Gervais, rector of Laval, and Dr. Alain Prujiner, the director of the Institute. For the organization of the special historical exhibit of material relating to the Second Quebec Conference, my appreciation goes to Robert Garon, conservateur des Archive nationales du Québec, and Gordon Burr, archivist of McGill University.

The support of the governments of Canada, the United States, and the United Kingdom, as well as the government of Quebec and the municipal government of Quebec City, ensured the success of the commemorations. The participation of the Right Honorable Raymond J. Hnatyshyn, former Governor General of Canada; the Honourable Michel Dupuy; H. E. Sir Nicholas Bayne, British high commissioner; Ivor Rawlinson, British consul general in Montreal; Marie T. Huhtala, U.S. consul general in Quebec City; the Right Honourable Martial Asselin, lieutenant-governor of Quebec; Bernard Landry, vice premier and minister of International Affairs, Quebec; Jean-Paul L'Allier, mayor of Quebec City; Jacques Joli-Coeur, chief of protocol, Ministère des Affaires internationales, Quebec; the late Claud Sirard; the Honorable Gilles Lamontagne; George Haynal, Department of Foreign Affairs and International Trade, Ottawa; former Principal and Vice Principal of McGill University, David Johnston and François Tavenas; the late Robert Vogel of the McGill Department of History; Professors Peter Hoffmann and Desmond Morton also of McGill; Philippe Borel, general manager of the Château Frontenac; Professor Terry Copp, Sir Wilfred Laurier University; Norman Rose of the Hebrew University of Jerusalem; Robert Bothwell, the University of Toronto; Dr. James Gibson; and Lord and Lady Jenkins was especially welcome. The armed forces of Canada also played an important role in the conference and commemorations. I am particularly grateful to General Alain Forand, Lieutenant Colonel J. J. Morneau, Captain Furlan, and the soldiers of the Royal 22 Regiment. I also wish to express my sincere appreciation to Robert Champagne, Robert Taylor, and Don Ives of Veterans Affairs Canada and the Canada Remembers program.

The commemoration of the Second Quebec Conference would not have been possible without major financial support from corporate sponsors, funding agencies, and institutions. In particular I note the contribution of the following: George Weston Limited; Hollinger Inc.; the Power Corporation of Canada; and Time Warner, Inc. The conference organizers also acknowledge the financial assistance of the Franklin and Eleanor Roosevelt Institute of New York; the Faculty of Arts, McGill University; the Department of Canadian Heritage; the Department of National Defence, Ottawa; the Department of Foreign Affairs and International Trade; Veterans Affairs Canada and Canada Remembers; the United States Embassy; the Consulate General of the United States in Quebec; the British Council; the British Consulate-General in Montreal; the British High Commission; the Ministère de la Culture et des Communications, Quebec; the Ministère des Affaires internationales, de l'Immigration et des communatés Culturelles, Quebec; Ville de Québec, and the Archives nationales du Québec.

My appreciation goes out to the staff of the Department of History at McGill University, under the capable direction of Georgii Mikula, as well as to the staff of the McGill Office of Government Relations. I also wish to thank Stèphane Guèvremont, the McGill student representative, for organizing the student delegation present at the conference. To Serge Durflinger, the editor's graduate colleague at McGill, a warm personal thanks for his wise counsel, steady hand, and unflinching assistance during the conference itself.

Finally, I would like to express my thanks to the speakers who so graciously accepted the invitation to share their knowledge and advance our understanding of this event and to those involved in the final preparations of this book—John F. Sears of the Roosevelt Institute, Michael Flamini at St. Martin's Press, and Anna Fisher of the Department of History, University of Prince Edward Island.

—David B. Woolner

FOREWORD

On September 11, 1944, on a beautiful fall morning just over half a century ago, Canadian Prime Minister William Lyon Mackenzie King left the Citadel, the stately summer residence of the Governor General of Canada, to make his way down the narrow winding streets of the historic walled city of Quebec to greet his two old friends, British Prime Minister Winston Churchill and U.S. President Franklin Roosevelt. The occasion was the Second Quebec Conference—the last major bilateral meeting between Churchill and Roosevelt in the series of conferences that had begun three years earlier in Placentia Bay off the coast of Newfoundland.[1] That first meeting had produced the Atlantic Charter, the set of guiding principles intended to govern international relations with the coming of peace.[2] Now, with the end of the war in Europe in sight, it was time for the two men to reflect on how the ideas of the charter might be applied in practice. It was also time to begin the serious business of mapping out the strategy for the final defeat of Japan.

Of all the major Allied summit meetings, the Second Quebec Conference is perhaps the one gathering that is most often overlooked in the historical panorama of World War II. Perhaps this is because much of what was discussed with respect to American, British, and Canadian strategy in the Far East was rendered unnecessary by the sudden surrender of the Japanese following the destruction of Hiroshima and Nagasaki. Perhaps, too, this is because much of what Churchill and Roosevelt discussed with respect to Europe and the postwar world was cast aside and forgotten with the onset of the Cold War. But a careful reading of the history of this conference can tell us much about the state of Allied relations in 1944, for although the promise of victory in Europe had led to great hopes for the future, it had also brought with it a whole new host of problems. What type of Germany would emerge from the ashes of the Third Reich? What would happen to U.S. military and economic aid to Britain now that the war in Europe appeared to be nearing its close? What role would the British and the Canadians play in the final assault on Japan and what was to become of the British Empire in the Far East? These are but a few of the serious questions that confronted the Allied leaders in September 1944 and given the acrimony that all previous attempts at their resolution had caused, Churchill concluded that the Second Quebec Conference was the most necessary meeting that he and the American President had had since the beginning of the war.[3]

The fiftieth anniversary of this important event seemed an appropriate moment to have a second look at the Second Quebec Conference. It also seemed an opportune time to examine the often overlooked Canadian contribution to the latter stages of the war. In the spring of 1994, therefore, a small group of individuals from McGill University, the Franklin and Eleanor Roosevelt Institute, and the Franklin D. Roosevelt Library; in association with l'Institut québécois des hautes études internationales from Laval University, began to organize what would become "The International Second Quebec Conference: A 50th Anniversary Commemoration." This event was held, much like the original, in the historic city of Quebec in the fall of 1994. It began with a moving tribute to the veterans of the war held at the Citadel, where Churchill and Roosevelt joined Mackenzie King for the duration of their stay. From there it moved on to an exhibition of wartime documents and photographs at the Archives nationales du Québec, and then to a *tour de ville,* arranged by the City of Quebec, which followed the same itinerary taken by Churchill, Roosevelt, and King in 1944. Other ceremonies, hosted by the British, American, and Canadian governments, as well as the Quebec government and the municipal government of Quebec City, provided the opportunity for further retrospection. The Director General of the Château Frontenac read an excerpt from the diary of Mrs. Neale, the wife of the former director general, who was in charge of the hotel in 1944, providing all of us with heartrending testimony of what it was like to be part of this extraordinary event. That most distinguished Canadian American, John Kenneth Galbraith, provided us with his unique perspective on the historical and economic dimensions of the conference, and with a view toward the future, the British consulate-general, the Franklin D. Roosevelt Library, and the Quebec government announced that the 1994 British Chevening Scholarship for the study of international relations would be granted to an outstanding student from Quebec in honor of the occasion.

In conjunction with the ceremonial aspects of the anniversary com-memoration, an academic conference was held at the Château Frontenac that included a host of speakers and scholars from Canada, Great Britain, the United States, and Israel. In attendance were a number of individuals who had participated in the original conference, along with more than a hundred students from Laval and McGill universities. For two days, this distinguished gathering debated and examined the significance of the Second Quebec Conference, the place of Canada in 1944-45, and the future of international relations in the North Atlantic. The major part of this book is drawn from these remarkable proceedings. They offer a new look at the state of Allied relations in 1944, including the important position of Canada, and provide a critical assessment of the historical significance of the Second Quebec Conference both during and after the war.

—David B. Woolner

NOTES

1. R. Edmonds, *The Big Three: Churchill Roosevelt and Stalin in Peace and War* (London, 1991), p. 380.
2. D. B. Brinkley and D. Farcey-Crowther, eds. *The Atlantic Charter* (New York, 1994), p. ix.
3. M. Gilbert, *The Road to Victory* (London, 1986), p. 936.

PART ONE

STRATEGY AND HIGH POLICY AT THE SECOND QUEBEC CONFERENCE

ONE

THE TWO-SIDED OCTAGON

ROOSEVELT AND CHURCHILL AT QUEBEC, SEPTEMBER 1944

WARREN F. KIMBALL

THE GREAT WORLD WAR II SUMMIT CONFERENCES provided an opportunity for major decisions without getting wrapped up in the red tape and bureaucratic caution that hems in leaders. The talks also offered contemporaries—and historians—a chance to step back from the frantic pace of wartime decision making and pull things together; a chance to figure out where they were, and where they wished to go. So it was with the Roosevelt-Churchill meeting in Quebec City in mid-September 1944—the Octagon Conference.

But historians assessing Octagon immediately have to confront an intimidating statement found in the basic U.S. source text, the *Foreign Relations* volume on the conference: "*There are . . . no American minutes or memoranda of conversation pertaining to most of the Roosevelt-Churchill meetings during the Second Quebec Conference.*"[1]

There are bits and pieces in this memoir and that diary of what the two leaders had to say, and the British records are a bit better, but the details— the nuances—of their personal talks are lost to history. Yet, in reconstructing what happened at Quebec and, more important, what happened that mattered, the intimate particulars of what went on between Franklin and Winston (as they called each other in private) become less important than what they did not discuss.

In part, what was not said was determined by who was not at the meetings. Canadian Prime Minister Mackenzie King, the ostensible host, was not there—having been firmly relegated just to appearances at social occasions. America's nominal partner in postwar East Asia, China's Chiang Kai-shek, was nowhere to be seen—in person or in proxy—nor were the leaders of any of the dozens of other United Nations, FDR's label for all those allied against the Axis powers. (Churchill and Roosevelt had worried that holding the First Quebec Conference in Canada would give the British Commonwealth and nations like Brazil and Chile a reason to demand seats—at least that was their excuse for excluding Mackenzie King from the formal talks at the first Quebec Conference.)[2]

Of course most conspicuous by his absence was Soviet leader Joseph Stalin. That was not because Churchill and Roosevelt failed to try to arrange another tripartite meeting. Battleships off Invergordon, Scotland, was FDR's favorite proposal for Eureka II (the Teheran meeting nine months earlier had been code-named EUREKA) until Stalin demurred. At that point Harry Hopkins, once the president's closest adviser and still someone who could touch chords in Roosevelt's thinking, warned that the Soviets and (he inferred) the American public might interpret a Churchill-Roosevelt meeting in England or Europe "as [to use Hopkins's phrase] a political meeting with Russia out in the cold."[3]

There were, of course, a number of important issues that needed to be resolved in autumn 1944. Many were military questions that required military answers—but those questions and answers also had political implications, implications that were accentuated by the approach of war's end. Octagon took place amid a general atmosphere of military optimism. The stated objective—the earliest possible unconditional surrender of Germany and Japan, to be accomplished (said Octagon's military conclusions) "in conjunction with Russia and other Allies"—seemed within reach.[4] The Anglo-Americans had broken out from Normandy and liberated northern France, including Paris. The Antwerp docks had been taken virtually unharmed; the Americans were in Liege a mere 20 miles from Germany, and had established a firm front running from the Moselle River in France to the Swiss border. All the while the strategic bombing campaign continued to rain destruction on German cities, accompanied by an equally heavy downpour of claims by Bomber Command and the U.S. Army Air Force that air attacks alone could drive the Germans to their knees.

On the Russian front, the Red Army, facing a German force twice the size of that in the west, had swept into Poland, reaching the outskirts of Warsaw; Finland, Bulgaria, and Romania—enemies of the Russians more than German allies—had surrendered; and the Soviets were poised to move toward western Czechoslovakia. The war in Europe will end by Christmas, trumpeted the rumor mill, which was supported by intelligence estimates.[5]

The Pacific War generated similar, if more restrained, optimism. No one questioned that the fight against Japan could prove long and costly (the first atomic device would not be exploded for another seven months). But the success of the U.S. Navy's island-hopping campaign, the planned invasion of the Philippines, and the repeated promise from Stalin that his forces would attack Japan after the German surrender added to the sense of impending victory.

Yet the major military questions could not be answered in straightforward terms of battlefield tactics and campaign strategies. Politics, which created a less optimistic atmosphere, had begun to move as quickly as the military lines. Both the British and the ever-impatient General George Patton predicted quick victory if they could launch a sharply focused single thrust into Germany. The Supreme Allied Commander in Europe, General Dwight Eisenhower, concerned about supply problems, insisted on his broad front approach.[6] Buried, not too deeply, was the political issue of getting into Germany, and specifically Berlin, before the Russians.

As early as March 1943, Hopkins had expressed fear that a defeated Germany would turn to communism and by the time of the First Quebec Conference five months later, Roosevelt decided to call for plans to ensure that the Anglo-Americans would get to Berlin *as quickly* as the Soviets.[7] Ostensibly, how to proceed against Germany in autumn 1944 was decided on military grounds. Shortly after Octagon ended, Eisenhower tested the sharp thrust thesis with the ill-fated Market-Garden operation in the Netherlands—the famous "bridge too far"—and then returned to his broad front strategy, a decision apparently validated later by the alarming, if very temporary, German success in the Battle of the Bulge—not at all the Christmas present American soldiers had hoped for. But Ike's campaign strategy fit FDR's grand politics. Trying to *beat* the Russians to Berlin flew in the face of the president's preference for confidence-building rather than confrontation with the Soviets. The race for Berlin generated no discussions or decisions at Quebec, but then Stalin was not there.[8]

In Italy, a British theater of operations once the Normandy invasion had taken place, Rome and Florence had been liberated or occupied (depending on whether one considered Italy an ally or a vanquished enemy). But Allied forces were stalled by terrain, weather, and stubborn German resistance. Dreams of an easy march to France and Austria once Italy surrendered had long since evaporated, and the August 1944 invasion of southern France, which Churchill had angrily opposed, had worked against any meaningful enlargement of the Allied effort in Italy. Nevertheless, Churchill continued to push for expanded operations, well aware that Italy was the last theater that offered an opportunity for a British-led victory. As his Chief of Staff, General Alan Brooke, put it, Churchill wanted "a purely British theatre where the laurels would be all ours."[9] The prime minister managed to retain the option of an amphibious attack on Istria (the peninsula at the head of the Adriatic, just south of Trieste), a proposal that U.S. Admiral Ernest King supported—to everyone's surprise (King, crankily anti-British, perhaps hoped to preclude the British from expanding their role in his beloved Pacific War).

In proposing a move into Istria, Churchill again put postwar politics ahead of military victory. It would, he argued, put the Allies in position to move toward Vienna and counter "the dangerous spread of Russian influence in this area"—the prime minister's famous and quixotic Ljubljana Gap strategy, deprecated even by his own military chiefs.[10] (In passing, one wonders what the Russians might have done in such circumstances— perhaps "liberate" Denmark, a possibility the British actually prepared for, then move into the Netherlands, and Belgium? Would a swap of Antwerp for Prague have improved Anglo-American security?)[11]

Actually, Churchill's proposals for military action in southeast Europe was aimed more at propping up British interests in Greece than at beating the Red Army to the prize. The night before Churchill called for an attack on the German "armpit" (toward Vienna from the Adriatic), he learned that the Russians had advanced more quickly into Bulgaria than expected. The reaction of both the prime minister and Foreign Secretary Anthony Eden was not concern for Bulgaria, but for British interests, with the foreign secretary proposing the immediate launching of operation MANNA—a landing in Greece. What mattered was not liberation, but who did the liberating. What the prime minister feared was that the Russians would take the prize—Greece, along with Hungary, Yugoslavia, and even Vienna— before the German "Siegfried" line in the west was broken: "However desirable militarily such a Russian incursion may be, its political effect upon Central and Southern Europe may be formidable in the last degree."[12]

Of course the "prizewinner" in the Pacific was a foregone conclusion, and the Americans assumed just that, whatever the niceties of arguments between Roosevelt and his military chiefs over international versus national accountability for the "trustees" of occupied Japanese territories.[13] With the war against Hitler moving toward its now-inevitable conclusion, Churchill and the British chiefs of staff became increasingly concerned about their nation's role in defeating Japan. Churchill, like Stalin, had promised throughout the war to shift British efforts to the

Pacific front as soon as Germany surrendered. And, like Stalin, he worried that British influence—her role as a Great Power—would be diminished, if not jeopardized, unless his majesty's forces had a visible part in the defeat of Japan. Wrapped up in that broad concern was Churchill's oft-stated desire that European (that is, British) troops liberate the Empire lest people in Singapore, India, and Burma conclude that, after all, Japanese propaganda was correct—Asians could stand on their own two feet. "Rangoon and Singapore are great names in the British eastern world," he told British General "Pug" Ismay, "and it will be an ill day for Britain if the war ends without our having made a stroke to regain these places."[14] Roosevelt quickly accepted Churchill's offer to put the British fleet at the disposal of the Americans once Hitler surrendered (prompting the droll comment that "at this point Admiral King was carried out"), but in private, the president sardonically dismissed the British offer with the comment: "All they want is Singapore back."[15]

Moreover, British proposals for operations in Asia were weakened by a curious interrelationship with the Italian theater. The primacy of the Normandy invasion plus the resources issue, particularly shipping and landing craft, consistently forced the choice between Italian and Southeast Asian operations—particularly since the Americans had little interest in either.[16]

In addition, plans for Southeast Asia pitted British preferences for operations in Burma against American insistence on providing relief for China. Winning the war was again subordinated to political aims; the British wanted to liberate their colonies, particularly Burma, while the Americans hoped to buttress the position of Chinese Kuomintang leader Chiang Kai-shek (even as FDR dispatched the so-called Dixie Mission to China in an effort to shoehorn the Chinese Communists and Nationalists into some sort of coalition).[17]

Despite the pervading optimism about the war, the military questions about Europe came with hidden political agendas that had to be considered in an atmosphere of Anglo-American frustration over the inability of the western Allied forces to provide even a cosmetically satisfying package of aid to the Warsaw rising. To Churchill's dismay, Roosevelt refused to participate in the romantic gesture of parachuting supplies from the west to the underground in Warsaw with aircraft that would then be forced to land and refuel on Soviet airfields despite Stalin's refusal to permit such aircraft to land. FDR feared such supply drops would accomplish nothing beyond pacifying domestic opinion—and he did not want to jeopardize ongoing negotiations allowing U.S. bombers to use Siberian airbases in connection with airstrikes against Japan. Moreover, Stalin was quite correct when he characterized the motives of the underground as an attempt "to seize power" rather than aid in the war against Germany, although they were hardly the "criminals" he labeled them.[18] But—as with the question of a race for Berlin—Stalin was not there.

The only two major political issues to surface and also generate decisions at Octagon—the reconstruction of both Britain and Germany after the war—seem to have been joined at the hip. The controversial Morgenthau Plan, with its call for returning Germany to its agricultural origins,[19] arose out of Roosevelt's firm belief that Germans, not just Nazis, had been "Prussianized" into a militaristic, warlike nation. U.S. Treasury Secretary Henry Morgenthau, Jr., said he wanted to make Germany like Denmark, "where the people, through small-scale farming, were in intimate association with the land and were peace-loving and without aggressive designs upon others."[20] Roosevelt and Morgenthau, like most New Dealers, accepted grand planning as the way to solve problems. Like the two Jeffersonian gentlemen farmers they pretended to be, Roosevelt and Morgenthau proposed returning the Germans to their agrarian origins to start all over again. Punishment for Nazis reflected the reaction of Morgenthau and the U.S. Treasury Department to the Holocaust; but reform reflected the long- range humanism of the New Deal in particular and Americans in general.[21]

Both American Secretary of State Cordell Hull and British Foreign Secretary Anthony Eden believed that an economically sound and self-supporting Germany was essential to the economic rehabilitation of Europe. Moreover, American and British prosperity depended heavily upon that recovery. The U.S. State Department put it in classic neomercantilist language: "German economic self-sufficiency for war must be replaced by an economy which can be integrated into an *inter-dependent world economy.*"[22] Moreover, State Department officials had warned that the Soviet Union would become a threat to world peace, thus the need to reintegrate Germany into "the projected world order," lest Moscow "establish a Russian hegemony in Germany." Such recommendations led the United States in the direction of just what Stalin suspected—a new version of a *cordon sanitaire* directed against the Soviet Union.[23] Roosevelt, firmly committed to his policy of turning uncivilized Bolsheviks into civilized Russians, never seriously considered that approach, relying instead on using the war to create a relationship of trust and cooperation.

On September 15, 1944, Roosevelt and Churchill initialed a memorandum that called for the elimination of "the war-making industries in the Ruhr and in the Saar" and the conversion of "Germany into a country primarily agricultural and pastoral in its character."[24] Churchill was ambivalent. When FDR mentioned the existence of groups in the United States and probably Britain who thought "evil could be eradicated from the

German makeup and the nation could be rejuvenated by a kindly approach to them," Churchill assured him that no such sentiments would be tolerated in the United Kingdom. But when Morgenthau laid out the specifics, the prime minister condemned the plan as "unnatural, unchristian and unnecessary," commenting that it would chain them to a dead body.[25] But with adviser Lord Cherwell conjuring up visions of new markets for British production, with Morgenthau pointedly discussing postwar aid to Britain (so-called stage II Lend-Lease), and the realization that a happy Roosevelt was more important than an unhappy Germany, the prime minister quickly changed his mind. After all, Britain desperately needed an extension of Lend-Lease into the postwar period, and an Anglo-American entente was fundamental to Churchill's long-term policies. Ever subject to extreme enthusiasms, Churchill switched from contemptuous opposition to strong support, so much so that it was he who suggested the word "pastoral," replacing weaker language.[26] Despite opposition from the Cabinet, particularly Eden, Churchill explained and supported the Morgenthau Plan when he met with Stalin in Moscow a month later.[27]

Whatever Roosevelt's own doubts about the feasibility of complete deindustrialization, the rest of Morgenthau's proposal seemed sound, particularly since FDR viewed the plan as a statement of general purpose rather than a precise policy directive. It fit in with previous Soviet statements, offered economic benefits to Britain, and promised the kind of broad reform of Germans and Germany that he believed necessary. It even offered a way out of having the American occupation zone in southern Germany, something FDR had opposed lest it turn into a lengthy entanglement in French domestic problems. Deindustrialization would eliminate German war-making potential, allowing American occupation troops to return home more quickly. Moreover, giving Britain the northwestern zone would leave them in charge of the difficult dismantling program in the most industrialized part of Germany.

The pastoralization of Germany eventually became a throwaway line in history books, not a reality. But the rest of the Morgenthau Plan—disarmament, denazification, dismemberment, and demilitarization—set Anglo-American policy toward Germany until the hidden agenda that became the Cold War displaced compromise, negotiations, and diplomacy. Nazi politicians, scientists, and spies ended up working for Washington, London, and Moscow; while the German military—East and West—rebuilt and rearmed in the service of their respective superpower. There remained only limited dismemberment, accomplished by redrawing Germany's boundaries, in the form of major territorial commitments to the Soviet Union, Czechoslovakia, and Poland in the east, to France in the west, and by the detachment of Austria from the Reich. Although the boundary details had been worked out at Teheran, that limited dismemberment remains—at least for the present—as one of two major Octagon legacies.[28]

The other Octagon legacy came in surroundings strikingly different from the grandeur and history of Quebec City. After the formal conference adjourned, Churchill and Roosevelt rejoined at the president's home in Hyde Park, overlooking the Hudson River just north of Poughkeepsie. In that comfortable, casual surrounding, the two agreed to perpetuate the Anglo-American monopoly on the Tube Alloys project—the atomic bomb. But if trust and cooperation were the keys to Roosevelt's goals, why keep the atomic bomb secret from the USSR? Roosevelt knew at least by September 1943 that Soviet espionage had penetrated the atomic project.[29] He knew that the Russians knew about the bomb, but did not tell them. Why not? (Perhaps Abbott and Costello asked an equally important question: did they know that he knew that they knew?)

Perhaps Roosevelt wished to maintain the image of secrecy lest Stalin demand access. Perhaps the president was reluctant to brag about something that had not yet been tested, and about which unsophisticated advisers remained skeptical. After all, in a world where the United States was jockeying with the USSR for position, false bravado could weaken his bargaining strength.

Another part of the answer may be that Roosevelt, like most nonscientists, did not comprehend the revolutionary potential of nuclear weapons. His key scientific adviser on atomic energy, James B. Conant, believed FDR had "only fleeting interest in the atom, and that the program never got very far past the threshold of his consciousness." He "really had no idea of the enormous importance of our [atomic] secrets." Interestingly, it appears Stalin was similarly ignorant.[30]

The easy answer is that the president was waiting for the right moment—when he could confront the Soviet Union with the new superweapon and gain effective political leverage. Was Roosevelt the first practitioner of atomic diplomacy? Do we have FDR, cold warrior?

But how to reconcile that with his consistent and persistent policy of trusting the Soviets in the hope of convincing them that the United States could likewise be relied upon? The likely answer is that the atomic bomb might work, and might not, but Franklin Roosevelt was firmly rooted in the practical present. He knew that Stalin had intelligence on the atom bomb project, so there was no secret. To tell the Soviets and then refuse to share the information would not quiet any of Stalin's suspicions and could lead to an open argument. Why make a decision until the decision had to be made? And there were so many other decisions to be made about the postwar world.

Where does that leave us with the Octagon summit—the two-sided Octagon? The military decisions reached could well have been settled without a face-to-face Churchill-Roosevelt meeting, even if the prime minister claimed that was his primary purpose for wanting the conference.[31] The major political agreement—on how to reconstruct postwar Germany—soon collapsed. The quid pro quo Churchill thought he had gotten for agreeing to the Morgenthau Plan—a continuation of Lend-Lease to aid British reconstruction—was never implemented. The prime minister's worries about spheres of influence-by-conquest (even though that was precisely what he hoped to do in Greece and the Pacific) prompted him to propose warning Stalin of "the political dangers of divergencies between Russia and the Western Allies in respect to Poland, Greece and Yugoslavia." Roosevelt—perhaps still following his postponement policy, perhaps unwilling to deal with such political issues in Stalin's absence—insisted that Octagon limit itself to military matters,[32] sending Churchill scurrying off to Moscow a month later to negotiate the ill-conceived "percentages" agreement with Stalin.

Despite the relative brevity and paucity of discussion at Quebec about politics, those issues hung like a cloud over the talks, driving home the reality of the sea change taking place: The USSR was now a great power; while the Anglo-American relationship, special as it was, did not allow creation of an Anglo-American entente *aimed* at containing the Soviets. The wartime alliance and Roosevelt's policy of cooperation took precedence. Moreover, regardless of whether Churchill and Roosevelt were (pick, Chinese menu - style, any one or combination of the following) wise, naive, realistic, realists, idealists, sick, opportunists, or realpolitikers, it is hard to escape the conclusion that, in 1944, any such Anglo-American entente would have achieved little or nothing. There was, after all, a stalemate in Italy and Market-Garden was about to fail in the Netherlands, thus ensuring that dreams of a German surrender by Christmas were not to be. The war in the Pacific found the British already scrambling to find enough troops to attack Singapore and the Americans counting on Soviet intervention in Manchuria. To what advantage an earlier declaration of Cold War? Perhaps the main result would have been the absorption of even more of Germany by the Red Army, the liberation of Denmark by the Soviets, and a swing toward the Low Countries. All that for Vienna and perhaps Prague?

As a summit meeting, the Quebec Conference was, in fact, unnecessary and perhaps counterproductive. Stalin was not the only absentee. The worlds of geopolitics and of ideals and ideas (revolutionary or not) required more than just Anglo-American discussions, as the United Nations Organization talks then going on at Dumbarton Oaks in Washington demonstrated. Not only were the Soviets needed, but so were all the other forces in the world that had no presence at Quebec—from decolonization (FDR spoke, but then counseled patience and a period of tutelage) to nationalism (again, FDR warned of problems in Serbia/Croatia even while he ignored those of French-speakers with his curious proposal for Wallonia).[33]

What Churchill and Roosevelt fundamentally did was to enjoy the beautiful city of Quebec, the hospitality of its people, and the elegance of the Château Frontenac while mulling over the great issues of the second world war. The decisions had to wait.

NOTES

1. U.S. Dept. of State, *Foreign Relations of the United States* [hereafter *FRUS* plus volume title] *The Conference at Quebec, 1944* (Washington, 1862-), p. 295 (italics added).

2. Churchill to Roosevelt, July 23, 1943, and Roosevelt to Churchill, July 24, 1943, in W. F. Kimball, ed., *Churchill & Roosevelt: The Complete Correspondence* (Princeton, 1984), vol. II, C-377 and R-323.

3. Hopkins to Roosevelt, July 26, 1944, *FRUS, Quebec, 1944*, p. 12.

4. That objective was reconfirmed in that language during Octagon; *FRUS, Quebec, 1944*, pp. 469-70.

5. C. C. Crane, *Bombs, Cities, and Civilians: American Airpower Strategy in World War II* (Lawrence KS, 1993), is a critical assessment of the limits of the strategic bombing campaign. For examples of intelligence over-optimism about the end of the war, see H. Feis, *Churchill, Roosevelt, Stalin* (Princeton, 1957), p. 396.

6. The Scheldt Rover estuary remained in German hands, making the port of Antwerp unusable.

7. Those ideas and the plans that followed (code-named Hadrian and Rankin), are found in the standard histories of the war, but particularly M. Matloff, *Strategic Planning for Coalition Warfare, 1943-1944* (Washington: Office of the Chief of Military History, 1959), pp. 225-27; G. Kolko, *The Politics of War* (New York, 1968), pp. 28-30, 315-17. See also the extensive files on Rankin in the Combined Chiefs of Staff files at the National Archives in Washington, D.C.; also memo by Hopkins, Mar. 17, 1943, *FRUS, 1943*, vol. III, p. 26, and pp. 13, 17, 22; *FRUS, Conference at Washington & Quebec, 1943*, pp. 910-11, 942.

8. Mackenzie King's notes indicate that Churchill expressed concern that the Russians might get to Vienna before the Anglo-Americans, but the venue was a luncheon with spouses as well as the Governor General of Canada present, making serious discussion improbable. Neither Roosevelt nor Churchill would comment on the race for Berlin; J. W. Pickersgill and D. F. Forster, *The Mackenzie King Record, 1944-1945*, vol. 2 (Toronto, 1968), p. 70.

9. As quoted in D. Reynolds, "Churchill and Allied Grand Strategy in Europe, 1944-1945" (Paper delivered at the Roosevelt Study Center/Roosevelt Institute Symposium on "World War II in Europe: the Final Year"), Roosevelt Study Center, Middelburg, the Netherlands, June 1-3, 1994. Symposium proceedings in press as *World War II in Europe: The Final Year,* ed. C. F. Brower (New York, 1998).

10. Churchill as paraphrased in *FRUS, Quebec, 1944,* p. 314 (meeting of Sept. 13, 1944). The thrust toward Vienna was dismissed as impractical at the time by his military and later by historians; see T. M. Barker, "The Ljubljana Gap Strategy: Alternative to Anvil/Dragoon or Fantasy?" *The Journal of Military History,* 56 (Jan. 1992): 57-85, and R. Edmonds, *The Big Three* (London, 1991), p. 378. An implausible variation on the soft-underbelly theme is M. W. Parish, *Aegean Adventures 1940-1943 and the End of Churchill's Dream* (Sussex, UK, 1993), who blames Roosevelt and the American military for preventing the implementation of Churchill's proposal for an attack through the Aegean into Rumania and Central Europe that, Parish claims, could have/or would have forestalled Soviet occupation of much of that area.

11. Fears that the Red Army would, in fact, liberate Denmark worried Churchill, which prompted Allied military planners to draw up plans to land paratroopers in Denmark. See T. Kaarsted, "Churchill and the Small States of Europe—The Danish Case" (Paper delivered at the conference "World War II in Europe: the Final Year." In press as *World War II in Europe,* ed. Brower, and M. Gilbert, *Winston S. Churchill, Road to Victory,* vol. VII (Boston, 1986), pp. 1299ff.

12. Churchill Minutes of Sept. 8, 1944; Gilbert, *Winston S. Churchill, Road to Victory,* p. 942.

13. Whatever the importance of such arguments for understanding Roosevelt's position on decolonization, both sides assumed that the decision was one that the United States, and the United States alone, had to make. On the trusteeship debate see W. F. Kimball and F. Pollock, "In Search of Monsters to Destroy," in W. F. Kimball, *The Juggler: Franklin Roosevelt as Wartime Statesman* (Princeton, 1991), chap. 7.

14. Churchill to Ismay, June 24, 1944, as quoted in Gilbert, *Winston S. Churchill, Road to Victory,* p. 834. *FRUS, Quebec, 1944,* p. 314, meeting of Sept. 13, 1944. See also Gilbert, *Winston S. Churchill, Road to Victory,* pp. 959, 963-66.

15. C. Pogue, *George C. Forrest Marshal: Organizer of Victory* (New York, 1973), p. 453; *FRUS, Quebec, 1944,* p. 350.

16. As the British official history put it: "the Far East and the Mediterranean had alternately been regarded, according to circumstances, as a source of supply for the other"; J. Erhman, *Grand Strategy, August 1943-September 1944,* vol. v (London, 1956), p. 394.

17. C. Thorne, *Allies at War* (New York, 1978), pp. 435-46.

18. Gilbert, *Winston S. Churchill, Road to Victory,* p. 925. The dispute over aid to Warsaw hardly broke Anglo-American unity, as suggested in ibid., p. 927. See

also A. Prazmowska, "Churchill and Poland," and W. F. Kimball, "'Matters for Academic Discussion': Churchill, Roosevelt and the Litmus Test for Postwar Europe," both in *Churchill, Europe, the Empire and the United States,* ed. R. A. C. Parker (London, 1995).

19.   *FRUS, Quebec, 1944,* pp. 466-67.

20.   Morgenthau, Memo of a Conference at Red Rice, Andover, England, Aug. 15, 1944, Harry Dexter White Papers, Box 7, Princeton University Library, Princeton, New Jersey. See also W. F. Kimball, *Swords or Ploughshares? The Morgenthau Plan for Defeated Nazi Germany* (Philadelphia, 1976).

21.   The formal plan came in early September 1944, after Morgenthau learned of War Department plans for "the gradual rehabilitation of peacetime industry," and the quick restoration "of the German civil government. . . . [so that] the machine works and works efficiently"; Morgenthau, Memo for the President, Aug. 25, 1944, Presidential Diaries, Morgenthau Papers, FDR Library [hereafter FDRL]. The War Department's primary purpose was not gentle treatment for the Germans, but rather a desire to promote law, order, efficiency, and the avoidance of political and economic responsibilities.

22.   Memo of the Executive Committee on Foreign Economic Policy, Aug. 14, 1944, *FRUS, 1944,* vol. I (Washington, 1966), p. 285. One of the more perceptive and penetrating presentations of American neomercantilist thinking as it pertained to postwar Germany is B. Kuklick, *American Policy and the Division of Germany: The Clash with Russia over Reparations* (Ithaca, NY, 1972). See Morgenthau, Memo to the President, "Suggested Post-Surrender Program for Germany," Sept. 5, 1944, *FRUS, Quebec, 1944,* pp. 101-06.

23.   The committee went on to recommend that, in order to create "an effective democracy in Germany," there had to be "a tolerable standard of living," "a minimum of bitterness against the peace terms," and "harmony of policy between the British and American Governments on the one hand and the Soviet Government on the other"; "The Political Reorganization of Germany," Recommendation of the Interdivisional Country Committee, Sept. 23, 1943, in *Postwar Foreign Policy Preparation, 1939-1945,* by H. A. Notter, Dept. of State Publ. 3580 (Washington, 1949), pp. 558-59.

24.   *FRUS, Quebec, 1944,* pp. 466-67.

25.   Gilbert, *Winston S. Churchill, Road to Victory,* p. 961; Lord Moran (Charles Wilson), *Churchill: Taken from the Diaries of Lord Moran* (Boston, 1966), pp. 190-95.

26.   Churchill's initial reaction is in a memo by H. D. White of a Conversation on Sept. 13, 1944, *FRUS, Quebec, 1944,* p. 326. The draft that Churchill revised is in ibid., p. 390. Earlier that summer, when Morgenthau told FDR that the British were "broke" and wanted to build up Germany so it could pay reparations, Roosevelt responded, "What do we want reparations for?" Not surprisingly, the Treasury secretary thereafter consistently presented German deindustrialization as a way to improve Britain's foreign trade and solve that nation's economic problems; Morgenthau memo of Conversation with

Roosevelt, Aug. 19, 1944, Presidential Diaries, pp. 1386-88, Morgenthau Papers, FDRL; see also Kimball, *Swords Or Ploughshares?*, pp. 38-41.

27. The two agreed that Britain should get the markets previously dominated by Germany, and that the defeated nation should not have a merchant fleet. Later claims of Soviet historians notwithstanding, Stalin's statements during these talks, as well as at Teheran and with Charles de Gaulle in December 1944, demonstrate his preference for a permanently partitioned Germany. British Cabinet and Foreign Office reactions included, among other arguments, suspicions that the Americans were trying to avoid a domestic political fight over postwar aid to Britain by providing new markets for Britain. See Minutes on Halifax to the Foreign Office, Sept. 14, 1944, No. 4941, FO 371/39080/ 4010, paper C12073/G18, PRO. Public Record Office, [hereafter PRO], Kew, England. Cabinet arguments that the Morgenthau Plan simply would not work are in PREM 3/192/1. Stalin's reaction is from the Records of the Meetings at the Kremlin, Moscow, Oct. 9-17, 1944 (Tolstoy), PREM 3/434/ 2, PRO.

28. But dividing what remained of Germany into independent states, an attempt to return to the world before Bismarck, was opposed by the State Department as well as the British as politically unsound and economically impractical.

29. According to Secretary of War Henry Stimson's Diary; J. Hershberg, *James B. Conant* (New York, 1993), p. 217.

30. Hershberg, *Conant*, p. 207. David Holloway speculates that the Soviet leadership may not have believed in the reality of the atomic bomb and illustrates how Stalin misused intelligence about the bomb; D. Holloway, *Stalin and the Bomb* (New Haven, 1994), 85-86, 90, 102-03, 115; D. Holloway, "The Atomic Bomb and the end of the Wartime Alliance," in *The Rise and Fall of the Grand Alliance, 1941-1945*, eds. Ann Lane and Howard Temperley (London and New York, 1995). But also see Gar Alperovitz, *The Decision to Use the Atomic Bomb* (New York, 1995).

31. Churchill wrote to his wife on Aug. 17, 1944: "This visit of mine to the President is the most necessary one that I have ever made since the very beginning, as it is there that various differences that exist between the Staffs, and also between me and the American Chiefs of Staff, must be brought to a decision." Martin Gilbert concludes that the prime minister had in mind that of three British forces (France, Italy, Burma), one was under U.S. command (France), and the other two were misemployed; Gilbert, *Winston S. Churchill, Road to Victory*, pp. 936-37.

32. *FRUS, Quebec, 1944*, p. 382.

33. Anthony Eden, *The Reckoning* (Boston, 1965), pp. 432-33; U.S. Dept. of State, *Post World War II Foreign Policy Planning: State Department Records of Harley A. Notter* [microfilm] (Bethesda, MD, 1987), 548-1, summary dated March 18, 1943 of a White House meeting on Feb. 22, 1943.

T W O

TOWARD THE POSTWAR SETTLEMENT
WINSTON CHURCHILL AND THE SECOND QUEBEC CONFERENCE

B . J . C . MCKERCHER

> This visit of mine to the President is the most necessary one that I have ever made since the very beginning [of the war], as it is there that various differences that exist between the Staffs, and also between me and the American Chiefs of Staff, must be brought to a decision.
> —Winston Churchill, August 1944[1]

BRITISH PARTICIPATION IN THE SECOND QUEBEC CONFERENCE was part of a diplomatic strategy followed by Winston Churchill, the British prime minister, to ensure Britain's international influence as the second world war world ended. By the summer of 1944, Churchill and his foreign policy and military advisers knew that the end of the struggle in Europe was approaching. The Normandy invasion in June, coupled with the speed of the Soviet Russian offensive in Eastern Europe in July and August, showed Germany's war effort to be crumbling. But the mastery of the Allied alliance on the battlefield augured ill for Britain's diplomatic strength and its strategic position in international politics once peace returned. American economic, financial, and manpower contributions to the war effort had given the United States the leading position in the western half of the alliance.

Moreover, the Americans were not averse to using their material strength to force the British to comply with Washington's wishes, something seen in the diplomacy that led to the cross-Channel invasion.[2] On the other hand, Red Army advances in Eastern Europe after 1943 were not designed simply to defeat Adolf Hitler's Germany. They were also geared to establish a postwar Soviet sphere of interest over the region, a situation that would give Russia a preponderant position on the continent while Germany was hobbled.[3] Already in the position of a "junior" partner in the alliance, Britain faced the unnerving possibility that after German defeat—and after Japan was vanquished—the United States and Soviet Russia would dominate in international councils. Accordingly, Churchill used his participation in the Second Quebec Conference as part of a deliberate design to provide Britain with the political strength to ensure that once peace returned, British interests in Europe and elsewhere were protected as much as possible from inroads by both Washington and Moscow.

Churchill had risen to the premiership on May 10, 1940 as the result of a political crisis in Britain following the German occupation of Norway. Six weeks later, after the success of German arms led to the defeat of France and the removal of Britain's chief ally on the continent, Britain stood alone against Nazi Germany and Fascist Italy. Admittedly, the independent Dominions remained at Britain's side; but their material and manpower contributions to the war effort were limited by the political caution of their leaders and, in the case of Australia and New Zealand, the need to consider Japanese ambitions in East Asia and the Pacific. Thus, as what amounted to a "warlord," Churchill endeavored to build up Britain's ability to resist an invasion of the home islands, shore up its position in the Mediterranean, and find some means to keep the predatory Japanese at bay in the Far East. Although his record is mixed, Churchill's determination to pursue these goals until the latter half of 1941 is well known.[4] The chance of a German cross-Channel invasion melted away after the British triumphed in the Battle of Britain and, after initial difficulties, the Italian advance on Egypt was stymied and thrown back. In the Far East, which had nothing to do with Churchill, the Japanese decided to prey upon a weakened France by establishing themselves in Indochina. Yet, while Britain was not defeated and its Empire was intact, all of these events showed the limitations of British power. Britain could prevent a German invasion, but it could not defeat a Germany that now dominated Western Europe. It could blunt an Italian offensive against Egypt but, after Hitler sent the Afrika Korps to aid his Fascist ally, it could probably not defeat the Axis in North Africa. And the situation in the Far East suggested that the security of the British Empire in East Asia and the

Pacific derived more from Japanese forbearance than any active British effort. By early June 1941, and especially after the debacle of Britain's support for Greece against Axis conquest—an intervention promoted by Churchill over the heads of his military commanders—Churchill's government confronted the dilemma of being engaged in a war that solitary Britain and its Dominion allies could not hope to win.

Then, between June and December 1941, Britain was unexpectedly handed powerful allies. In late June, Hitler stupidly embarked on a war of conquest against Soviet Russia; six months later, the avarice of the Japanese leadership saw Tokyo launch a war of aggression in East Asia and the Pacific Ocean to acquire the British and Dutch eastern empires, Australia and New Zealand, and American holdings in the region.[5] The year after June 1941 was not an easy one for this new coalition of Allies: a brutal winter and concerted Russian military action slowed but did not stop the German advance; Japan's offensive was only blunted by the Americans in May and June 1942 in the battles of the Coral Sea and Midway (but after Japanese forces unexpectedly captured Singapore, the Malayan Peninsula, Burma, and the Philippines); and the Axis remained in North Africa despite concerted British and Imperial air and ground operations.[6] Over the next two years, along with the Normandy invasion, the war gradually turned in Allied favor.[7] In Russia, after the German defeat at Stalingrad, the Red Army began pushing the Wehrmacht back toward Central Europe and the Balkans. In the Far East, the Americans inaugurated an island-hopping campaign that produced a slow Japanese retreat across the Pacific, a struggle augmented by British and Chinese operations against Japanese forces on the mainland of Southeast and East Asia. And, with Axis forces swept out of North Africa by British Empire and American forces by mid-1943, and Mussolini overthrown in Italy, the western Allies were fighting their way up the Italian peninsula.

Following Pearl Harbor, Britain and its new allies built up a cohesive alliance against their European and East Asian enemies. In the west, after Churchill conferred in Washington in December 1941-January 1942 with the American president, Franklin Roosevelt, an Anglo-American Combined Chiefs of Staff was created to devise and execute a unified strategy.[8] Although the Russians were not involved thereafter in determining western Allied operations, Churchill and Roosevelt ensured that Stalin and his advisers were fully apprised of Anglo-American planning and strategy: the Russians conducted their own war, but did so aware of the intentions of the British and Americans.[9] Beyond the military and naval side of the war, the three Allied leaders used high-level diplomacy to reduce intra-alliance friction and begin planning the structure of the postwar world. Meeting at Casablanca in January 1943, Churchill and

Roosevelt agreed on the invasion of Sicily, the strategic bombing of Germany, and the transfer of British forces to the Far East after the war in Europe ended—at the last minute, Stalin decided to remain in Russia to oversee the final defeat of the German army at Stalingrad.[10] Nine months later at Teheran, all three leaders met together for the first time.[11] With the tide of battle turning against the Axis and Japan, and the decision made to coordinate the Anglo-American cross-Channel invasion with a major Red Army offensive in Eastern Europe, war aims dominated discussions. Out of these Big Three deliberations, there came agreement to begin establishing the framework of a new international organization to maintain peace and security. Following preliminary discussions, Allied negotiations to this end were launched at Dumbarton Oaks, Virginia, in August 1944. The Dumbarton Oaks conference began while other inter-Allied deliberations were underway at Bretton Woods, New Hampshire; these other talks were also born out of Roosevelt's initiative, in this case to establish a monetary fund and a world bank to obviate in future the international financial anarchy that had supposedly marked the 1930s.[12]

In the three years between the German attack on Russia and the Normandy invasion, the British ability to shape Allied military and diplomatic policies diminished. During his December 1941-January 1942 meetings with Roosevelt, and building on British experience in fighting total war for more than two years, Churchill succeeded in getting the Americans to adopt the so-called peripheral strategy.[13] Instead of building up western Allied forces in Britain to launch as soon as possible a cross-Channel invasion, it was agreed that they would be concentrated in the Mediterranean: to drive the Axis out of North Africa before attacking the Italian mainland and, thereby, establishing a foothold on the continent by which the final assault on Germany could be mounted. Though the American president did not need much coaxing because of the Russian predicament, Churchill also succeeded in getting Roosevelt to accept a Europe first strategy. This entailed defeating Germany and Italy before bringing the full strength of the Allied alliance to bear on Japan. The Russians, however, decried the peripheral strategy, seeing it as inadequate to divert German forces westward. Stalin and Vyacheslav Molotov, his foreign minister, thereafter constantly demanded a cross-Channel second front, the delay of which strained Moscow's relations with London and Washington.[14] At Teheran, when it was obvious that the Italian campaign would not bring quick victory, Stalin told his two colleagues that he would delay his summer 1944 offensive until after a cross-Channel invasion. Roosevelt understood the situation, with the result that Churchill had to acquiesce in his partners' determination to establish a second front in France—and accept an

American supreme military commander, General Dwight Eisenhower.[15] If not clear already, the making of this major strategic decision demonstrated that Britain had become junior to the United States and Soviet Russia.

Britain's weakening political influence within the Allied alliance had not occurred suddenly in November 1943. Much of this situation had to do with the parlous state of British finances.[16] Until the fall of its French ally in June 1940, Britain's financial position had been onerous rather than acute. The French supplied the bulk of the anti-German coalition's armed forces on the continent; Britain, most of its naval and financial resources; and the Roosevelt administration had done what it could to smooth the way for Anglo-French purchases in the United States. Still, in the year after June 1940, British financial sinews enervated. Alone against the Axis, and with minimal Imperial pecuniary support, London stretched every fiscal resource to keep British and Imperial forces in the field. Only Roosevelt's decision in late 1940 to give massive material assistance to Britain via the Lend-Lease program kept the British war effort going—and, along with American financial aid, especially after Pearl Harbor, Churchill's government came to rely on American supplies of war materiel, other industrial goods, and agricultural production to survive and fight. Seizing the chance to capitalize on Britain's weakness, the Americans unabashedly drove hard bargains over trade policy, the purchase of British overseas investments, and the control of merchant shipping. As Roosevelt and his advisers gained greater confidence in their ability to conduct war, and as American troops participated in the fighting in the Mediterranean theater, these economic and financial advantages began to be translated into political pressure on the Churchill government. The Teheran decision about a second front and the selection of an American supreme commander to oversee the Normandy invasion represented a watershed in the relationship of the two English-speaking powers. Therefore, as 1944 progressed, little question existed that Washington stood as the locus of power in Anglo-American relations, and that Roosevelt would seek to put an American imprimatur on the emerging postwar international structures so to benefit the United States when peace returned.

The Anglo-Russian relationship differed in that the achievements of the Red Army against the Wehrmacht after January 1943 suggested that with German defeat, the Russians might dominate in Eastern Europe.[17] But as the war had yet to be won in the summer of 1944, the simple fact was that the Red Army was tying down the bulk of German forces and, with heavy casualties, inflicting grievous materiel and manpower losses on them. Since in wartime victory on the battlefield translates into a stronger foreign policy, this fact gave Stalin political clout within the Allied alliance. Although receiving substantial amounts of material aid from

Britain and the United States, Stalin's armies were forcing the Germans to retreat from Soviet Russia. Coupled with the possibility that Stalin might seek a separate peace with Hitler once the Germans were pushed back beyond the pre-1941 Russian borders[18]—in 1939, the two dictators had cynically concluded the Nazi-Soviet Nonaggression Pact—this fact gave Stalin a louder voice in Allied councils. A case in point was his tough stance at Teheran about delaying his 1944 offensive until after a cross-Channel invasion began. Again, just as in the case of British relations with the United States, those with Russia passed a watershed in November 1943. German defeat at the hands of the Russians would constitute a major threat to the balance of power in Europe and, depending on what Russian forces might achieve in southeastern Europe, also in the Balkans and the eastern Mediterranean. The growing ascendancy of the Red Army in its war with Germany presented Churchill with the unpalatable possibility of a postwar Russia that could seriously threaten British security and British claims to Great Power status.

In this way, by the summer of 1944, the military and economic strength of Britain's two major allies, and the political leverage this gave them within the alliance, signaled to Churchill and his advisers that Britain would have a significantly reduced international position once peace returned. Given that the Americans had arrogated for themselves the leadership of the war against Japan—and jealously guarded that leadership[19]—what was true of Europe and the Mediterranean would be doubly so for East Asia and the Pacific. It is crucial to understand that Churchill was a late convert to the concept that close Anglo-American relations would be helpful to Britain in protecting its leading position among the Great Powers.[20] Until the late 1930s, and especially in the 1920s, he had been extremely critical of the United States and its foreign, naval, and international financial and trade policies. Only when Britain needed support in opposing the Axis powers in the late 1930s, and particularly after the war in Europe erupted in September 1939, did he see the value of building strong Anglo-American bonds. This recognition led him to establish a personal relationship with Roosevelt beginning in October 1939, through which he labored to obtain the maximum American support for Britain's war effort.[21] By the same token Churchill had been a consistent critic of the Bolshevik regime in Russia since 1917 and, until early 1941, he never wasted an opportunity to use his political influence to frustrate a regime that he thought brutal and aggressive. But as his famous remark in June 1941 attests—that "If Hitler invaded Hell, I would at least make a favourable reference to the Devil in the House of Commons"[22]—the necessities of war made Stalin his ally.

By the early summer of 1944, Churchill and his senior foreign policy and armed forces advisers saw clearly the difficulties of working within the alliance on an unequal basis with the Americans and Russians and, by extension, what it presaged for the postwar period. For instance, before Teheran, when the Russians with American support pressed for their concept of the second front, Churchill expressed concern about the disaster that might befall the western Allies if a cross-Channel invasion failed. Roosevelt's representative to whom Churchill confided his anxiety, Harry Hopkins, thought Churchill "obstreperous."[23] It unnerved the prime minister and his inner circle that "to the Americans the P.M. is the villain of the piece; they are far more sceptical of him than they are of Stalin." Equivalent sentiments emerged in the Foreign Office over what seemed continual British yielding to Washington. Thus, in July 1944, after Roosevelt outmaneuvered the British over recognizing the Free French movement under Charles de Gaulle as the legitimate government of liberated France, the foreign secretary, Sir Anthony Eden, told a confidant that he was "getting fed up with referring everything to the U.S.A. 'Can't we really have a foreign policy of our own?' Anything referred to the U.S.A. is at once blocked by Hull [the secretary of state] or President who are afraid of anything being done at all except by themselves."[24] Eden's permanent under-secretary, Sir Alexander Cadogan, had greater detachment but was equally concerned at the exercise of American strength at British expense. In discussing the Allied amphibious invasion of southern France—code-named, first, "Anvil" and, then, "Dragoon"—he remarked: "I gather P.M. has had to give way to [the] Americans . . . I am not *sure* this is wrong but it is heartbreaking."[25]

Involving much more than the French question, the British difficulty came from their perception that their influence over Allied policy was slipping from their grasp. By July 1944, a series of strategic questions concerning the final defeat of Germany, the answers for which would have a profound impact on Britain's place in the postwar constellation of international power, had yet to be resolved. No doubt existed that the cross-Channel invasion, code-named Overlord, had improved Anglo-American relations with Soviet Russia. But with the Americans now flexing their diplomatic muscle over a range of issues in the West, such as policy toward the Free French, and with the Red Army moving into Eastern and Central Europe and toward the Balkans, there was every chance that Britain could be left behind in shaping the face of postwar Europe. And weakness in Europe could influence unfavorably the British position in East Asia when British forces came to reoccupy lost colonies. Unless Churchill took the initiative of capitalizing on British advantages on the battlefield, transforming them into strong foreign policy, Washington and Moscow would dominate the peace settlement. With the western Allies entrenched in northern France by July, Churchill moved to garner a position of influence for Britain in the postwar world. His efforts centered on two issues: ensuring that British forces in the Mediterranean theater had a major role both in achieving victory in Italy and in expanding the war into the Balkans and southern Germany; and getting Britain its due in the eventual occupation of defeated Germany. Every British military and diplomatic gain along the southern littoral of the Mediterranean would help revive Britain's prewar position as the leading Power in that region, let alone make easier the defense of vital sea lanes to the eastern reaches of the Empire. Respecting Germany, the greater the British role in the occupation regime that the three Allied powers imposed on its enemy, the greater the say London would have in postwar continental affairs.

Three months before D-Day, Churchill had sought a meeting with Roosevelt "not so much [because] . . . there are new departures in policy to be taken but there is a need after more than 90 days of separation [since Teheran] for checking up and shaking together." Roosevelt demurred, citing slight illness but, really, wanting to avoid a disagreement with Churchill over carrying out the cross-Channel invasion.[26] Although Churchill continued to seek a meeting with the president, nothing came of his overtures until late June 1944. At that time, the Combined Chiefs of Staff were deliberating in London—the better to be near the fighting; and in these discussions, the British and American staffs were divided over essential Allied strategy in Western Europe and the Mediterranean. Based on assessments from Eisenhower's headquarters, the American chiefs were concerned about the success of both the operations in northern France and the proposed Anvil landings.[27] To this end, the Americans advocated stripping the Allied armies in Italy of manpower and resources, transferring them to the other two fronts, and leaving only enough forces in Italy to defend the gains made. The British disagreed. As Churchill informed Roosevelt on June 28: "The deadlock between our Chiefs of Staff raise most serious issues. Our first wish is to help General Eisenhower in the most speedy and effective manner. But, we do not think this necessarily involves the complete ruin of all our great affairs in the Mediterranean, and we take it hard that this should be demanded of us."[28] He had already broached a face-to-face meeting with the president at Quebec City, where they had met in August 1943 prior to Teheran; and his concern about the seeming muddle in which the western Allies found themselves was impressed on both Hopkins and John Winant, the American ambassador at London.[29] Although the immediacy of this specific problem abated somewhat by early July, the broad strategic problem of where western Allied forces should fight—and in what strength—needed to be addressed at the highest level. Roosevelt accepted Churchill's invitation, and planning for what became an Anglo-American summit at Quebec began.

For Churchill, this meeting provided an opportunity to push for British-led military operations in Italy and the Balkans that could be translated into strengthening his diplomatic hand when he, Roosevelt, and Stalin finalized the occupation of Germany, the structure of the new international security and financial organizations, the general European settlement, and the plans for the defeat of Japan. Eden had already laid before the Cabinet the difficulties that any Soviet Russian advance into the Balkans would create for Britain once peace returned; and the pungency of his assessment lay in the very real possibility that, as had occurred after World War I, the Americans might take a major role in establishing the postwar European order and then avoid assuming any obligations.[30] The British had to confront the possibility that they might in time face the Russians alone in Europe, thus, any gains they could make now would better protect their interests after hostilities ceased. Accordingly, in the War Cabinet in early July, Churchill told his ministers that because of the exploits of the Red Army, Britain would have to accept Russian domination of Romania and Bulgaria; however, British force could be brought to bear on both Yugoslavia and Greece to keep them within the British sphere.[31]

Such an attitude—a return to the old balance of power—underscored the need to prevent any weakening of British and Imperial forces in Italy under the command of General Sir Harold Alexander. Churchill's strategic idea involved a defeat of German forces entrenched in northern Italy; and, with this accomplished, an offensive into Yugoslavia via an amphibious landing on the Istrian peninsula at the head of the Adriatic Sea could be mounted. Along with operations against German-occupied Greece, the British could prevail in these two Balkan states and, via the Ljublyana gap, push north through the Alps into Austria, with Vienna as the goal. In this, it has to be admitted, Churchill's military advisers, principally General Sir Alan Brooke, the chief of the Imperial general staff, did not share the prime minister's sanguinity about the Ljublyana option.[32] However, for Churchill at this juncture, the political side of war-making dominated its operational component. Similar attitudes touched proposed policies for occupied Germany—and, after 1938, Austria had been absorbed into Hitler's Reich. The Allied occupation of defeated Germany, the zones for which were then the subject of intra-Allied negotiations, were to be discussed at Quebec.[33] Britain had to do everything to enhance its postwar interests on the continent and in the Mediterranean. Adding to the lure of this southern strategy was the fact that the British, not the Russians, had long been aiding the Yugoslav Communist resistance commanded by Marshal Josip Broz Tito against their German occupiers.[34] Admittedly, a competing royalist partisan movement led by General Draža Mihailović also existed in Yugoslavia, and some concern existed in British quarters, chiefly the Foreign Office, about the chance of Tito aligning with the Russians.[35] Undeterred, Churchill moved in the summer of 1944 to give Britain the leading role in Yugoslavia. Hence, when Roosevelt inadvertently sent an American military mission to meet with Mihailović, Churchill forced its recall with the argument that: "We are endeavouring to give Tito the support and, of course, if the United States back Mihailovic [sic], complete chaos will ensue . . . we lay the scene for a fine civil war."[36] Admittedly, the British position in Yugoslavia might have been somewhat tenuous. But in the aftermath of Teheran, Roosevelt had told Churchill that "I am absolutely unwilling to police [liberated] France and possibly Italy and the Balkans as well."[37] With the Russians pressing from the east and the Americans concerned more with the campaign in northern France, Churchill moved to exploit his opportunities in Italy and the south.

These intertwined issues preoccupied Churchill and his advisers in the two months before the Second Quebec conference convened on September 11. Of course, other matters were also to be addressed during this summit: the occupation and treatment of defeated Germany, Anglo-American economic relations, and the war in East Asia and the Pacific.[38] Yet, while weighty, these questions seemed of lesser moment for Churchill when considering the importance he placed on continuing the war in Italy with the maximum of number of troops, ships, and airplanes. And this importance increased when an unexpected crisis developed in early August over Russian policy toward Poland.

Claiming sovereignty over Poland despite the German occupation of their country, a Polish government-in-exile had established itself in London in 1940.[39] During the next four years, despite being ostensible allies in the anti-Axis coalition, relations between this body and Stalin's regime worsened because of historical hatreds on each side, the Russian demand for a slice of eastern Polish territory, and, most important, the discovery in 1943 of graves containing massacred Polish officers who had been captured by the Russians in 1940. Although Stalin denied Soviet culpability for the massacre—he accused the Germans—the London Poles blamed the Russians. Moscow severed formal relations with the government-in-exile and, in late July 1944, when the Red Army liberated part of eastern Poland, recognized a committee of pro-Soviet Communist Poles in situ in Lublin as the legitimate government of reborn Poland. Seeking to recapture the political initiative, the London Poles authorized their resistance movement to rise in rebellion in Poland to defeat the Germans and, thereby, establish the exiles' claim be the legitimate government of the country. On August 1, with the Red Army nearby, an uprising against the Germans began in Warsaw. However, the Russians withdrew; they refused to let the Anglo-Americans air-drop supplies to the resistance (claiming disingenuously that their airfields were not yet ready); and they allowed the Germans to crush the uprising and, thereby, weaken the political claims of the exiled government. Of course, the Germans were also enfeebled, something that helped the Red Army when its offensive recommenced at the end of September.

Throughout August and into the first days of September, Churchill attempted to win Roosevelt's support to pressure Stalin to allow material support to reach the insurgents.[40] He failed. Unwilling to create a Russo-American rift at this crucial stage of the war—he would need Red Army assistance to defeat Japan after Germany fell—Roosevelt even refused to append his name to a toothless Anglo-American request that Stalin allow the airdrop. "I do not consider it advantageous to the long range general war prospect," he wired Churchill, "for me to join with you in the proposed message to [Stalin]."[41] By September 5, a week before the second Quebec conference convened, the president closed the matter: "The problem of relief for the Poles in Warsaw has therefore unfortunately been solved by delay and by German action and there now appears to be nothing we can do to assist them."[42] If any doubt existed before this message, the prime minister now knew that British interests in the last phase of the war and afterward would be overshadowed by Russian and American strength unless he translated British success at arms into a stronger voice in Allied councils.[43] Quebec would give him the opportunity to do so.

Anglo-American discussions at Quebec occurred in an atmosphere of bonhomie and goodwill that flowed from the personal relationship developed by Roosevelt and Churchill since the autumn of 1939. Yet, underneath the veneer of civility lurked mutual suspicions and a degree of distrust fostered by competing visions of how best to defeat Germany and Japan and win the resultant peace. Both leaders arrived on September 11 and, after perfunctory formalities, Churchill began preparing for his formal meetings with Roosevelt, which were to begin two days later. His observations on the general military situation showed that the British-led southern European campaign and that in Southeast Asia to capture Burma and Singapore were connected. At this juncture, it was crucial to get the maximum British and Imperial forces ready for a joint airborne-amphibious attack on Rangoon—code-named Dracula.[44] Such preparations involved freeing up three divisions from northern Burma as well as the transfer of forces from southern Europe after the anticipated success in Italy. But the Burmese operation would only be preliminary to the recapture of Singapore. He made this plain in a minute dated September 12: "[Singapore] is the Supreme British objective in the whole of the Indian and Far Eastern theatres. It is the only prize that will restore British prestige in this region, and in pursuing it we render the maximum aid to the United States operations by engaging the largest number of the enemy in the most intense degree possible and at the earliest moment."[45] Putting aside the assistance that British forces could give the Americans, the reestablishment of the British Empire in East Asia remained central to the political influence that London hoped to enjoy in the region once the war ended.

In this context, the sooner Istria was taken and a British bridgehead established, the sooner Dracula could be launched—Churchill and his advisers reckoned that the Rangoon operation could not begin until early 1945 at the earliest. The British, therefore, had to press for American support in southern Europe. Essential to this support was the transfer of 60 landing craft capable of carrying tanks from Dragoon to northeastern Italy; these vessels had to be prevented from being transferred to northern France. On September 11-12, the possibility of a weakening German position in both Italy and the Balkans intensified Churchill's determination to get the maximum resources to achieve the conquest of Istria. On September 12, he sent Roosevelt intercepts of German communications that suggested that orders had been given to German forces "which declares that a complete withdrawal from Italy and the Balkans has been ordered."[46] Though these reports were inaccurate—only some German forces were to be evacuated—the fact remained that Wehrmacht ability to hold this vital region had diminished significantly. The chances for Britain to attain laurels on the battlefield were at hand. They had to be pursued, the more so as they could be transformed into a stronger voice at the diplomatic bargaining table that shaped the postwar order.

These considerations lay at the fore in British diplomacy at Quebec, a diplomacy that had two dimensions: one involving discussions between the British and American commanders in the Combined Chiefs of Staff, and the second involving talks between Churchill and Roosevelt. On the afternoon of September 12, just as Allied forces were approaching the northwestern frontier of Germany, the Combined Chiefs of Staff held their first and most important meeting to discuss a series of outstanding issues before they consulted Churchill and Roosevelt.[47] Although they covered a range of topics including the coordination of the Anglo-American–Soviet Russian war effort and the control of strategic bomber forces in Europe,[48] the most crucial matters dealt with the situation in the Mediterranean and the Far East. In this the British believed they made a signal achievement.[49] The landing craft for the Istrian operation would not be transferred north until the situation in Italy was clarified, and a date for such a decision was set for a month hence—October 14. Along the same lines, the Americans accepted a British proposal that a sizable British and Imperial naval force would be transferred to the Far East to assist General Douglas MacArthur, the Supreme Allied Commander, in his final offensive against Japan.[50]

Brooke and his British colleagues had to convince the prime minister that any British and Imperial naval forces sent to the Pacific would have to be put under MacArthur's command. As Brooke recorded in his diary: ". . . we had an ordinary Chiefs of Staff meeting to discuss latest minute by P.M. on Pacific strategy. He is gradually coming around to sane strategy, but by Heaven what labour we have had for it!"[51] Importantly, as Churchill's biographer points out: "Churchill's principal point in this minute, not however mentioned by Brooke in his diary, was that Britain's 'own thrust' was to be against Rangoon, as a preliminary to a 'major attack' on Singapore."[52] The British prime minister had no desire to share his strategic objectives with his American allies unless he had to do so. And at that same meeting with the British chiefs, Churchill laid out his intention to have British forces on the continent "revert to an independent command" once Germany surrendered. There would be no question of British occupation forces in Germany or elsewhere continuing under the command of Eisenhower or some other American general after hostilities ceased.

The reason for the American service chiefs not opposing British desires in the Mediterranean and Southeast Asia seems to have derived from their need to concentrate more on the conduct of the war in the regions they judged important for their interests; and, as a corollary, there existed a willingness to divert British forces to theaters of operations of less importance to the United States. To this end, evidence exists that with Roosevelt's support, General George Marshall, the chairman of the American Joint Chiefs of Staff, was moving at this time to leave Southeast Asia as a British sphere of command in return for an American free hand in the final phase of the Pacific war against Japan.[53] By the same token, Admiral Ernest King, the naval chief and an unbending anglophobe, endorsed the Istrian operation. His support surprised the British; but, as Warren Kimball points out in chapter 1, King probably wanted to divert as many British forces as possible away from the Pacific to minimize London's contribution in the final defeat of Japan. For his part, despite the existence of an American informal empire in Latin America, Roosevelt entertained an abiding distaste for colonialism. He had no desire to see American power employed to revive the British and other European overseas empires.[54] As he told his Secretary of the Treasury Henry Morgenthau, who accompanied him to Quebec, he suspected that Churchill was being less than truthful with him about issues like the parlous state of British national wealth.[55] As it was in this question, so it probably was with the military side of the war. The British would do anything to acquire as much American material and other aid as they could to revive their country's leading position as a Great Power. Little hard evidence exists to show the workings of the president's mind—a problem for both his contemporaries and historians;[56] however, he seems to have supported Churchill's desires in the Mediterranean and Southeast Asia at Quebec because it was the path of least resistance when he had more important matters to deal with such as American relations with Soviet Russia, the shape of the new international security and financial organizations, and the treatment of defeated Germany and Japan.

Over the next several days, Churchill and Roosevelt, and the Combined Chiefs, gave form to the general principles of the Mediterranean and Southeast Asian strategies agreed to on September 12.[57] Although still intent on supporting Eisenhower's armies in his broad attack on western Germany via the path established after Normandy, the Americans agreed that: "If General Eisenhower indicates that he does not require a part or all of the U.S. forces now in Italy, they should then be utilized to clear the Germans from Italy and to assist British forces in operations to the north-eastward toward Vienna." Moreover, the transfer of the American 12th Air Force from Italy to France "should be dependent on the progress and outcome of the present offensive in Italy." Along with their own considerable forces in that theater—and with British forces preparing to land in Greece after concurrent negotiations with the Greek government that were completed at Caserta on September 26[58]—the British position in the Mediterranean was strengthened considerably. This had added piquancy given that the Red Army had made unexpectedly quick progress in its invasion of Bulgaria; hence, for Churchill and Eden, who "were afraid that Russia would go into Bulgaria, Yugoslavia, and Greece and never get out," taking the offensive in the Balkans as soon as possible remained critical. In terms of the Far East, despite Marshall's desire to eliminate the American presence in the British-led Southeast Asia Command, he and his colleagues agreed to reinforce British forces in Burma with an air commando group and a combat cargo group. The only discordant note in this process occurred on September 14 when King "lost his temper entirely and was opposed by the whole of his own Committee"[59] over the decision to have British and Imperial naval forces operate with MacArthur in the Pacific. While these differences were papered over the next day in a meeting between King and Admiral Sir Andrew Cunningham,[60] King's discomfort at British involvement in the Pacific theater did not abate. Such involvement might give them greater influence in the postwar East Asian balance of power. After the conference ended, he told a friend "that the British should be told what they can get, not [asked] what they want."[61]

In this way, Churchill had helped to resolve the strategic differences that had existed before the conference between the British and American staffs in a way that had the potential of giving Britain greater influence in the postwar settlements in Europe and the Far East. But there developed for the British an unforeseen problem when Roosevelt presented Churchill with a plan devised by Morgenthau for the treatment of defeated Germany.[62] Roosevelt's animosity for the Nazi regime had reached new levels by mid-August 1944, when he told Morgenthau: "We have got to be tough with Germany and I mean the German people, not just the Nazis. You have either to castrate the German people or you have got to treat them in such a manner so they can't go on reproducing people who want to continue the way they have in the past."[63] Morgenthau shared Roosevelt's sentiments. He had recently been, however, on a financial mission to London. When he pointed out that the British wanted "to build up [postwar] Germany so that she can pay reparations," the president was unmoved. He opposed any notion of reparations, a problem that had undermined his economic diplomacy when he first took office in 1933. The result was the Morgenthau Plan.[64] In simplest terms, this scheme envisaged the complete disarmament of Germany; it posited the dismantling and removal of almost all German heavy industry to destroy the country's war-making potential and the transfer of those industrial components to those countries that Germany had devastated in the war; of that industry which remained, largely in the Ruhr Valley, part would be internationalized and part would be turned over to the French; outside the Ruhr, the remainder of the country would be divided into a northern and a southern state, where the basis of their economies would be agricultural. There would be no question of the Germans paying reparations—thereby removing the kind of question that had bedeviled Germany's relations with the Allied victors after 1919—and the Germans would be able to construct democratic institutions after the Nazis and their supporters had been purged.

The presentation of this plan to Churchill at a dinner meeting on September 13 proved to be the basis of the second dimension of British diplomacy at Quebec.[65] Despite Morgenthau emphasizing its economic and financial benefits for Britain—"Morgenthau wanted to close down the Ruhr to help British exports, especially steel"—Churchill immediately argued against it. He found nothing to quarrel with concerning the disarming of Germany, but he thought it impolitic "to prevent her living decently" after denazification and disarmament. He also reckoned that the British people "will not stand for the policy you are advocating," and he quoted Edmund Burke when he countered that: "You cannot indict a whole nation." According to Moran, an unnamed American replied "that Germany should be made to return to a pastoral state, she ought to have a lower standard of living." Roosevelt's only serious interjection was to repeat an argument marshaled by Stalin at Teheran almost a year before: "a factory which made steel furniture could be turned overnight to war production." After more than three hours of, in Moran's words, "wild talk [in which] only the P.M. seemed to have his feet on the ground," it was agreed that Morgenthau would go over the plan the next day with Lord Cherwell, one of Churchill's senior advisers.

Cherwell had supported Morgenthau's plan at the September 13 dinner meeting and, in his discussions with the secretary the next day, he expressed surprise "at Churchill's attitude."[66] Morgenthau opined that his experience with Hull and Eden suggested that both foreign ministers would support this initiative, at the basis of which was a simple question: "Do you want a strong Germany and a weak England or a weak Germany and a strong England?" Cherwell, who also in this meeting discussed the continuation of American Lend-Lease aid to Britain in the interim between the defeat of Germany and that of Japan, needed little convincing. He promised to broach the Morgenthau Plan to his political master in a "more attractive" way. Later that day, when Cherwell and Morgenthau met with Churchill and Roosevelt, Cherwell pressed the idea that Germany's war-making capacity had to be eliminated, he argued that the postwar German standard of living would be higher than that under Hitler's regime when so many resources were diverted to the armed forces, and that British export trade would benefit.[67] Churchill had supposedly been briefed on the work of the intra-Allied committee looking at the creation of occupation zones in Germany, which ran contrary to the basic thrust of Morgenthau's ideas;[68] but, seeing the financial benefits that could accrue to Britain by severely restraining Germany's industrial capacity, he endorsed the plan. The question is why did he reverse himself and accept these proposals, which would weaken Germany vis-à-vis Soviet Russia and make the postwar balance of power on the continent more difficult? As Churchill's biographer is uninstructive in seeking an answer, one needs to turn to Churchill's memoirs for an explanation.[69] Churchill later argued that there were two reasons for his change of opinion. The first derived from his desire to see the continuation of Lend-Lease aid after Germany's defeat: "[T]he President, with Mr. Morgenthau—from whom we had so much to ask—were so insistent that in the end we agreed to consider it." In this way, British support of the plan was a quid pro quo for continued American economic aid, which would be crucial for the final phase of the war against Japan and the reestablishment of the British Empire in East Asia. The second reason stemmed from the anti-German temper of the times: "[A]t that time, when German militarism based on German industry had done such appalling damage to Europe, it did not seem unfair to agree that her manufacturing capacity need not be revived beyond what was needed to give her the same standards of life as her neighbours [which lacked such industries]." Indeed, the next day, on September 15, Roosevelt and Churchill met with Morgenthau, Eden, Cherwell, and Cadogan to discuss the treatment of Germany.[70] Seeking to show his commitment to the plan, he dictated the final conference memorandum summarizing the deindustrialization of Germany.[71]

Despite Churchill's and Roosevelt's endorsement of the plan, senior members of the British and American governments were appalled at its contents. Henry Stimson, Roosevelt's secretary of war, a former Republican secretary of state, and one of the few senior American political leaders who thought in strategic terms, argued against destroying "a natural and necessary asset for the productivity of Europe."[72] Stimson's critique occurred privately, after preconference discussions with Roosevelt. Eden, on the other hand, took his own prime minister to task on September 15 in front of Roosevelt and Morgenthau.[73] "I did not like the plan," he recorded in his diary, "nor was I convinced that it was to our national advantage." He went on: "I said so, and also suggested that Mr. Cordell Hull's opinion should be sought for. This was the only occasion I can remember when the Prime Minister showed impatience with my views before foreign representatives. He resented my criticism of something which he and the President approved, not I am sure on his account, but on the President's."

Supported by the War Office in London, Eden was actually articulating the long-standing view of the Foreign Office in this matter: Britain had to work to reestablish a workable balance of power on the continent after peace returned; and, in this equation, a viable Germany remained essential.[74] With the usual American moralizing against the tenets of "old diplomacy," Morgenthau had earlier disparaged British policy toward postwar Germany because of its deleterious affect on the Soviet Russians: "Russia feared we and the British were going to try to make a soft peace with Germany and build her up as possible future counter-weight against

Russia."[75] He was correct, at least as far as the Foreign Office was concerned, in wanting a strong, democratic postwar Germany able to withstand Russian pressures—the Warsaw rising was in its final phase during the Quebec Conference. And it was such attitudes that informed British policy concerning the zones of occupation for defeated Germany.

After Teheran, intra-Allied bodies, chiefly the European Advisory Commission, had grappled the nettled problem of the Allied occupation of Germany. By early August 1944, several decisions had been agreed on by British, American, and Russian negotiators: Soviet Russia would occupy eastern Germany, the British, northwestern Germany, and the Americans, the southwestern part; Berlin would have a separate tripartite occupation; each of the three Powers would appoint commanders in chief for their zones in Germany and Berlin; these commanders would occupy and administer their zones and would make major decisions in two committees of commanders in chief, one for Germany and one for Berlin.[76] In discussions at Quebec, involving both the senior civilian leaders and the Combined Chiefs, some modifications concerning the proposed British and American zones were made to the August agreement. In this the British and Americans had different objectives, which they both pursued successfully in making an adjustment to the proposed occupation regime.

The Americans had been unhappy with the location of their proposed zone. Because American troops would be landlocked, the American Joint Chiefs wanted "access to northwestern sea ports and passage through the British controlled area."[77] The British chiefs conceded to this sensible requirement, and the port of Bremen, which could handle 10,000 tons of goods a day, was allocated to American control.[78] For his part, Roosevelt wanted to ensure that the American zone and its line of communications to the North Sea coast was not contiguous with French territory. The president not only had a pathological dislike for de Gaulle—which created difficulties in Anglo-American diplomacy toward the Free French movement—but some evidence exists to suggest American fear of a postwar revolution in France.[79] Additionally, Roosevelt seems to have wanted to establish a cooperative atmosphere in which postwar Anglo-American - Russian relations could develop—such ideas also underscored his support for the Dumbarton Oaks talks. On the eve of the Quebec Conference, he agreed with Morgenthau, who commented: "There are two kinds of people—one like Eden who believes we must cooperate with Russia and that we must trust Russia for the peace of the world, and there is the other school, which is illustrated by the remark of Churchill who said, 'What are we going to have between the white snows of Russia and the White Cliffs of Dover?' . . . what Churchill did mean at that time was a strong Germany. So the President said, 'I belong to the same school as Eden.'"[80] The construction of an administrative structure to run the zonal occupation of a demilitarized and divided Germany would help to provide the basis for that atmosphere of cooperation.[81]

Churchill and his advisers, on the other hand, sought as free a hand as possible in postwar Germany; and, except for the premier's embrace of the Morgenthau Plan, they seemed to be on the threshold of achieving this at Quebec. In one sense, despite their division over the merits of the plan, both Churchill and Eden were united in their desire to ensure that London had a voice in determining how policy toward defeated Germany should be devised and implemented. Tied to both having British forces on the continent "revert to an independent command" once hostilities ceased and the British zonal commanders sitting as equals with their American and Russian counterparts, the occupation regime would give London that voice. There can also be little doubt that Churchill wanted American forces to remain in Europe after the war ended, the better to contain Soviet Russian power and limit Moscow's influence on how the postwar continent should evolve.[82] But Roosevelt had earlier made noises about pulling out of Europe as soon as possible after the war.[83] This unpleasant possibility could be obviated by the American contribution to the occupation regime in Germany. Should, however, the Americans decide to withdraw, the British needed insurance against the Russians, then seeking to shape the emerging political regimes in Poland and the other areas they were liberating in the east. A revived France that could help counterbalance Soviet Russia offered possibilities for the British. At Quebec, Eden lobbied Roosevelt and Churchill to recognize de Gaulle's Free French as the legitimate government of liberated France.[84] Although Roosevelt successfully resisted the foreign secretary's blandishments over this issue at that juncture, Eden got the two leaders to agree that "the matter [of formally recognising the French Committee of National Liberation as the provisional government of France] should be kept constantly under review."[85] Just at this moment in London, French diplomatists were lobbying a receptive Foreign Office for a separate French occupation zone in postwar Germany.[86]

Churchill left Quebec certain that he and his advisers had ensured Britain's international influence as the second world war world ended. British-led military operations in Italy, the Balkans, and Southeast Asia had the potential to translate into a stronger voice in the councils of the Allied Powers when Germany and Japan were defeated.[87] Although his acceptance of the Morgenthau Plan suggested that much more punishment would be meted out to the Germans than he at first envisaged, he had been able to trade his initials on this document for continued Lend-Lease aid after the war in Europe ended. Moreover, the British ensured their formal equality with the Americans and Russians within the occupation regime in defeated Germany, an equality that would give independent British military commanders latitude on the continent and British political leaders in London a major voice in the councils that determined the postwar order on the continent. And, if the French could be brought into the occupation regime, the British ability to manipulate better the European balance of power would be amplified and the chance to restrain Russian ambitions improved. Of course, Roosevelt and his advisers had protected their own interests at Quebec. They had shielded their leading role in the Pacific War against Japan. They had given minimal material support to the British theater of operations in the Mediterranean—60 landing craft and some ground and air forces—while keeping the maximum Anglo-American forces in the continuing offensive against Germany's western borders. They had ensured access to the sea for their eventual zone of occupation in defeated Germany. And, in Roosevelt's case, he had gained Churchill's support for a "hard peace" in Germany that would assist in establishing what he thought would be a good working relationship with the Soviet Russians once peace returned.

Churchill's strategy to ensure Britain's postwar international influence continued in the months following Quebec. Immediately after the conference ended, Roosevelt entertained Churchill at his estate at Hyde Park, New York. On September 18-19, the two leaders discussed a number of matters including the ongoing development of the atomic bomb.[88] It was possible that this weapon, which when it was ready had the explosive equivalent of 20,000 tons of TNT, would be available for use by the summer of 1945. Because of the supposed imminence of German defeat, the Allies could use it against Japan in the final phase of the war. Despite the Americans having contributed most to the development of this weapon in manpower and finance—and it was being made in facilities in the United States—the British and Canadians were providing important scientific aid and the uranium required to make the explosive. Churchill and his advisers understood the enormous potential of atomic energy, both its military implications and the possibilities of its peacetime use.[89] At Hyde Park, therefore, the British prime minister was able to win Roosevelt's agreement that: "Full collaboration between the United States and the British Government in developing Tube Alloys [the code name of the atomic bomb project] for military and commercial purposes should continue after the defeat of Japan unless and until terminated by joint agreement."[90] In Churchill's mind, he had helped create another diplomatic device to extend Anglo-American cooperation into the postwar period. Moreover, he felt that he had assured the British government's influence in the continued development of atomic energy.

Just as crucial as the American dimension of Churchill's diplomatic strategy was that concerning Soviet Russia. The Russian question had preoccupied the British and Americans at Quebec, both the immediate problem of the Warsaw rising and the long-term relationship that Stalin's regime would have with its two chief western allies.[91] Red Army advances into the Balkans and Central Europe in September 1944 convinced Churchill and Eden that an approach to Moscow was required to assure that the emerging postwar order in Europe did not develop to British disadvantage. After the war, a Soviet Russia that dominated most of the continent would diminish Britain's ability to protect its security, economic and financial, and political interests. It became incumbent, therefore, for Churchill to balance his efforts with Roosevelt at Quebec with others with Stalin. These issues concerned Churchill in the days after Quebec and, on September 29, he informed Roosevelt: "Anthony and I are seriously considering flying there [Moscow] very soon. . . . Our two great objects would be, first, to clinch his [Stalin's] coming in against Japan and, secondly, to try to effect a friendly settlement with Poland. There are other points too about Greece and Yugoslavia which we would also discuss. We should keep you informed of every point."[92] Roosevelt entertained mixed feelings about Churchill's proposal: he deprecated a high-level meeting that he could not attend (he was in the midst of the 1944 general election); yet, he wanted to do everything possible to ensure good relations with Stalin that he believed had been tarnished since Teheran over the Polish question, the Dumbarton Oaks talks, and other issues.[93] He, thus, supported the Churchill-Stalin talks but would not allow a senior administration official to participate. By such action, he could disavow any agreements his two partners might reach that he opposed.

The story of the subsequent Anglo-Russian meetings, held in Moscow from October 10 to October 18, 1944, and code-named Tolstoy, is well known.[94] Along with Eden and Molotov, Churchill and Stalin moved to settle the Polish issue, they discussed the war against Japan, and they gave preliminary shape to postwar spheres of influence in Central and Eastern Europe and the Balkans. This latter point was the most important in terms of determining the shape of postwar Europe and, from the British vantage, of providing Britain with political and strategic advantages in southern Europe and the Mediterranean once the war against Germany ended. The crucial point came when Churchill proposed suddenly and informally that the three major Allies determine amongst themselves "percentages" of dominance in Romania, Greece, Yugoslavia, Hungary, and Bulgaria. Despite the odd nature of dividing Allied influence by "percentages,"[95] the proposal constituted a realistic effort by Churchill that recognized both the Red Army's successes by 1944 and the fact that Stalin was going to ensure pliant, pro-Soviet regimes in those regions liberated by Russian force of arms. It was a simple matter of realpolitik that portended much about the postwar balance of power in Europe. The Russians would dominate in the interior of the continent, including the interior of the Balkans and along the Black Sea coast of Bulgaria to the Straits but not beyond. The British, with American concurrence, would dominate on the Balkan littoral, including the Yugoslav coast, which Molotov conceded. Although there was some adjustment of the original percentages— for instance, the Russians received dominance in Hungary—and although Stalin promised Churchill his support for democratic elections in the divided countries and Poland, the die was cast.[96]

Churchill informed Roosevelt of what had transpired: "It is absolutely necessary we should try to get a common mind about the Balkans, so that we may prevent civil war breaking out in several countries when probably you and I would be in sympathy with one side and U.J. ['Uncle Joe' Stalin] with the other."[97] Reaching an equivalent compromise concerning Poland was more difficult. The Red Army was pushing the Germans out of Poland, and the Moscow-supported Lublin committee was in place. Bowing to the inevitable and swallowing his distaste for Stalin's response to the Warsaw rising, Churchill forced the head of the Polish government-in-exile in London to find the political means to create a coalition government in liberated Poland with the Lublin committee. Naturally, Churchill empha-sized the "preliminary" nature of all of these discussions to Roosevelt, which would be "subject to further discussion and melting-down with you." But the president offered no comment on the "percentages agreement," and he did not seem to care much about the fate of the Polish exiled government.[98] His principal concern centered on defeating Germany as soon as possible, the recognition of a French government, and the need to assure good western Allied relations with Russia while a tripartite summit involving the three leaders was being planned for the new year.

By late October 1944, Churchill believed he had accomplished a great deal diplomatically for Britain since the summer. In this, the second Quebec Conference appeared as a watershed. His need to have British forces take the leading role in the southern Mediterranean and Southeast Asian campaigns had been achieved. The zones of occupation for Germany had been decided to the extent that all that was needed thereafter was fiddling with the minutiae of its administrative apparatus—and, for the Foreign Office, there was the very great possibility that the French would become involved as a means to counterbalance the Russian threat. British forces in postwar Europe, especially those in Germany, were to revert to British command. Churchill had also won Roosevelt's approval for "full collaboration" between Britain and the United States over postwar development of atomic energy. And, in Eastern and

Central Europe and the Balkans, the postwar British position seemed to be further entrenched after Tolstoy. Indeed, in tandem with Churchill's aspirations for the Istrian operation and the Caserta agreement with the Greeks, the framework had been built that would allow for a significant British voice in postwar Mediterranean affairs, this while excluding the Russians from the region. Of course, diplomacy is a two-way street. Roosevelt had shielded his strategic vision of how to defeat Germany, while winning Churchill's support for the Morgenthau Plan. American military commanders had protected from undue British interference their Pacific strategy for the final thrust against Japan. Stalin had been given a free hand in Eastern and Central Europe, while his determination to achieve a Polish settlement to his liking had been given a British blessing. Churchill understood all of this, but he believed he had done the best he could in a difficult situation. He put his feelings about Britain's postwar role with the United States in his congratulations on Roosevelt's re-election in early November: "I feel that you will not mind my saying that I prayed for your success and that I am truly thankful for it. This does not mean that I seek or wish for anything more than the full, fair and free play of your mind upon the world issues now at stake in which our two nations have to discharge their respective duties."[99] Here was the focus of Churchill's crowded mind as the defeat of the Allied enemies in Europe and the Far East loomed: Britain and the United States should continue to work together to bring about effective international peace and security, but they would do so as full partners.

The difficulty for Churchill after November 1944 was that events were beyond his control. To a large extent, nearly all the gains that he believed he had achieved at Quebec were compromised before the war in Europe ended in May 1945. The British advance into southern Austria was blunted by the inability of Allied arms to win a decisive victory in Italy and effective German military resistance. At the same time, the anticipated defeat of Germany did not occur in the few weeks envisaged in the optimistic atmosphere of Quebec. German forces continued to fight effectively on the Reich's western borders for several months, a situation compounded when the Wehrmacht launched a counterattack in Belgium in December 1944 that required substantial Allied forces to repel. As the war proceeded against Germany in the north, Washington continued to support Eisenhower in maintaining his broad front from the English Channel south to Switzerland. In addition, Roosevelt was convinced by Stimson and others of the false promise offered by the Morgenthau Plan. Accordingly, he dropped it. While this action did not undermine the agreements on the zonal division of Germany, it did mean that one of the bases of postwar Anglo-American relations, to which Churchill had agreed at Quebec, had been compromised. Along with the lack of British battlefield successes in Italy and in southern Germany, the potential volume of the British voice in postwar Allied councils had been reduced. More important, Roosevelt died suddenly on April 12, 1945. This sad event deprived Churchill of a receptive, if not always congenial, ear at the highest levels in Washington; his personal relationship with the new president, Harry Truman, was formal and never close. And flowing from this change in leadership in the United States, the Anglo-American relationship was transformed. Soon after he took office, Truman decided to cancel Lend-Lease aid to American allies, including Britain, and he arbitrarily abrogated the Hyde Park agreement on joint Anglo-American development of atomic energy. In the Far East, under Truman's leadership, the Americans pushed ahead with their assault on Japan; this was a campaign in which Britain, though British-led forces recaptured Burma, Singapore, and Hong Kong, was clearly the junior partner and in which Washington and MacArthur determined policy alone.

None of this is to say that everything Churchill sought via his diplomatic strategy to ensure Britain's international influence was lost: Britain had a major role in the occupation regime in Germany and Berlin; its armed forces on the continent reverted to British command after Germany's surrender; the spheres of influence in Central and Eastern Europe and the Balkans, which Churchill had worked out with Stalin in October 1944, were confirmed at the last Big Three meeting at Yalta in February 1945; Churchill managed to get French occupation zones in Germany, Berlin, Austria, and Vienna; and British forces liberated those crucial colonial holdings in Southeast and East Asia as a precursor to what the prime minister hoped would lead to the reassertion of Britain's Imperial presence in that region. How much Britain would have been able to achieve in late 1944 if there had been no second Quebec Conference is moot. Yet, it is certain that that conference had a central position in Churchill's diplomatic effort to find a significant postwar role for Britain in its evolving relationship with both the United States and Soviet Russia as the Second World War was ending. It is just as certain that its results were at once his great accomplishment and his great frustration.

NOTES

1. Churchill to his wife, Aug. 17, 1944, quoted in M. Gilbert, *Winston S. Churchill, Road to Victory* vol. VII (London, 1986), p. 936.
2. P. Böttger, *Winston Churchill und die Zweite Front, 1941-1943: Ein Aspekt der britischen Strategie im Zweiten Weltkrieg* (Frankfurt, 1984); W. S. Dunn,

Second Front Now—1943 (Maxwell, AL: 1980); M. Stoler, *The Politics of the Second Front: American Military Planning and Diplomacy in Coalition Warfare, 1941-1943* (London, 1977). Compare to A. P. Dobson, *U.S. Wartime Aid to Britain, 1940-1946* (London, 1986); G. C. Herring, "The United States and British Bankruptcy, 1944-1945: Responsibilities Deferred," *Political Science Quarterly,* 86 (1971): 332-44.

3. L. Kettenacker, "The Anglo-Soviet Alliance and the Problem of Germany, 1941-1945," *Journal of Contemporary History,* 17 (1982): 435-58; T. Sharp, *The Wartime Alliance and the Zonal Division of Germany* (London, 1975); A. Polonsky, "Polish Failure in Wartime London: Attempts to Forge a European Alliance, 1940-1944," *International History Review,* 7 (1985): 519-60.

4. The rest of this paragraph is based on A. Best, *Britain, Japan, and Pearl Harbor: Avoiding War in East Asia, 1936-1941* (London, 1995); D. I. Hall, *The Birth of the Tactical Airforce: British Theory and Practice of Air Support in the West, 1939-1943* (Oxford D. Phil., 1998), chapters, 5, 7, 9; R. D. S. Higham, *Diary of a Disaster: British Aid to Greece, 1940-1941* (Lexington, KY, 1986); M. Knox, *Mussolini Unleashed, 1939-1941: Politics and Strategy in Fascist Italy's Last War* (Cambridge, 1982); P. Lowe, "Winston Churchill and Japan, 1914-1942," *Proceedings of the British Association for Japanese Studies,* 6 (1981): 39-48; K. A. Maier, H. Rohde et al., *Germany and the Second World War: Germany's Initial Conquests in Europe,* vol. II (Oxford, 1991), especially see K. A. Maier, "The Battle of Britain," pp. 374-407; G. Weinberg, *A World at Arms. A Global History of World War II* (Cambridge, 1994), 122-263.

5. J. Erickson and D. Dilks, eds., *Barbarossa: the Axis and the Allies* (Edinburgh, 1994); A. Hillgruber, "Der Hitler-Stalin-Pakt und die Entfesselung des Zweiten Weltkrieges: Situationsanalyse und Machtkalkül der beiden Pakt-Partner," *Historisches Zeitschrift,* 230 (1980): 339-61; R. Spector, *Eagle Against the Sun: The American War Against Japan* (New York, 1985), pp. 1-183; Weinberg, *World at Arms,* pp. 264-309.

6. L. Allen, *Singapore 1941-1942* (London, 1984); A. Draper, *Dawns Like Thunder: The Retreat from Burma 1942* (London, 1987); J. Erickson, *The Road to Stalingrad* (London, 1975); B. Pitt, *The Crucible of War: Western Desert 1941* (London, 1980); G. W. Prange, *Miracle at Midway* (New York, 1982); H. P. Willmott, *Empires in the Balance: Japan and Allied Strategies to April 1942* (Annapolis, MD, 1982).

7. L. Allen, *Burma. The Longest War* (London, 1984); W. B. Breuer, *Operation Torch: The Allied Gamble to Invade North Africa* (New York, 1985); C. D'Este, *Decision in Normandy* (New York, 1983); J. Erickson, *The Road to Berlin: Continuing the History of Stalin's War with Germany* (Boulder, CO, 1983); J. Mabire, *Stalingrad: la bataille décisive de la Deuxième Guerre Mondiale, julliet 1942-février 1943* (Paris, 1993); E. Morris, *Circles of Hell: The War in Italy, 1943-1945* (London, 1993); R. Spector, *Eagle Against the Sun,* pp. 184-416.

8. A. Danchev, *Very Special Relationship: Field Marshal Sir John Dill and the Anglo-American Alliance, 1941-1944* (London, 1986); J. B. Duroselle, "Le conflit stratégique anglo-américain de juin 1940 à juin 1944," *Revue d'histoire*

moderne et contemporaine, 10 (1963): 161-84; M. Howard, *Grand Strategy: August 1942-September 1943*, vol. IV (London, 1974); M. Matloff and E. M. Snell, *Strategic Planning for Coalition Warfare, 1941-1942* (Washington, 1953). Compare to F. J. Harbutt, "Churchill, Hopkins and the 'Other' Americans: An Alternative Perspective on Anglo-American Relations, 1941-1945," *International History Review*, 8 (1986): 236-62.

9.   R. Beitzell, *The Uneasy Alliance: America, Britain and Russia, 1941-1943* (New York, 1972); R. Dallek, *Franklin D. Roosevelt and American Foreign Policy, 1933-1945* (Oxford/New York, 1979), pp. 317-405; G. Gorodetsky, *Stafford Cripps Mission to Moscow, 1940-1942* (London, 1982); S. M. Miner, *Between Churchill and Roosevelt: The Soviet Union, Great Britain, and the Origins of the Grand Alliance* (London, 1988); K. Sainsbury, *Churchill and Roosevelt at War: The War They Fought and the Peace They Hoped to Make* (Basingstoke, UK, 1994).

10. Dallek, *Roosevelt*, pp. 369-85; Howard, *Grand Strategy*, chapter 13.

11. K. Eubank, *Summit at Teheran* (New York, 1985); P. D. Mayle, *Eureka Summit: Agreement in Principle and the Big Three at Teheran, 1943* (London, 1987).

12. For instance, see R. C. Hilderbrand, *Dumbarton Oaks. The Origins of the United Nations and the Search for Postwar Security* (London, 1990). Compare to D. C. Watt, "Every War Must End: War-Time Planning for Post-War Security, in Britain and America in the Wars of 1914-1918 and 1939-1939," *Transactions of the Royal Historical Society*, 28 (1978): 159-73.

13. For instance, see Churchill memoranda, Dec. 16-20, 1941, Jan. 10, 1942, Stimson [U.S. secretary for war] memorandum "A Suggested Analysis of the Basic Problems," Dec. 20, 1941, all U.S. Dept. of State, *Foreign Relations of the United States* [hereafter *FRUS*, plus volume title]. *The Conferences at Washington, 1941-1942*, and *Casablanca, 1943* (Washington, DC, 1968), pp. 21-37, 44-47, 220-28. Compare to J. R. M. Butler, *Grand Strategy: June 1941-August 1942*, vol. III, part II (London, 1964), pp. 349-401.

14. Böttger, *Zweite Front;* Dunn, *Second Front;* Stoler, *Second Front.*

15. Mayle, *Eureka*, 30-39, 63-64, 80-82, 162; K. Sainsbury, *The Turning Point: Roosevelt, Stalin, Churchill and Chaing-Kai-Shek, 1943. The Moscow, Cairo, and Teheran Conferences* (Oxford, 1985), pp. 217-80.

16. This paragraph is based on W. K. Hancock, *British War Economy* (London, 1949); M. M. Postan, *British War Production* (London, 1952); R. S. Sayers, *Financial Policy, 1939-1945* (London, 1956). Compare to C. Barnet, *The Audit of War: The Illusion and Reality of Britain as a Great Nation* (London, 1986); A. P. Dobson, *U.S. Wartime Aid to Britain, 1940-1946* (London, 1986); W. F. Kimball, *The Most Unsordid Act: Lend-Lease, 1939-1941* (Baltimore, MD, 1969); K. Smith, *Conflict Over Convoys: Anglo-American Logistics Diplomacy in the Second World War* (Cambridge, 1996).

17. Except where noted, this paragraph is based on W. Deakin, et al., eds., *British Political and Military Strategy in Central, Eastern and Southern Europe in 1944* (London, 1944); R. Garson, "The Atlantic Alliance, Eastern Europe and the

Origins of the Cold War: From Pearl Harbor to Yalta," in *Contrast and Contention: Bicentennial Essays in Anglo-American History*, eds. H. C. Allen and R. Thompson (London, 1976); Kettenacker, "Anglo-Soviet Alliance"; Polonsky, "Polish Failure"; T. Sharp, "The Origins of the 'Teheran Formula' on Polish Frontiers," *Journal of Contemporary History*, 12 (1977): 381-93.

18. H. W. Koch, "The Spectre of a Separate Peace in the East: Russo-German 'Peace Feelers', 1942-44," *Journal of Contemporary History*, 10 (1975): 532-47; B. Martin, "Deutsch-Sowjetische Sondirungen über einen separaten Friedenschluss im Zweiten Weltkrieg: Bericht und Dokumentation," in *Felder und Vorfelder russicher Geschichte: Studien zu Ehre von Peter Schiebert*, eds. A. Hillgruber and G. Schramm (Freiberg, 1985), pp. 280-308.

19. E. P. Hoyt, *How They Won the War in the Pacific: Nimitz and his Admirals* (New York, 1970); H. Millington, *American Diplomacy and the War in the Pacific* (New York, 1972); C. Thorne, *Allies of a Kind: The United States, Britain and the War Against Japan, 1941-1945* (London, 1978); D. Van der Vat, *The Pacific Campaign: World War II, the U.S. - Japanese Naval War* (London, 1992).

20. B. J. C. McKercher, "Churchill, the European Balance of Power and the USA," in *Winston Churchill. Studies in Statesmanship*, ed. R. A. C. Parker (London, Washington, 1995), pp. 42-64.

21. W. F. Kimball, "Wheel within a Wheel: Churchill, Roosevelt, and the Special Relationship," in *Churchill*, eds. R. Blake and W. R. Louis (Oxford, 1994), pp. 291-307; D. Reynolds, "Roosevelt, Churchill, and the Wartime Anglo-American Alliance, 1939-1945: Towards a New Synthesis," in *The "Special Relationship": Anglo-American Relations Since 1945*, eds. H. Bull and W. R. Louis (Oxford, 1989), pp. 17-41.

22. J. W. Wheeler-Bennett, *Action This Day: Working with Churchill* (London, 1968), p. 89. See J. Beaumont, *Comrades in Arms: British Aid to Russia, 1941-1945* (London, 1980); P. M. H. Bell, *John Bull and the Bear: British Public Opinion, Foreign Policy, and the Soviet Union, 1941-1945* (New York, 1990); M. Kitchen, *British Policy Towards the Soviet Union During the Second World War* (Basingstoke, UK, 1986); Miner, *Between Churchill and Roosevelt.* Compare to V. G. Trukhanovskii, *British Foreign Policy During World War II, 1939-1945* (Moscow, 1970).

23. This and the next sentence are from Moran [Churchill's doctor] Diary, Nov. 25, 1943, in Lord Moran, *Churchill. Taken from the Diaries of Lord Moran. The Struggle for Survival 1940-1965* (London, 1966), pp. 141-42.

24. Hardy [Eden's private secretary] Diary, July 15, 1944, in *The War Diaries of Oliver Hardy* ed. J. Harvey (London, 1978), p. 348.

25. Cadogan Diary, June 30, 1944, *The Diaries of Sir Alexander Cadogan, O.M., 1938-1945*, ed. D. Dilks (London, 1971), p. 644. (Emphasis in original.)

26. Churchill Telegram to Roosevelt, Mar. 18, 1944, and reply, Mar. 20, 1944, both *FRUS, The Conference at Quebec 1944* (Washington, 1972), pp. 3-4. Compare to Dallek, *Roosevelt*, p. 468.

27. SHAEF Memoranda, "Release of Shipping and Craft from Operation 'Neptune,'" June 12, 1944, "The Employment of Mediterranean Forces in Aid of 'Neptune,'" June 12, 1944, are both annexes in Combined Chiefs of Staff [hereafter CCS] Meeting 164, June 13, 1944, in CCS "Octagon Conference September 1944. Papers and Minutes of Meetings, Octagon Conference and Minutes of Combined Chiefs of Staff Meetings in London, June 1944" [microfilm edition: National Archives, Washington, DC]. Neptune was the code name of the assault phase of Overlord.

28. Telegram, Churchill to Roosevelt, June 28, 1944, in *Churchill & Roosevelt. The Complete Correspondence: Alliance Declining, February 1944 - April 1945,* vol. III, ed. W. F. Kimball (Princeton, 1984), pp. 212-13. Compare to Telegram, Churchill to Roosevelt, June 28, 1944, enclosing Prime Minister and Minister of Defence Memorandum, "Operations in the European Theatres," no date, and reply, June 29, 1944, ibid., 214-23.

29. Telegram, Churchill to Roosevelt, June 20, 1944, *FRUS Quebec,* 8. See Winant to Roosevelt, July 3, 1944, Churchill to Hopkins, July 19, 1944, both Roosevelt Map Room MSS, Roosevelt Library, Hyde Park, NY [hereafter Roosevelt MR] 11.

30. Eden memorandum, "Soviet Policy in the Balkans," June 4, 1944, WP(44)304, Cabinet Archives, Public Record Office, Kew [hereafter CAB] 66/51.

31. War Minutes [hereafter WM] (44)88, July 7, 1944, CAB/65 [Public Record Office microfiche edition].

32. Brooke Diary, June 1944, in A. Bryant, *Triumph in the West, 1943-1946. Based on the Diaries and Autobiographical Notes of Field Marshal The Viscount Alanbrooke, K.G., O.M.* (London, 1959), pp. 222-23.

33. Sharp, *Zonal Division,* pp. 56-89.

34. P. Auty and R. Clogg, eds., *British Policy towards Wartime Resistance in Yugoslavia and Greece* (London, 1975); M. Wheeler, *Britain and the War for Yugoslavia, 1940-1943* (Boulder, CO, 1980).

35. Eden memorandum, "Soviet Policy in the Balkans," June 4, 1944, WP(44)304, CAB 66/51.

36. Telegram, Churchill to Roosevelt, Sept. 1, 1944, and reply, Sept. 3, 1944, both Kimball, *Churchill & Roosevelt,* vol. III, p. 306, 309.

37. Telegram, Roosevelt to Churchill, Feb. 7, 1944, in W. F. Kimball ed., *Churchill & Roosevelt. The Complete Correspondence: Alliance Forged, November 1942 - February 1944,* vol. II (Princeton, 1984), p. 709.

38. For instance, see the Hull Memorandum to Roosevelt, Aug. 28, 1944, enclosing three memoranda on policy recommendations for the treatment of Germany, May 31, Aug. 5, Aug. 22, 1944, British Treasury Memorandum, Aug. 14, 1944, Wickard [secretary of agriculture] to Roosevelt, Aug. 23, 1944, British Chiefs of Staff Memorandum, no date, Joint Chiefs of Staff to Hull, Aug. 29, 1944, all *FRUS, Quebec, 1944,* pp. 48-76, 159-60, 162-63, 244-46, 252-53.

39.   This paragraph is based on J. Coutouvidis and J. Reynolds, *Poland 1939-1947* (New York, 1986), pp. 91-102; A. Polonsky, *The Great Powers and the Polish Question 1941-45. A Documentary Study in Cold War Origins* (London, 1976), pp. 31-37; idem., "Polish Failure in Wartime London: Attempts to Forge a European Alliance, 1940-1944," *International History Review*, 7 (1985): 519-60; J. T. Tomasz, *Revolution From Abroad: The Soviet Conquest of Poland's western Ukraine and western Byelorussia* (Princeton, 1988).

40.   For instance, Churchill Telegrams, (3) Aug. 18, Aug. 23, (3) Sept. 4, 1944, Kimball, *Churchill & Roosevelt*, vol. III, pp. 281-83, 292-93, 309-12.

41.   Roosevelt to Churchill, Aug. 26, 1944, ibid., III, p. 296.

42.   Telegram, Roosevelt to Churchill, Sept. 5, 1944, ibid., p. 313.

43.   Compare to W. S. Churchill, *The Second World War*, vol. VI (London, 1954), p. 124.

44.   Gilbert, *Churchill*, vol. VII, p. 954.

45.   Churchill Minutes, Sept. 12, 1944, quoted in ibid., p. 955.

46.   Churchill to Roosevelt, Sept. 12, 1944, Kimball, *Churchill & Roosevelt*, vol. III, p. 321. The American Joint Chiefs had the same information from their sources in neutral Switzerland; see Part 5 of CCS Meeting 172, Sept. 12, 1944, in CCS "Octagon Conference." Compare to Gilbert, *Churchill*, vol. VII, pp. 955-56, including n.5.

47.   CCS Meeting 172, Sept. 12, 1944, in CCS "Octagon Conference."

48.   See "Progress of Operations Report, Supreme Commander, Allied Expeditionary Force" (SCAF 78), Sept. 10, 1944, Combined Chiefs of Staff telegram to Supreme Headquarters, Allied Expeditionary Force (FACS 78), Sept. 12, 1944, both ibid.

49.   "[The first meeting] went off most satisfactorily and we found ourselves in complete agreement with [the] American Chiefs of Staff."; from Brooke Diary, Sept. 12, 1944, in Bryant, *Triumph*, p. 272.

50.   British Chiefs of Staff Memorandum, "British Participation in the War Against Japan," no date (but probably Sept. 14, 1944), and United States Chiefs of Staff, "British Participation in the War Against Japan," no date (but most likely Sept. 14, 1944), both ibid.

51.   Brooke Diary, Sept. 12, 1944, in Bryant, *Triumph*, p. 272.

52.   Gilbert, *Churchill*, vol. VII, p. 957.

53.   C. Thorne, *Allies of a Kind: The United States, Britain, and the War Against Japan, 1941-1945* (Oxford, 1978), p. 529.

54.   W. R. Louis, *Imperialism at Bay: The United States and the Decolonization of the British Empire, 1941-1945* (Oxford, 1978), pp. 356-57. Compare to K. Clymer, "Franklin D. Roosevelt, Louis Johnson, India, and Anticolonialism: Another Look," *Pacific Historical Review*, 57 (1988): 261-84; S. M. Habibuddin, "Franklin D. Roosevelt's Anti-Colonial Policy towards Asia: Its Implications for India, Indo-China, and Indonesia (1941-45)," *Journal of Indian History*, 53 (1975): 497-522; M. S. Venkataramani and B. K. Shrivastava, *Roosevelt, Gandhi, Churchill: America and the Last Phase of India's Freedom Struggle* (New Delhi, 1983).

55. Morgenthau Diary, Sept. 9, 1944, Morgenthau MSS [Roosevelt Library, Hyde Park, NY].

56. Compare to Dallek, *Roosevelt*, 467-78, which discusses the second Quebec Conference. His notes do not contain one archival source that shows Roosevelt's strategic thinking.

57. Except where noted, this paragraph is based on CCS meetings 173-176, Sept. 13-16, 1944, CCS memoranda, "Assumption of Command of 'Dragoon' Forces by Supreme Commander, Allied Expeditionary Force" (CCS 674), Sept. 11, 1944, "A Combined Memorandum on Troop Movements, Covering the Period October 1944 to March 1945" (CCS 675/1), Sept. 13, 1944, "Future Operations in the Mediterranean. Memorandum by the United States Chiefs of Staff" (CCS 677 and 677/1), Sept. 12-13, 1944, "Planning Date for the End of the War Against Japan. Memorandum by the British Chiefs of Staff" (CCS 678), 13 Sept. 1944, "Planning Date for the end of the War Against Japan" (CCS 678/1), Sept. 19, 1944, all CCS "Octagon Conference"; and "Meeting of the Combined Chiefs of Staff with Roosevelt and Churchill, September 13, 1944," "Meeting of the Combined Chiefs of Staff with Roosevelt and Churchill, September 16, 1944," both *FRUS, Quebec, 1944,* pp. 312-18, 377-83.

58. Weinberg, *World at Arms,* p. 727.

59. Brooke diary, Sept. 14, 1944, in Bryant, *Triumph,* p. 274.

60. "King-Cunningham Meeting, September 15th, 1944," *FRUS, Quebec, 1944,* pp. 350-54.

61. Thorne, *Allies of a Kind,* p. 416.

62. Treasury Department Memorandum, "Suggested Post-Surrender Program for Germany," Sept. 1, 1944, *FRUS, Quebec, 1944,* pp. 86-90. Compare to White [U.S. Treasury] Minute to Morgenthau, Sept. 1, 1944, with enclosures, especially. "Directive for Military Government in Germany under Phase I," "Political Guide," "Economic Guide for Germany," "Financial Guide for Germany," in Morgenthau Diary, Morgenthau MSS.

63. Morgenthau Diary, Aug. 19, 1944, ibid.

64. W. F. Kimball, *Swords or Ploughshares? The Morgenthau Plan for Defeated Germany, 1943-1946* (Philadelphia, 1978).

65. "Roosevelt-Churchill Dinner Meeting, September 13, 1944," *FRUS, Quebec, 1944,* pp. 324-328. There is no official record of this meeting, thus, the *FRUS* editors reconstructed it from the diaries of Moran and Admiral William Leahy, a Roosevelt adviser, a reminiscence of Morgenthau published in 1947, as well as U.S. Treasury and State Department records.

66. "Morgenthau-Cherwell Meeting, September 14, 1944," ibid.

67. Cherwell Memorandum, Sept. 14, 1944, ibid.

68. Colville [Churchill's private secretary] diary, Sept. 12, 1944, in J. Colville, *The Fringes of Power: 10 Downing Street Diaries 1939-1955* (New York/ London, 1985), p. 513. Compare to Sharp, *Zonal Division,* pp. 56-89.

69. See Gilbert, *Churchill,* vol. VII, pp. 961-62. Compare to Churchill, *Second World War,* vol. VI, pp. 156-57.

70. "Roosevelt-Churchill Meeting, September 15, 1944," *FRUS, Quebec, 1944,* pp. 360-62.
71. "Memorandum Initialled by President Roosevelt and Prime Minister Churchill," Sept. 15, 1944, ibid., pp. 466-67.
72. Stimson "Memorandum for the President," Sept. 9, 1944, in Morgenthau Diary, Morgenthau MSS.
73. "Roosevelt-Churchill Meeting, September 15, 1944," *FRUS Quebec 1944,* p. 362.
74. L. Woodward, *British Foreign Policy in the Second World War,* vol. V (London, 1976), pp. 226-27.
75. "Roosevelt-Churchill Dinner Meeting, September 13 1944," *FRUS Quebec, 1944,* pp. 327-28.
76. "Draft Protocol on the Zones of Occupation in Germany and the Administration of Greater Berlin," Aug. 3, 1944, ibid., pp. 386-88. Compare to B. Kuklick, *American Policy and the Division of Germany. The Clash with Russia over Reparations* (Ithaca, NY/London, 1972), pp. 19-46; Sharp, *Zonal Division,* pp. 56-89.
77. "Meeting of the Joint Chiefs of Staff . . . September 16, 1944," *FRUS, Quebec, 1944,* pp. 372-74.
78. Part 4 of CCS Meeting 176, Sept. 16, 1944, in CCS "Octagon Conference."
79. "Tripartite Luncheon Meeting, September 12, 1944," *FRUS Quebec, 1944,* p. 306. On the French question during the war, see J.-P. Cointet, "Les relations entre de Gaulle et le Gouvernement brittanique durant la seconde guerre mondiale," *Revue Historique,* 268 (1982): 432-52; F. Kersaudy, "Churchill and de Gaulle," in Parker, *Churchill,* pp. 124-34; D. S. White, "Charles de Gaulle et Franklin Roosevelt. Les chemins de la discorde," *Espoir,* (1974): 20-44.
80. Morgenthau Diary, Aug. 25, 1944, Morgenthau MSS.
81. "We won over the 'Zones' question." In Harvey Diary, Sept. 24, 1944, Harvey, *Diaries,* p. 357.
82. A year earlier, Churchill had proposed to Roosevelt "maintaining the Combined Anglo-American-Chiefs of Staff after the war 'on, say, a ten-year footing'"; three months after the Quebec Conference, "the P.M. said that after the war he was going to resign and devote himself to promoting good US - British relations." Both in Gilbert, *Churchill,* vol. VII, pp. 495-96, 1106.
83. Dallek, *Roosevelt,* p. 433.
84. Lord Avon [A. Eden], *The Eden Memoirs. The Reckoning* (London, 1965), p. 477.
85. "Minute by President Roosevelt and Prime Minister Churchill," 15 Sept. 1944, *FRUS, Quebec, 1944,* p. 469.
86. See Harvey Diary, Sept. 24, 1944, in Harvey, *Diaries,* pp. 357-58.
87. Compare to Eden's report to the War Cabinet, in WM (44)123, Minute 7, in Confidential Annex, CAB 65. It is recorded therein: "The Deputy Prime Minister [Clement Attlee] thought the outcome of the Quebec Conference

was a matter for great satisfaction, and he felt sure that the War Cabinet would wish to convey their congratulations to the Prime Minister."

88. Gilbert, *Churchill*, vol. VII, pp. 969-70; Dallek, *Roosevelt*, pp. 469-72.

89. Generally, see M. M. Gowing, *Britain and Atomic Energy, 1939-1945* (London, 1965).

90. "Aide-Mémoire Initialled by President Roosevelt and Prime Minister Churchill," Sept. 19, 1944, *FRUS, Quebec, 1944*, pp. 492-93, plus notes.

91. For example, State Department memorandum, "Anglo-American-Russian Relations," undated, State Department memorandum, "U.S. Relations with the Soviet Union," undated, Telegram, Harriman to Hopkins, Sept. 9, 1944, all ibid., pp. 190-93; British Chiefs of Staff Memorandum, "Machinery for Coordination of United States-Soviet-British Military Effort" (CCS 618/3), Sept. 12, 1944, Secretaries' note, "Machinery for Coordination of United States-Soviet-British Military Effort" (CCS 618/9), Sept. 12, 1944, both in CCS "Octagon Conference."

92. Telegram, Churchill to Roosevelt, Sept. 29, 1944, Kimball, *Churchill & Roosevelt*, vol. III, pp. 340-41. On Churchill and Eden's concern, see E. Barker, *British Policy in South East Europe during the Second World War* (London, 1976), p. 143; Gilbert, *Churchill*, vol. VII, pp. 978-84; L. Woodward, *British Foreign Policy in the Second World War*, vol. III (London, 1971), pp. 148-49.

93. Dallek, *Roosevelt*, p. 478.

94. Except where noted, the following paragraph is based on Barker, *British Policy*, pp. 140-47; Churchill, *Second World War*, vol. VI, pp. 226-43; P. G. H. Holdich, "A Policy of Percentages? British Policy and the Balkans after the Moscow Conference of October 1944," *International History Review*, 9 (1987): 28-47; P. Papastratis, "The Anglo-Soviet Balkan Agreement and Greece," in A. L. Macrakis, et al., *New Trends in Modern Greek Historiography* (Hanover, NH, 1982); A. Resis, "The Churchill-Stalin Secret 'Percentages' Agreement on the Balkans, Moscow, October 1944," *American Historical Review*, 83 (1978): 368-87; J. M. Siracusa, "The Meaning of TOLSTOY: Churchill, Stalin, and the Balkans, Moscow, October 1944," *Diplomatic History*, 3 (1979): 443-63; idem., "The Night Stalin and Hitler Divided Europe: The View from Washington," *Review of Politics*, 43 (1981): 381-410.

95. Romania (Russia 90 percent; the others, 10 percent); Greece (Britain, in accord with the United States, 90 percent; Russia 10 percent); Yugoslavia and Hungary (a 50 percent split each); and Bulgaria (Russia 75 percent; the others 25 percent). In Churchill, *Second World War*, vol. VI, p. 227.

96. For the implications concerning Yugoslavia, see A. Lane, *Britain, the Cold War and Yugoslav Unity, 1941-1949* (Brighton, England, 1996), pp. 47-48.

97. Telegram, Churchill to Stalin, Oct. 11, 1944, Kimball, *Churchill & Roosevelt*, vol. III, p. 353.

98. See Telegrams, Roosevelt to Churchill, Oct. 19, 22, 1944, ibid., pp. 363-64, 365-66. Compare to Dallek, *Roosevelt*, pp. 479-80.

99. Telegram, Churchill to Roosevelt, Nov. 8, 1944, Kimball, *Churchill & Roosevelt*, vol. III, p. 383.

THREE

HAPPILY ON
THE MARGINS

MACKENZIE KING AND CANADA AT
THE QUEBEC CONFERENCES

J. L. GRANATSTEIN

THE LATE CHARLES P. STACEY was Canada's most distinguished military historian, the official historian of the Canadian Army in the Second World War and, moreover, the author of the best book on Canadian policy in that war.[1] He was also no admirer of wartime Prime Minister William Lyon Mackenzie King[2] and, in the context of this commemoration of the Quebec Conference of 1944, a stern critic of his failure to press for a role in the negotiations over strategy between the United States and Britain. "At the two Quebec conferences," Stacey wrote, "Canada played merely the part of host, providing the whisky and soda, and was not admitted to the strategic discussions. But King was amply photographed with Churchill and Roosevelt, and few Canadians realized the true facts."[3]

Stacey's damning words suggest that the Canadian prime minister was interested only in the appearances, desirous merely that the Canadian public see him with his betters. They imply as well that King was little more than a fearful colonial, afraid to press Canada's case for equality of status or for a proper voice on the leaders of the Anglo-American alliance. No one can deny that there is more than a little truth in these charges, which have formed a part of the historical interpretation of Canada's war.

What Canadian historians, including Stacey, have not asked, however, is whether Canada had a legitimate claim to direct representation in the discussions at Quebec. Did the national contribution to the war merit such a place? Would representation at Quebec square with the Canadian arguments for application of the "functional principle" to representation in international organizations? And what consequences might have arisen with other allies had Canada participated? I will argue that the provision of whisky and soda in the historic city of Quebec was all to which Canada was entitled. Even so, by his presence, as well as his Cabinet colleagues and military staff, Mackenzie King, in fact, both acquired information and influenced events out of all proportion to Canada's role in the war.

The issue of Canadian representation at the Quebec discussions first arose when Quadrant, the 1943 meeting of Prime Minister Winston Churchill and President Franklin D. Roosevelt, was being arranged. In mid-July 1943, just after the Allies had landed in Sicily and just after the Canadian government had to fight very hard to ensure that its division-size representation in the assault received recognition in the official communiqués, Churchill indicated by telegram that he wanted to meet the president in the near future in Quebec. Mackenzie King discussed the suggestion with his Under-Secretary of State for External Affairs Norman Robertson and the British High Commissioner to Canada Malcolm MacDonald. King indicated that he had prepared a reply "cordially approving the idea," but Robertson "said immediately he thought my own position would have to be very carefully considered." MacDonald agreed and, feeling it would be embarrassing for King to raise this with Churchill, volunteered to do so to "make it quite clear that it would be a mistake to have the meeting at Quebec unless [King] were more than in the position merely of host to Churchill and Roosevelt in the eyes of the people." Very friendly with Robertson, a highly intelligent official,[4] and close to Mackenzie King (who had dandled this son of Ramsay MacDonald on his knee when he was a child), MacDonald was as full of warm feelings toward Canada as his suggestion indicated. Clearly, the high commissioner had succumbed to "localitis," the disease that often afflicts ambassadors who become advocates for the country to which they are accredited rather than for their own nation.

The prime minister, however, was dubious about the idea—"to try to get Churchill and Roosevelt to agree to this would be more than could be expected of them. They would wish to take the position that jointly they have supreme direction of the war. I have conceded them that position." In Mackenzie King's view, it would be enough if he was the host and was with them all the time they were in Quebec. Then the conference "would be regarded as between the three, as in fact it would be, in large part, without having the question raised too acutely or defended too sharply." But under the urgings of MacDonald and Robertson, King ultimately agreed to let MacDonald send a telegram to London on July 20 that set out his under-secretary's proposal.[5] "I know that Mr. Mackenzie King is assuming that in any meeting on Canadian soil he would be present throughout as host and that he would also be a party in discussions," the high commissioner said. Of course, there would be full opportunity for private Anglo-American talks, and King did not want to cause difficulties over the position of the other and absent Commonwealth premiers. Still, MacDonald added, "it would be extremely embarrassing politically" if King seemed to be "less than a fairly full partner in a meeting in Canada."[6]

Churchill grasped the matter and, in his reply on July 23, he suggested that King and the Canadian Chiefs of Staff participate in plenary sessions of the political and military discussions, a situation that would not prevent he and Roosevelt and their Combined Chiefs of Staff from having such private discussions as they wished.[7] As King noted in his diary, it was "quite clear Churchill saw the need of Conference appearing to be an Anglo-American-Canadian conference."[8]

But when the British leader put this plan to President Roosevelt, the American leader saw "insuperable difficulties in the Canadian Chiefs of Staff attending meetings of the Combined Chiefs of Staff." That would be sure to lead to demands from Brazil and China and other Allied and Commonwealth countries for representation on the Combined Chiefs.[9] This, as we shall see, was a line of argument Canadians had heard frequently before. Moreover, if the Canadians persisted, Roosevelt suggested to his friend Leighton McCarthy, the Canadian minister to the United States, he might not come to Quebec at all and would, if necessary, move the conference to Bermuda.[10] Rightly alarmed, King drew back from any suggestion that he or the Canadian chiefs ought to be directly involved, and he told Cabinet ministers, officials, and (through the Canadian minister in Washington) the president, that this did not upset him. The important thing "was to have the meeting held at Quebec. That, of itself, would cause all else to work out satisfactorily."[11] As Stacey put it, "King's anxiety not to give Roosevelt one moment's uneasiness is almost comic." He goes on to add that the Canadian "was not interested in a share in discussing strategy, about which he knew nothing."[12] This greatly overstates matters in my view, but if it was Stacey's position that King knew nothing about strategic questions, why then should the Canadian leader have pressed for a seat at the table? Why not be satisfied with the role of host?

In fact, again contrary to Stacey who suggested that Canadians had no more to do with the actual Quebec Conference "than if it had been held in Timbuctoo,"[13] King did achieve much more than the provision of Scotch and soda. To start, Churchill proposed that the British and Canadian Chiefs of Staff meet and added that he and King "can confer formally on various important Imperial questions which are outstanding." King informed his Cabinet War Committee of this, took them to Quebec with him, and important discussions duly occurred.[14] There would also prove to be ample opportunity for Mackenzie King to have private discussions at Quadrant with both the prime minister and the president.[15]

The simple truth is that King had understood what was involved in the meeting at Quebec City in August 1943 better than Robertson or Mac-Donald. The leaders of the Anglo-American alliance had delicate issues to discuss—including further action against Italy and the timing of the invasion of France—and could not afford to let Canada, a spear-carrier in the middle rank of the Allied chorus—inside the room when they were being considered. The Combined Chiefs of Staff similarly could not allow the Canadian Chiefs to attend meetings and successfully maintain their barrier to representation of the lesser allies. Of course, King knew that his role as host and the widespread circulation of photographs in the press would be helpful to him and his government, but he and his ministers, officials, and officers also received full value from their attendance at Quebec. They were kept up-to-date on much of the Anglo-American military and political discussions, including subjects ranging from postwar world organization, the sharing of information on the development of the atomic bomb in which Canada was a junior, but heavily involved, partner,[16] and policy to international civil aviation, aside entirely from bilateral discussions they held with their British and (less frequently) with their American counterparts. It is almost certainly true that Canadians knew more of Allied strategic plans after Quadrant than any other of the lesser Allies. Admittedly, there was much they could not find out.[17]

Above all, as Mackenzie King had grasped at once, the Quadrant Conference served Canadian domestic purposes. In the summer of 1943, the country was weary of the war it had been involved in for four years, tired of restrictions and rationing, and awaiting with increasing trepidation the heavy casualty tolls yet to come. The Liberal government was at its lowest point in popular esteem (in September, Canadian Institute of Public Opinion polls showed it with only 28 percent support), and the fragile unity between French and English Canadians was wearing thin as complaints from Quebec about French Canadians being denied their share of field commands and contracts clashed head on with English Canada's boiling resentment that francophone enlistments were well below the average elsewhere.[18] The Quebec Conference distracted and inspired the country, and the prominent place accorded Mackenzie King, even if only in photographs, conveyed the sense that Canada was a valued partner in the Allied effort. That had to help.

One of the most important discussions Mackenzie King had during the Quebec Conference of 1943 was with Churchill on August 10. "I got a good chance both at dinner and after to speak of my problem which is Canada's problem—namely having a voice in all matters pertaining to the war."[19] There is, to be sure, a certain irony in King, having carried self-abnegation to the point he had in making the arrangements for Quadrant, raising this matter in private discussion with Churchill. In fact, however, his was a recurrent Canadian theme.

For purely domestic reasons, King had hung back from pressing Britain for much of a share in the direction of the war after September 1939.[20] In the prime minister's view, the memory of the divisions of the Great War, and the abhorrence of conscription for overseas service in what many in 1940s Quebec still persisted in viewing as an Imperial war, demanded that French Canada receive delicate handling. One aspect of this was that he not visit Britain, so that none could suggest that the Imperial War Cabinet of the earlier conflict had been re-created. Moreover, the fact that King was not invited to the Churchill-Roosevelt Atlantic Charter meeting of August 1941 and did not visit London for the first two years of the war called into question another of the public perceptions he had fostered, namely that Canada was the indispensable linchpin between Britain and the United States.[21]

The pressures on Canada soon increased even further. The United States' entry into the war in December 1941, an undoubted blessing for the hard-pressed British Commonwealth, pushed Canada into the background even further, and there was an almost schizophrenic response in Ottawa as events developed. On the one hand, there was great satisfaction that Britain and the United States were now working hand in glove; on the other, Ottawa felt left out as a result of the new Anglo-American unity that confirmed Canadian diplomats' secondary status. After Churchill visited the United States in December, the two Great Powers set out to coordinate their war effort. The Combined Chiefs of Staff Committee was set up to run the military war effort, while a series of combined boards coordinated the economic struggle. No Canadian seriously sought a place with the Combined Chiefs of Staff—the country's military contribution, large though it was in Canadian terms, was merely a small part of a vast array.[22] But Canada's economic war effort was a different matter, and Ottawa was shocked that its material contribution to the war was simply assumed.

Canada was producing vast quantities of food and raw materials and, by the beginning of 1942, its factories had hit their stride, and war production moved out of the shops and across the Atlantic in a torrent.[23]

And Canada had received very little for all its efforts. It had been completely shut out of the direction of the war by an ungrateful London and Washington. Was Canada's war production now to be allocated by the new Boards without so much as a by-your-leave to Ottawa?

It fell to Hume Wrong to draft the response to the Anglo-American affront to Canadian prestige. The minister-counselor at the Washington Legation was the most clearheaded member of the Department of External Affairs, and he understood that Canada had been omitted in substantial part because "the Government has hitherto adopted in these matters what may unkindly be called a semi-colonial position. . . . We have tended . . . to be satisfied with the form rather than the substance."[24] From the sidelines to which Canada had relegated itself, Wrong found the way out when he suggested the governing principle that should apply for Canada and other lesser allies in relations with the Great Powers: "each member of the grand alliance should have a voice in the conduct of the war proportionate to its contribution to the general war effort. A subsidiary principle is that the influence of the various countries should be greatest in connection with those matters with which they are most directly concerned."[25]

As yet there was no name for this idea (which drew on studies of functionalism then circulating through academe), though its formulation clearly marked the beginning of the middle power concept that Canada would later champion during the rest of the war and into the postwar era. Canadians nonetheless began using this argument regularly. The first charge came in July 1942 when Ottawa, the most important Allied producer of foodstuffs after the United States, tried to secure a seat on the Combined Food Board, the Anglo-American agency designed to allocate food supplies. Consulted first, London replied with the infuriating argument that membership "would not make for technical efficiency" and offered support only for Canadian membership on the much less important Combined Production and Resources Board. Prime Minister Mackenzie King, showing what one disgruntled diplomat called "the strong glove over the velvet hand,"[26] overrode his advisers and accepted the offer; Canada became a member of the Combined Production and Resources Board, one of the combined boards without much of a role.

But in March 1943, the Canadian government renewed its claim for a seat on the Combined Food Board. Again the British were reluctant, now countering Ottawa with the argument that if Canada won a seat, Australia and Argentina would demand one too. The infuriated Canadians responded that when those countries produced as much food as Canada, the second-largest food-producing Allied nation, they too would be entitled to a place on the Combined Food Board. Not until October, after much hard bargaining and threats that Canadian financial aid to Britain would cease unless Canada received its due, London and Washington finally conceded. Canada accepted membership on the board, the only smaller nation to win such status.

Victory here was hard to repeat, however. Created in 1942, the United Nations Relief and Rehabilitation Administration was the Allies' organization designed to distribute aid to liberated territories. Canada was expected to be one of the major contributors, but the Great Powers had also decided that Canada was to have no seat on the senior directing committee of UNRRA. The "Americans might not like the British side overweighed by Canadian representation,"[27] Whitehall officials said. Such a response was guaranteed to get Ottawa riled, its officials convinced that Canada was a nation in its own right and no mere British satellite. The maneuvering went on for months, and British, American, and Soviet stalling led Ottawa to put Hume Wrong's doctrine into principled phrases. In a diplomatic note in January 1943, the Canadians pressed their argument "that no workable international system can be based on the concentration of influence and authority wholly in bodies composed of a few great powers to the exclusion of all the rest. It is not always the largest powers that have the greatest contribution to make to the work of these bodies. In international economic organizations such as the Relief Administration representation . . . can often be determined on a functional basis and in our view this principle should be applied whenever it is feasible."[28]

The position had been spelled out, and Canada continued to argue its case with vigor for another three months. Unfortunately, when the British pressed King to yield, offering a place on UNRRA's supplies committee and representation on the key policy committee whenever supply questions were discussed, the prime minister yet again conceded, fearing the ill-will of the Great Powers. King was likely correct, for he had no stomach to try to bring UNRRA crashing down, almost the only alternative. As it was, Canada gave 1 percent of its GNP to UNRRA in 1943. Similar sums followed in future years.

UNRRA was a test case for Canada. It had argued its case with great vigor and lost. But the functional principle on which the government had stood its ground was worth reiteration. On July 9, 1943, just a month before the first Quebec Conference, King explained the Canadian conception of functionalism to Parliament and the Canadian people: "A number of new international organizations are likely to be set up as a result of the war. . . . In the view of the government, effective representations on these bodies should neither be restricted to the largest states nor necessarily extended to all states. Representation should be determined on a functional basis which will admit to full membership those countries, large or small, which have the greatest contribution to make to the particular object in question."[29] Simply put, this meant that if, for example, Canada produced a significant share of the world's food or if it held a crucial place in civil aviation, the Great Powers could not deny it a voice in decisions on those subjects because Canada itself was not a Great Power.

Did the functional principle as enunciated by King in Parliament in July entitle Canada to a place at the table at Quebec in August? Norman Robertson and Malcolm MacDonald presumably thought it did, but Mackenzie King did not. The prime minister was right, not the under-secretary and the high commissioner. Functionalism should have qualified Canada for a key role in UNRRA and on the various economic combined boards. It did not, despite the country's very substantial military contribu-tion, entitle Canada to a place on the Combined Chiefs of Staff. By what right, therefore, was Canada entitled to have its Chiefs of Staff sit with the Combined Chiefs at Quebec? By what right did the functional principle entitle Mackenzie King, the leader of a nation of just over 11 million people, to sit as an equal with Churchill and Roosevelt for strategic discussions on the course of the war? What Canada was entitled to, what all the lesser Allies were entitled to, was control over the disposition of their military and economic resources and full consultation on all broad questions of policy. That Canada did not always achieve these does not take away from the fact that the Dominion had no valid claim to representation at Quebec. Mackenzie King, in other words, was truer to the government's functional principle than his advisers, and if he recognized that the most that he, his government, and Canada could get from the Quadrant Conference was publicity and bilateral meetings, that was enough for him. The provision of whisky and soda was cheap at twice the price for those rewards which helped encourage the Canadian war effort—and the Liberal government.

When Mackenzie King learned on August 12, 1944, that Churchill and Roosevelt again wished to meet in Quebec the next month, he was instantly agreeable. "I supposed they would expect me to act as host as I did before," he said to Britain's deputy high commissioner. "If so, I shall be very happy to so act." The idea of another conference in Canada delighted the prime minister, in part because, as he noted, it "gives a further reason why there should be no immediate haste with an election." The main reason, however, was that "I shall really enjoy I think being at Quebec with the President and Churchill. Besides nothing could be more interesting than the questions which will be discussed and to be so completely on the inside in relation to all of them would mean a great deal. Moreover the close relationship of Churchill, the President and myself cannot fail to be of help to me politically. Altogether I greatly welcome the prospect."[30]

Important questions were to be discussed at Octagon, as the second Quebec Conference was code-named, relating to the end of the war in Europe—which in August 1944 looked to be approaching with some speed—the prosecution of the war against Japan, the continuing development of the atomic bomb, and the establishment of a postwar world organization. From Canada's point of view, the most important of these issues requiring immediate decision was the Pacific War and the question of if and how Canada would participate.

That question had been under consideration in Ottawa for some months, with the military services and the politicians preparing their arguments and counterarguments.[31] For Canada, the Pacific theater was largely terra incognita, and Canadian eyes, except to some extent in British Columbia, remained firmly fixed on Europe.[32] Moreover, the hasty decision in the fall of 1941 to accede to a British request to send an understrength brigade to garrison Hong Kong—a force lost to a man when the Crown colony fell to the Japanese on Christmas Day, 1941—had left Canadians unhappy about the Far Eastern war and some less than pleased with British stewardship of it. There was almost no public desire, in other words, for a major role in the Pacific. Against this, however, was the sense of duty that impelled the government, a feeling that Canada's fine record in the war could not be allowed to be jeopardized by too scant a contribution.

Whether the United States wanted a Canadian contribution to the final phase of the war against Japan—or even a British one—was also uncertain until the Quebec Conference. The U.S. Navy, in particular, was markedly unenthusiastic about any British participation in the coming assault on Japan. London, on the other hand, had its own reasons for wanting to be in at the kill, and it most definitely wanted substantial Canadian air, ground, and sea participation to help bolster its position. The three Canadian defense ministers and their Chiefs of Staff generally agreed, making plans for a very large contribution, though there were serious concerns in the Cabinet War Committee about where and how to participate. The prime minister, for one, was dead set against participation in the Southwest Pacific, convinced that jungle warfare was unlikely to prove Canada's metier. Nor did he want Canadian forces to work with Britain in reimposing colonialism on the Imperial possessions that had been incorporated into Japan's Greater East Asia Co-Prosperity Sphere. "I held very strongly to the view that no government in Canada once the war in Europe was over," King told his ministers, "would send its men to India, Burma and Singapore to fight . . . and hope to get through a general election successfully. That to permit this would be to raise at a general election, a nation-wide cry of Imperial wars versus Canada as a nation."[33] With the last national elections having been held in March 1940, King had to go to the polls in the near future, and Quebec, the heart of his party's strength, remained restive, and all the more so since Maurice Duplessis' autonomist and *nationaliste* Union Nationale had just been returned to power in provincial elections in August 1944. At the second Quebec Conference, Mackenzie King would make sure that Duplessis "was given as much recognition as possible," his aide J. W. Pickersgill later recalled, for he realized "that if a crisis arose there would be an unfriendly government in Quebec ready to fish in troubled waters."[34]

On September 6, 1944, a few days before the second Quebec Conference began, the Cabinet made the basic decisions about future participation in the war against Japan, although King took the view that Canada had to know the Anglo-American plans before Canada's role was definitively determined.[35] He noted in his diary that "all were agreed Canada should participate. Seemed to be a consensus of view of having one division prepared to go to Japan; one to remain as army of occupation in Europe. Navy to be cut down 50%. The contribution of the Air Force to be made smaller than [the 58 squadrons originally] contemplated."

The formal decision was that Canadian forces would "participate in the war against Japan in operational theatres of direct interest to Canada as a North American nation, for example in the North or Central Pacific, rather than in more remote areas such as Southeast Asia." Reflecting the prime minister's view, the scale and form of the contribution were to be definitively decided after the Quebec meeting,[36] subject to the Americans allowing Canada and Britain in at the kill.

The Canadian ideas went to the meeting the Cabinet War Committee had with Churchill and the two countries' Chiefs of Staff in Quebec on September 14. The prime minister's position had stiffened even further on confining Canadian participation to the North Pacific; indeed the day before he had told one of his ministers "that I would have to consider whether I could allow my name to be associated with a Canadian Ministry that would go that far . . . If it was decided our forces had to fight in southern Asia, I would have to say as Prime Minister, I could not agree to such a policy and would have to leave it to other Members of the Government to carry it out."[37]

King explained his position to Churchill—carefully noting as one politician to another that he faced a general election and everything had to be considered in the light of that event—and Churchill accepted it. As King recorded the discussion, the British prime minister "made quite clear that he did not expect the Canadians to fight in any tropical region . . . our men should not be expected to go into the South Pacific."[38] Thus, when the British leader offered a Royal Navy fleet to share in the assault on Japan and President Roosevelt accepted it, Churchill then added that Canada wanted to participate in the north Pacific. This was also agreed in principle. King confirmed all this in a private talk with the president that same evening. "I feel immensely relieved in my mind as a result," King wrote. "I can now see the road pretty clear ahead, first of all as to our contribution in the Pacific; there is no reason why it should be made one that would be costly in life."[39] Conscription, the shibboleth against which King had struggled for five years, in other words, could not become essential because of the commitment of a single division to the war in Asia.[40] Moreover, the decision to participate in this way meant that the Canadian infantry division allocated for the invasion of Japan, if not the naval and air contributions that were to be under overall British command, was destined to serve under American command and with a U.S. Army table of organization and U.S. weapons.[41] This was a major departure for the country and yet another sign of the way global power had shifted during the war. Those decisions over the Pacific War were the major ones that directly concerned Canada at Quebec.

Mackenzie King also had ample opportunity to talk with Churchill and Roosevelt during the meetings on a host of topics. For example, the Canadian prime minister had persuaded Roosevelt and Churchill to agree to accept honorary degrees from McGill University at a special convocation on September 16. At a lunch just before the ceremony, King made a major interjection with the president, speaking out very strongly against Roosevelt's plan to have an international conference on world organization a week before the American presidential elections in early November. The Canadian leader knew the details of the Dumbarton Oaks Great Power proposals on international organization (made public only on October 10), and he feared that their being put before smaller countries might hurt the president's reelection campaign, or so King argued. "That once it was learned that the four great powers . . . were to have the main authority of the Council to tell other nations what other contributions they might have to make in carrying out the decisions of the Council, there would almost certainly be strong objection on the part certainly of the small nations. . . . I pointed out that in Canada the nationalist feeling would be aroused in opposition to the proposals. . . . That what I feared was that with so many persons in the States of foreign descent, they would all likely side with anyone who became champions of the smaller nations."

It was not, of course, only Canadian "nationalist feeling" that resisted the Big Four's attempt to seize all power for themselves with their proposals—King's own government had led and continued to lead the attack against this position. Nonetheless, Churchill and Anthony Eden, present for this well-meaning Canadian advice on how to fight the American election, agreed with Mackenzie King, adding that they believed this conference "might really injure" the president's chances of reelection.[42] Roosevelt then departed, no doubt puzzled and gratified in equal part by the tactical advice he had received, and the second Quebec Conference was over.

Before Churchill left for home, he and King spoke at length on the role and manner in which Canada had played its part in the war. Churchill waxed eloquent, as the Canadian noted in his diary, about how "you have been so fine about letting England lead, not making it difficult for us by insisting always on several having direction. I said it had been difficult to maintain my position at times but that as long as I knew we were being consulted and getting informed on new policies and were able to speak about them before they were settled, I thought it was much better before the world to leave the matter of leadership in the hands of the President and himself. He said that had meant everything in the effecting of needed co-operation."[43] Whether Canada was always consulted and informed and whether it always had the opportunity to speak out before decisions were implemented might well be questioned, but of King's sincerity here there can be no question. The functional principle, in his view, entitled Canada to be treated seriously when it had the capacity to make a major contribution, as was certainly the case on economic and relief matters. But on grand strategy, it was different. On such questions, the Canadian prime minister was happily on the margins, most interested in contributing what little he could to facilitating the progress of the war.

Hanging back was not the stuff of nationalist myth, not the bold course. But it was the practical, sensible, and correct position—and doubly so as King (who knew this better than anyone) could not have crashed the table at Quebec City in 1943 or 1944 in any case. That Mackenzie King also received the opportunity to influence events and undoubted political benefits from his limited role at Quadrant and Octagon was a very large bonus, well worth the contribution of even the largest quantities of whisky. When his government won reelection in June 1945, thanks in substantial part to surprisingly heavy support from Quebec voters, he knew that his policy had been the right one.

NOTES

1. C. P. Stacey, *Arms, Men and Governments: The War Policies of Canada 1939-1945* (Ottawa, 1970).
2. For the fullest expression of Stacey's view of King, see his *A Very Double Life: The Private World of Mackenzie King* (Toronto, 1976).
3. C. P. Stacey, *Canada and the Age of Conflict: 1921-1948. The Mackenzie King Era,* vol. II (Toronto, 1981), p. 334. Much the same phrasing, happily omitting the dreadful use of "true facts" (which was most uncharacteristic of Stacey's ordinarily splendid prose), was used in his *Mackenzie King and the Atlantic Triangle* (Toronto, 1976), p. 58.
4. See on Robertson, J. L. Granatstein, *A Man of Influence: Norman Robertson and Canadian Statecraft 1929-1968* (Ottawa, 1981). There is as yet no satisfactory study of MacDonald's important tenure in Canada.
5. National Archives of Canada, W. L. M. King Papers, King Diary, July 19, 1943; J. W. Pickersgill, ed., *The Mackenzie King Record: 1939-44,* vol. I (Toronto, 1960), pp. 527-28.
6. J. F. Hilliker, ed., *Documents on Canadian External Relations: 1942-1943,* vol. IX [hereafter *DCER* plus volume number] (Ottawa, 1980), p. 253.
7. Ibid., pp. 253-54.
8. King Diary, July 23, 1943.
9. *DCER,* vol. IX, p. 255.
10. King Diary, July 24, 1943; U.S. Dept. of State, *Foreign Relations of the United States Conferences at Washington and Quebec 1943* [hereafter *FRUS* plus volume title], (Washington, 1970), p. 397.
11. King Diary, July 24, 1943.
12. Stacey, *Mackenzie King and the Atlantic Triangle,* p. 58.
13. Stacey, *Arms, Men and Governments,* p. 182.
14. *DCER,* vol. IX, p. 254; NAC, Privy Council Office Records, Cabinet War Committee Meetings, Aug. 10, 1943.
15. Pickersgill, *Mackenzie King,* vol. I, pp. 534ff.; *DCER,* vol. IX, pp. 256-58.
16. On this subject, see Robert Bothwell's books, *Eldorado: Canada's National Uranium Company* (Toronto, 1984) and *Nucleus: The History of Atomic Energy of Canada Limited* (Toronto, 1988).
17. See, for example, *DCER,* vol. IX, pp. 256-58, and the account of Lt. Gen. Maurice Pope, *Soldiers and Politicians: the Memoirs of Lt.-Gen. Maurice A. Pope* (Toronto, 1962), pp. 221ff. Pope's report on the 1943 conference (pp. 228-31), however, demonstrates how much he did uncover.
18. Norman Hillmer put it well in his description of the 1944 Quebec meeting: "the Prime Minister's eye was on another Quebec . . . more interested in the defence of Canada than the salvation of Europe." "Canada as an Ally" (address delivered at the Society for Military History, Kingston, Ont., May 22, 1993). The usual assessment is that French Canada contributed less than 20 percent

of military manpower though its population represented more than 30 percent of the Canadian total.

19. King Diary, Aug. 15, 1943. Stacey acknowledges these discussions in *Arms, Men and Governments,* p. 183.

20. Before the war (at the Imperial Conference of 1937, for example), King had successfully resisted every effort by London, Canberra, and Wellington to achieve defense coordination prior to the outbreak of hostilities. His argument was based on the need to preserve Canadian unity and on the principle that each part of the Empire was primarily responsible only for its own defense.

21. See J. L. Granatstein, "The Man Who Wasn't There: Mackenzie King, Canada, and the Atlantic Charter," in *The Atlantic Charter,* eds. D. Brinkley and D. R. Facey-Crowther, (New York, 1994), pp. 115ff.

22. The Canadian armed forces enlisted 1.1 million men and women out of a population of less than 12 million. This produced the First Canadian Army of five divisions and two armored brigades, plus additional units in North America; the Royal Canadian Navy, the fourth largest Allied navy, which escorted half of all convoys across the North Atlantic; and the Royal Canadian Air Force that, in addition to running the British Commonwealth Air Training Plan that trained 131,000 aircrew, operated 85 squadrons while also providing tens of thousands of aircrew for the Royal Air Force.

23. So great was the flow that in 1942 the Canadian government gave Britain a gift of a billion dollars worth of war supplies, a testimony to Canada's support for the war effort and to its recognition that England could not pay for all it needed. Similar gifts, called Mutual Aid in an effort to allay widespread French-Canadian concerns that Britain was getting something for nothing, were repeated until the end of the war, amounting in all to $3.5 billion—or approximately one-fifth of Canada's total war costs. To put these numbers in context, the GNP in 1945 was $11 billion.

24. Department of External Affairs, Ottawa, [hereafter DEA], External Affairs Records [hereafter EAR], File 3265-A-40C, Wrong to L. B. Pearson, Feb. 3, 1942. See also J. L. Granatstein, "Hume Wrong's Road to the Functional Principle," in *Coalition Warfare,* eds. K. Neilson and R. Prete (Waterloo, Ont., 1983), pp. 53ff.

25. EAR, File 3265-A-40C, Wrong to N. A. Robertson, Jan. 20, 1942.

26. King Papers, L. B. Pearson Memorandum, Mar. 18, 1943, ff. C241878.

27. King Diary, July 30, 1942.

28. DEA, File 2295-G-40, Memorandum, Robertson to King, Jan. 18, 1943.

29. House of Commons, *Debates,* July 9, 1943, p. 4558.

30. King Diary, Aug. 12, 1944.

31. A useful collection of documents on this subject are collected in *DCER,* vol. X, pp. 368ff.

32. Canada, King said later, "had not an acre of land or property in the Orient," and B. Greenhous et al., *The Crucible of War: The Official History of the Royal Canadian Air Force,* vol. III (Toronto, 1994), notes, "Canadians thought not one whit about the Pacific and the war against Japan" (p. 106).

33. King Diary, Sept. 13, 1944.
34. J. W. Pickersgill, *Seeing Canada Whole: A Memoir* (Toronto, 1994), p. 239.
35. King Diary, Aug. 31, 1944.
36. C. P. Stacey, *Arms, Men and Governments,* p. 58.
37. King Diary, Sept. 13, 1944.
38. Ibid., Sept. 14, 1944; Cabinet War Committee Minutes, Sept. 14, 1944.
39. King Diary, 14 Sept. 1944.
40. During his stay in Quebec City, King made a speech at the city's Reform Club in which he spoke indiscreetly about how he had prevented conscription and how, with the war all but won, it would never be imposed. This provoked a sharp reaction from his Defence Minister J. L. Ralston. In fact, by late October the First Canadian Army in northwest Europe was desperately short of infantry reinforcements and King saved his government only through desperate maneuverings. See J. L. Granatstein, *Canada's War: The Politics of the Mackenzie King Government, 1939-1945* (Toronto, 1990), pp. 333ff.
41. *DCER,* vol. X, pp. 419-20, details meetings between the Canadian Chief of the General Staff and Gen. G. C. Marshall on Sept. 16, 1944, to discuss details of Canadian army participation with the U.S. forces. See on this and the conference generally, Pope, *Soldiers and Politicians,* pp. 241ff. The Canadian air contribution to the Pacific war is exhaustively detailed in Greenhous, et al., *The Crucible of War,* pp. 106ff. and more concisely in Hillmer, "Canada as an Ally," 10ff.
42. King Diary, Sept. 16, 1944.
43. Ibid., Sept. 17, 1944.

FOUR

COMING TO GRIPS WITH THE "GERMAN PROBLEM"
ROOSEVELT, CHURCHILL, AND THE MORGENTHAU PLAN AT THE SECOND QUEBEC CONFERENCE[1]

DAVID B. WOOLNER

There can be no peace on earth—no security for any man, woman, or child, if aggressor nations like Germany and Japan retain any power to strike at their neighbors.

It is not enough for us to say "we will disarm Germany and Japan and *hope* that they will learn to behave themselves as decent people." Hoping is not enough.

—Henry Morgenthau Jr.,
in an address to the British people, August 16,1944[2]

I cannot treat as realistic the suggestion that such an area [as the Ruhr] in the present economic condition of the world can be turned into a nonproductive "ghost territory" when it has become the center of one of the most industrialized continents in the world, populated by peoples of energy, vigor and progressiveness. . . .

Such methods, in my opinion, do not prevent war; they breed war.

—Henry Stimson, September 5, 1944[3]

THE DISCUSSIONS AT THE SECOND QUEBEC CONFERENCE are perhaps most famous for having brought about one of the most controversial policy battles of the Second World War, involving a key issue—the postwar planning for Germany—and an unlikely figure, U.S. Treasury Secretary, Henry Morgenthau, Jr. This policy battle erupted with the introduction of the so-called Morgenthau Plan, which was endorsed by Churchill and Roosevelt in a memorandum issued at the Second Quebec Conference on September 15, 1944. The Morgenthau Plan was controversial because it demanded nothing less than the deindustrialization of Germany through the removal or destruction of her physical plant, what Churchill in the September 15 memorandum referred to as "pastoralization," and which the *New York Times* later interpreted as the postwar conversion of Germany "into a nation of small farms."[4] The plan also called for the disarmament, dismemberment, and denazification of the Reich and the swift punishment of all Germans involved in war crimes. But it was Morgenthau's call for deindustrialization—in short the destruction of the Ruhr and the Saar regions of Germany—that sparked the most controversy and led to a heated battle over postwar planning among Churchill's and Roosevelt's top advisers.[5]

The question at the core of this controversy was how to solve "the German problem"—the widespread belief that the existence of a powerful and united Germany was incompatible with world peace. The formal title of Morgenthau's proposal—"Program to Prevent Germany from Starting a World War III"—makes this eminently clear.[6] Underlying Morgenthau's demand for the dismemberment and deindustrialization of the German state, lay the conviction that the German people themselves, and not merely the Nazis, were inherently aggressive and militaristic and must be punished for their crimes against humanity. In the eyes of Morgenthau and many of his fellow countrymen, the Germans were responsible for the outbreak of two world wars, had engaged in unspeakable atrocities against the Jews and others, and would more than likely cause a third world war if the character of the German people and nation was not thoroughly reformed. As a sensitive and humane individual and a Jew who was deeply outraged by the Holocaust, Morgenthau believed that it was not enough simply to disarm Germany. One also had to recast the German soul, to root out the evil that had led to the rise of Nazism and the subsequent drive to establish a racially pure Aryan empire based on the Eurasian continent. The Morgenthau Plan represented a serious attempt to come to terms with these difficult questions—motivated in part by the belief that the world would never be free from the fear of war until the twin evils of German Nazism and Prussian militarism were permanently destroyed. The conversion of Germany into a pastoral state, therefore, was not merely a reflection of the desire to deindustrialize Germany and hence destroy her war-making potential, it was also an attempt to reform the German character and transform the once powerful German nation into a small collection of simple, peace-loving, agrarian democracies.[7]

To a certain extent, both Roosevelt and Churchill supported Morgenthau's sentiments about the need for a "harsh peace." Like Morgenthau, both leaders had been appalled by reports detailing Hitler's plans to systematically murder the entire Jewish population of Europe as well as other racial or ethnic groups deemed unworthy of life by the Nazis.[8] The two leaders also agreed that the German people as a whole must be held accountable for the crimes committed under the Nazi banner and that following the war all traces of Nazism and Prussian militarism must cease to exist. The reform of the German character, therefore, was also very much on the minds of Roosevelt and Churchill and even before Morgenthau first enunciated his ideas for the peace both men had come to the conclusion that the German people must suffer as a consequence of their actions. This would require the complete disarmament and total defeat of the enemy—as evidenced by the call for "unconditional surrender"—the denazification of German society, reparations—at least as far as Churchill was concerned—to help with the overall reconstruction of Europe, the punishment and summary execution of leading Nazi officials and officers, and eventually, the breakup of the German state itself.[9]

Prior to the summer of 1944, however, none of these ideas had been worked out in any great detail and there remained wide areas of disagreement between Churchill and Roosevelt as to the manner and degree to which these items might be carried out. Churchill, reflecting the prevailing view of his government, for example, was more enthusiastic about the prospect of collecting reparations from Germany than was Roosevelt. Churchill also believed that Prussia and Prussian militarism were at the core of the German problem, and as such, tended to place greater emphasis on the need to eliminate Prussian influence from German society. Moreover, although the two leaders came to an agreement in principle with Soviet Premier Joseph Stalin at the 1943 Teheran Conference on the need to partition Germany after the war, no final decision on this matter had been taken. The defeat of Germany still seemed a long way off, and the three men had varying opinions as to the best means to accomplish this goal. Roosevelt, for instance, suggested the breakup of Germany into five or more states (plus two additional regions placed under international control), while Churchill, more concerned than his American counterpart about the expansion of Soviet influence into Central and southeastern Europe, proposed the creation of a Danubian Federation from parts of southern

Germany, Austria, and Hungary.[10] Churchill also proposed the separation of East Prussia from the bulk of Germany proper, in part as a means to do away with the Prussian menace. Stalin cared less for means than for ends. The important thing, he insisted, was that whatever shape or shapes Germany took after the war (and Stalin preferred the breakup of Germany into as many states as possible), she must never again be allowed to wage war. This would require, at the very least, rigid control of her industry and the complete occupation of the country by the Allies. All in all, however, with the Normandy invasion still looming on the horizon, there seemed to be no pressing need to issue precise directives on how best to solve the German problem. Hence, the question of partition was referred to the newly created European Advisory Commission, or EAC, which had been established in London following the October 1943 meeting of the Allied foreign ministers in Moscow, and concerns over matters such as reparations and the control of German industry were left largely in abeyance.[11]

This lack of direction from the top on how best to proceed with Germany following the war had important consequences in both London and Washington. The inability of the Big Three to come to a consensus on the specifics of postwar German policy did not stop officials in both capitals from developing plans for the treatment of Germany after the war. As a consequence, a number of different institutions became involved in developing plans for postwar Germany, each with its own agenda. Moreover, the tendency for both Roosevelt and Churchill to try to divorce military matters from political affairs meant that much of the planning that did go on proceeded in a kind of vacuum, largely cut off from the ideas being considered at the highest levels of government. So long as the defeat of Germany remained somewhere in the distant future, this lack of communication did not pose a serious problem. But by August 1944, following the successful Allied drive across northern France in the wake of the Normandy invasion, when it suddenly appeared that German resistance might collapse and that the Allies might in fact take possession of Germany in a matter of weeks, the need for concrete proposals on the treatment of defeated Germany became an urgent matter. Suddenly, a whole host of proposals concerning postwar German policy began to emerge, particularly from the War and State departments in Washington, and the Foreign Office in London. Most of these plans, however, bore little or no resemblance to the discussions that had gone on among Roosevelt, Churchill, and Stalin at Teheran, or the ideas that would shortly be enunciated by Morgenthau at the Second Quebec Conference. As a consequence, a furious debate would soon break out among a number of key institutions and individuals over how best to solve the German problem.

As noted, it was Morgenthau's involvement in this question that precipitated this debate. Yet, it must be remembered that prior to the summer of 1944 neither the Treasury Department nor Secretary Morgenthau had had much to do with the planning for postwar Germany. To this point, in fact, Morgenthau remained largely unaware of the work that had gone on at the War Office and the State Department, or for that matter at the British Foreign Office, over the future of the Reich. But on August 6, 1944, while on an airplane en route to London to discuss currency policy in liberated France, Morgenthau was handed a memorandum on the State Department's economic policy for postwar Germany written by U.S. Secretary of State Cordell Hull's chief economic adviser, Leo Pasvolsky, which he found deeply disturbing. Hull was the Roosevelt administration's leading Wilsonian. He was a firm believer in the third of Wilson's famous Fourteen Points, which called for the removal of international barriers to trade and the establishment of a new world commercial order based on the multilateral application of traditional American capitalism. Hull also believed, like Wilson, that economic nationalism was one of the primary causes of war and that the establishment of this new world order would lead to peace, prosperity, and the expansion of democracy. Hull's convictions were enhanced by his experience in the 1930s. To a large extent Hull blamed the onset of the Great Depression and the subsequent rise of fascism on restrictive trade practices. He abhorred the British system of imperial preference (which granted preferential treatment to goods traded within the British empire), and was equally contemptuous of the Nazis' drive for autarky. Indeed, in his view, both of these closed economic systems had contributed to the spread of global violence and were in part responsible for the seemingly inexorable march toward war that so characterized the international relations of the 1930s.[12]

The outbreak of World War II, however, created what one historian has called "a uniquely hopeful situation," for it provided a set of circumstances, such as the economic dependence of Great Britain on the United States, in which the American multilateralists led by Hull could force their economic vision for the future on their allies and enemies alike and hence "eliminate forever the war-producing conditions of the thirties."[13] One consequence of this situation was the decision by Hull to use the negotiation of the 1942 Lend-Lease Consideration Agreement as a means to force Great Britain to adopt less restrictive trade practices after the war.[14] The same drive to reshape the British Commonwealth in the American economic image can be found in the State Department plans for postwar Germany. Here too, from a very early date, the State Department, under Hull's guidance, worked feverishly on plans to reintegrate the defeated state into the new, multilateral, interdependent economy.[15]

By 1943, a special group of Hull's planners led by Pasvolsky had come to a number of important conclusions about how this goal was to be achieved. In the first place, it was imperative to avoid the enforced breakup of Germany. Partition, they believed, would create economic ruin in Central Europe. This would weaken the overall continental economy, reduce the purchasing power of the average European, and ultimately mean the loss of a vital market for surplus American goods. Moreover, because of the high degree of "economic, political and cultural integration in Germany" it was also assumed that dismemberment would stimulate German nationalism and lead to a renewed drive for unification.[16] The fragmentation of Germany, therefore, could only be maintained by "external force." This would create bitterness among the German people (bitterness made all the more intense by economic hardship), and provide those individuals opposed to the peace with "a ready-made program of national resurgence" of the type practiced by the Nazis in the 1920s and '30s. Such a repetition of the mistakes made at Versailles, which Hull's planners regarded as a harsh peace, had to be avoided. Hence partition was a bad idea, both politically and economically, for it might lead to a situation that represented the very antithesis of what the department hoped to achieve in the postwar world.[17]

The State Department memorandum that Secretary Morgenthau was handed while en route to London reflected this thinking. It insisted, for example, that following the defeat, German industry must be restored and/ or maintained (subject to the destruction of certain selected war industries), and that the German people must have "a tolerable standard of living."[18] This would allow for the reintegration of Germany into the world economy and create an environment conducive to the development of democracy, thus making it possible for Germany to rejoin the community of civilized nations "as envisaged by the Atlantic Charter."[19] The recovery of the German economy would also facilitate the restitution of property stolen by the Nazis, and make it possible for Germany to pay *limited* reparations in the form of goods from current production. The latter would be used to help with the reconstruction of Europe. This would speed up the recovery process and render the establishment of the new postwar multilateral system more likely. The State Department did not oppose the separation of certain border areas, such as Alsace Lorraine or East Prussia, from Germany proper, but it argued that the enforced breakup of the core state of Germany should be avoided on the grounds that it would cripple the European economy and rekindle German nationalism.[20]

Morgenthau sharply disagreed with the assertion that the German people might be rehabilitated through their participation in a new

Wilsonian economic order. He also felt the State Department's call for the retention and restoration of the German state and its industries bordered on criminal negligence, even if all or part of those industries were initially used to supply reparations for reconstruction. Indeed, the lessons that Morgenthau drew from Versailles differed sharply from those of his counterparts at the State Department. The 1919 demand for reparations, for example, led in his view to the creation of an industrial base that merely facilitated Germany's rapid rearmament in preparation for World War II. The treaty also failed to address the fundamental issue at hand— the fact that Germany was an aggressor nation that had to be controlled. The problem with the Treaty of Versailles, then, was not that it was too hard, but rather that it was too soft.

Angered by what he had read, Morgenthau resolved to make further inquiries about a whole host of issues concerning the future of Germany upon his arrival in London. He soon discovered that Allied policy on this issue was anything but coherent. On the one hand, for example, Morgenthau learned that the European Advisory Commission, which had been instructed at Teheran to study and make recommendations on the future of Germany, had been proceeding in its work on the assumption that Germany would remain a unified state following the war. From his discussions with British Foreign Secretary Anthony Eden, however, Morgenthau learned that this assumption stood in direct contradiction to the wishes of Roosevelt, Churchill, and Stalin, who had agreed in principle at the Teheran Conference that Germany should be dismembered.[21] Morgenthau also concluded (somewhat erroneously) that British opinion on Germany "fell into two main camps," one, led by Sir John Simon, the British chancellor of the exchequer and other Tories, that favored a "soft policy" based on allowing Germany to be built up after the war, "partly as a potential market, partly as a counterweight to Russia," and a second, led by Eden, who argued that a soft peace would be counterproductive as it would "arouse Russian suspicions and make postwar cooperation among the three powers more difficult."[22] It appears that Morgenthau interpreted Eden's remarks as an endorsement of his own view that Germany should be dismembered and deindustrialized. But this was not the case. As the quintessential British diplomat, Eden probably gave his guest the impression that he was on "his side," particularly on the question of the punishment of German war criminals. But in his talks with Morgenthau, Eden remained silent on the issue of dismemberment and deindustrialization, and while he was adamant on the need to avoid a confrontation over postwar German policy with Russia, he was also on record as being opposed to the enforced breakup of Germany's core state and in fact favored the limited rehabilitation of German industry following the war.[23]

In addition to his discussions with members of the EAC and Eden, Morgenthau also met with General Eisenhower and other officials from the civilian branch of the Supreme Headquarters, Allied Expeditionary Forces, London (SHAEF). Here, Morgenthau discovered that the State Department was not alone in advocating the rehabilitation of the German economy after the war. This was also the position adopted by the U.S. War Department, the Combined Chiefs of Staff, and SHAEF. In fact, under the direction of the former two bodies, the Civil Affairs Division of SHAEF had developed the "Handbook of Military Government for Germany" which, among other things, called on the Allied occupying forces to preserve the centralized German administrative system, to provide for the revival of German agriculture, to import food and other supplies, and to retain and rehabilitate enough light and heavy industry to make Germany self-supporting and also to keep the whole European economy on a relatively even keel.[24] Similar to Pasvolsky's memorandum, the handbook also insisted that the Germans were to have a relatively high standard of living, including "an average food supply of 2000 calories per person per day," which, it noted, "was more than their neighbors could expect."[25] Of course, the primary concern of the military planners was to ensure an efficient and orderly period of occupation free from civil unrest. But these short-term plans had long-term implications, particularly with respect to the rehabilitation of German industry.

Shocked by what he had learned, Morgenthau vehemently protested these findings to General Eisenhower, the Supreme Commander of SHAEF, whom the secretary met while on a brief tour of northern France. There are conflicting reports about just what was said during these discussions. According to Morgenthau, Eisenhower strongly supported the need for a harsh peace, so much so that Morgenthau later claimed that Eisenhower had given him the idea for the Morgenthau Plan. Certainly, there is no question that Eisenhower admitted that the German people must not be allowed to escape "a personal sense of guilt" and that Germany's war-making power must be eliminated.[26] It is also true that, much like the case with Eden, Morgenthau interpreted Eisenhower's remarks as a personal endorsement of his ideas.[27] But Eisenhower's response to the German problem was more subtle and pragmatic than Morgenthau supposed. Eisenhower may have hated the Germans—and in 1944 and 1945, he was not alone in this—but he could also be flexible and magnanimous.[28] He opposed the policy of unconditional surrender, for example, on the basis that it might prolong the war, and at the Potsdam Conference in July 1945, informed U.S. President Truman that "the rehabilitation of the Ruhr was vital to . . . [U.S.] interests."[29]

In August 1944, however, amid the death and destruction of northern France and the nightly havoc created in London by the launch of Hitler's V-1 rockets, these fine distinctions were lost. Convinced from his discussions with Eisenhower, Eden, and others, that there was a body of opinion that favored the harsh treatment of Germany after the war, and that this consensus stood in sharp contrast to the whole thrust of the policies advocated by the State and War departments in Washington and the EAC in London, Morgenthau decided that he must act. To him, it was inconceivable that these institutions were promoting policies that would enable the German people to carry on with the business of rebuilding their lives and country in a manner not unlike that of their ravaged neighbors. Morgenthau believed that the entire German nation had been engaged in a lawless conspiracy against the most basic tenets of human decency. To allow such a nation to escape unpunished was not only immoral, but dangerous, for plans such as these did nothing to solve the German problem, but simply left unanswered the fundamental question of the incompatibility of German unity and power with world peace.

Morgenthau returned to Washington on August 18, 1944, determined to do something about the discoveries he had made in London. He was well aware that recent Allied successes on the battlefield meant that there was an urgent need for policy directives on postwar Germany, and furthermore, that there was every likelihood that Roosevelt and Churchill might discuss the issue at the Second Quebec Conference scheduled for September. It was critical, therefore, that he act immediately if he was to have any chance of reshaping Allied policy toward Germany along harsher lines. Morgenthau's first task was to convince the president of the validity of his ideas, and over the course of the next three weeks, Morgenthau would meet repeatedly with Roosevelt in an attempt to convince the latter that the Germans deserved harsh treatment after the war. Morgenthau had a close personal relationship with Roosevelt, who was a longtime friend and neighbor in Dutchess County, New York.[30] Morgenthau would use this relationship to his full advantage when pressing his ideas, but Roosevelt did not need much convincing. As a schoolboy who frequently spent his summer holidays in Germany, and as assistant secretary of the Navy during World War I (where German submarines first introduced the world to the deadly perils of unrestricted submarine warfare), Roosevelt had already developed an antipathy for the German people that became more intense with the outbreak of World War II. The president also felt that his youthful exposure to German culture meant that he possessed a keen understanding of the German mind, which, he believed, had been poisoned by its exposure to the cult of militarism.[31] Much to his satisfaction, Morgenthau soon discovered that Roosevelt shared many of his concerns about the postwar treatment of Germany. The president agreed that "we had got to be tough with the Germans," and he appeared genuinely concerned when Morgenthau pointed out the apparent inconsistencies in Allied policy that the Treasury secretary had discovered in London. Roosevelt also made it clear that he opposed the rehabilitation of the German economy and had no interest in collecting reparations.[32] Indeed, after reading the War Department's handbook (which Morgenthau brought to the White House) with its plans to maintain or rehabilitate essential governmental and economic services in Germany (so as to ensure that "the machine works and works efficiently"), Roosevelt sent a scathing letter to his Secretary of War Henry Stimson, demanding information on "how . . . [the book] came to be written and who approved it." Roosevelt also insisted that all copies of the handbook should be withdrawn immediately, pending its revision, for in the president's view, the whole tone of book was flawed. "It gives the impression," he wrote, that "Germany is to be restored just as much as the Netherlands or Belgium," with the people "brought back as quickly as possible to their pre-war estate." This was wrong, for it was "of the utmost importance," he continued, "that every person in Germany should realize that this time Germany is a defeated nation. I do not want them to starve to death but, as an example, if they need food to keep body and soul together beyond what they have, they should be fed three times a day with soup from Army soup kitchens. That will keep them perfectly healthy and they will remember that experience all their lives."

Roosevelt also made it clear that he was concerned about a tendency toward a "soft peace," which had become prevalent among certain circles in London and Washington. Such ideas, he insisted, had to be rejected. He could see "no reason" in fact, "for starting a WPA, PWA or CCC for Germany when we go in with our Army of Occupation."[33] On the contrary: "Too many people here and in England hold to the view that the German people as a whole are not responsible for what has taken place—that only a few Nazi leaders are responsible. That unfortunately is not based on fact. The German people as a whole must have it driven home to them that the whole nation has been engaged in a lawless conspiracy against the decencies of modern civilization."[34]

Roosevelt's sympathy for Morgenthau's objections to the State and War departments plans for postwar Germany bolstered the latter's resolve to press his demands for what was now being called "a harsh peace." Accordingly, Morgenthau decided to appoint a special committee of Treasury representatives, including Harry Dexter White, John Pehle, and

Ansel Luxford, to draft a Treasury plan for postwar Germany. He also engineered the creation of a special Cabinet Committee on Germany composed of himself, Secretaries Hull and Stimson, and presidential adviser Harry Hopkins, which was given the task of looking into the German problem so as to be able to make recommendations to the president on the issue prior to his departure for the Quebec Conference.[35]

With great urgency, White and Pehle were instructed to devote all of their energies to developing the Treasury plan, which Morgenthau hoped would be adopted by the newly created Cabinet Committee on Germany as its own. Morgenthau insisted that the two men should not be afraid to make the plan "as ruthless as is necessary," particularly as they were dealing with the question of how to attack the German mind, of how to handle a people who had been "inculcated with . . . fanaticism."[36] At one point, in fact, Morgenthau even suggested that it might be necessary to remove all of the children of SS men under the age of six from Germany—perhaps to Africa—as a means of preventing them from being poisoned by the ideas of their parents.[37] But when it came to the practical side of implementing Morgenthau's instructions, both White and Pehle found themselves confronting some very difficult problems. Morgenthau repeatedly insisted, for example, that the chief industrial regions of Germany, the Ruhr and the Saar, must be "completely put out of business." After studying this question, however, White concluded that this would present the Allies "with about fifteen million out of eighteen million people who . . . will have nothing to do."[38] As an alternative, White reverted to the idea, previously put forward by the State Department, of allowing the Ruhr and the Saar to continue as industrial areas under international control, with the goods produced in these regions being seized by the Allies as reparations for use in the reconstruction of Europe. But Morgenthau flatly rejected any proposal that contemplated the survival of German industry—even if the goods produced were to be used as reparations. The temptation to build up German industry so as to increase the level of compensation would be too great. Hence, Morgenthau insisted that there could be no reparations from current production. It would be far better and safer, he opined, if the war-ravaged states of Europe sought compensation by simply carrying off whole factories. When White questioned the secretary as to the fate of the surplus population and the ability of the president to sell such a program to the public, Morgenthau reiterated Roosevelt's suggestion that hungry Germans could be fed from the army's soup kitchens. Moreover, the secretary went on:

> [T]he only thing . . . I will have any part of, is the complete shut down of the Ruhr. . . . Just strip it. I don't care what happens to

the population. . . . I would take every mine, every mill and factory and wreck it. . . . I am for destroying it first and we will worry about the population second. . . . Sure it . . . seems a terrific task; it seems inhuman; it seems cruel. We didn't ask for this war; we didn't put millions of people through gas chambers, we didn't do any of these things. They have asked for it.

    Now, what I say is, for the future of my children and grandchildren I don't want these beasts to wage war. I don't know any other way than to go to the heart of the thing, which is the Ruhr, and I am not going to be budged. I can be overruled by the President, but nobody else is going to overrule me.[39]

With their objections disallowed, White, Pehle, and other Treasury officials completed the draft which would become the Morgenthau Plan. As noted, the formal title given the document was the "Program to Prevent Germany from Starting a World War III." In language that was clear and unequivocal, the plan detailed a course for the dismemberment, deindustrialization, denazification, and demilitarization of Germany. It also included a map (presented as "Appendix A"), and a second addendum ("Appendix B"), which discussed the punishment and treatment of war criminals. Among the specific provisions contained in the main body of the document was a call for the complete destruction of the entire German armaments industry, as well as the removal or ruination of all those industries "which are basic to military strength." Hence, the industrial plant of the Ruhr and surrounding areas, which the plan termed "the cauldron of wars," was to be carried away for distribution among those countries devastated by the war. Items that could not be moved were to be destroyed, or "reduced to scrap, and allocated to the United Nations"—all within six months of the cessation of hostilities.[40] In keeping with the above, and in an effort to prevent the preservation of German industry, the plan also prohibited long-term or recurrent reparations and insisted that restitution shall only be effected by the transfer of existing German resources including whole factories and territories. Trade and capital imports were to be strictly controlled for a period of at least 20 years. In addition, the Allied military government was forbidden from assuming any responsibility for the German economy, and was not to take any measures designed to maintain or strengthen it, except as was necessary for military operations. Furthermore, in an effort to avoid long-term military and political commitments to Europe (which FDR and the American public opposed), as well as to allow for the speedy transfer of U.S. troops to the war against Japan, the long-term occupation of Germany was to be handled, not by the major Allies, but by her continental neighbors.[41] With respect to the physical makeup of the German state following the war, the plan reiterated the nearly ubiquitous call for the separation of East Prussia from the rest of Germany; it also called for France to receive the Saar and adjacent territories, for the Ruhr and surrounding industrial areas to become "an international zone," and for the remaining portion of pre-1937 Germany to be divided into two independent states— one northern and one southern.[42] The plan also encouraged social reform and political decentralization. All German radio stations, newspapers, and other publications, for example, were banned until adequate controls and further programs were formulated; all schools and universities would remain closed until new textbooks, teachers, and curricula were found or developed; and to "facilitate partitioning and to assure its permanence," the military authorities were instructed to dismiss all policy-making officials of the central government and deal primarily with local authorities.[43]

In the appendix entitled "Punishment of Certain War Crimes and Treatment of Special Groups," the plan insisted that the Allies draw up a list of "arch-criminals" who, once identified, would be summarily executed, as Churchill had suggested.[44] It also called for the death penalty for all those who had caused the death of another in violation of the rules of war, in reprisal for the action of others, or because of a person's "nationality, race, color, creed, or political conviction." Membership in such organizations as the SS, the Gestapo, and other Nazi security groups would render an individual liable for reconstruction service in labor battalions employed in devastated areas outside Germany.[45] Emigration was prohibited. And in an effort to destroy the Prussian aristocracy, all large landholdings were to be broken up and distributed among the peasants, while the system of primogeniture and entail was to be abolished.[46]

Taken together, the Morgenthau Plan presented a succinct formula for the complete overhaul of modern industrial Germany. The core of this effort was based on the destruction of the Ruhr and the dismemberment of the German state. This would virtually guarantee that Germany would no longer have the means to threaten world peace. But there was much more to the plan than the mere destruction of German heavy industry and the breakup of the Reich. Morgenthau firmly believed that the "will to war" was deeply ingrained in the German psyche. The German character, therefore, had to undergo some sort of metamorphosis if the German people were ever to join the community of civilized nations. This would require punishment and reform, and Morgenthau was adamant that only his proposals, with their call for a return to the land, would be able "to redeem this virile, capable people from their worship of force and their lust for war."[47] Indeed, as a "gentleman farmer," Morgenthau, much like his more famous neighbor, remained a firm believer in the Jeffersonian ideal—the myth that the pursuit of small-scale agriculture was good for the soul. Such ideas, in fact, were quite prevalent in New Deal America, where Arthurdale and other experimental communities were established as part of the reform impulse that grew out of the misery of the Great Depression.[48] By returning the Germans to their agrarian roots, then, Morgenthau sought to provide them with the opportunity to rediscover the common good and respect for human decency that both he and Roosevelt felt had been lacking in the last three generations.

In spite of Roosevelt's obvious sympathy for his ideas, Morgenthau was well aware that the president had not as yet decided on a definitive policy for postwar Germany. It was also likely that the Treasury secretary's plan would face considerable opposition from other members of the government, particularly Hull and Stimson, and that there would be an intense period of bureaucratic wrangling before the White House finally arrived at a decision. Not one to tempt fate, Morgenthau continued to meet regularly with Roosevelt in the days and weeks leading to the Quebec Conference, stressing repeatedly that the German people deserved harsh treatment.[49] Morgenthau also expanded his argument in favor of a harsh peace by skillfully linking the question of Great Britain's postwar economic position with that of the survival of German industry. Morgenthau had long been aware that Roosevelt was concerned about this issue, and that the matter would more than likely be discussed at the upcoming Quebec Conference. Indeed, while in London, Morgenthau had been informed by Churchill that England was "broke" and would not be able to carry on with the war against Japan or recover economically from the supreme effort to defeat Nazi Germany without a massive infusion of American aid.[50] Britain had hoped to receive this help by extending the terms of the Lend-Lease agreement to cover the time involved in the defeat of Japan. She had also hoped that the terms of "Stage II"—the British phrase for the extension of Lend-Lease for the period between the defeat of Germany and the surrender of Japan—would be written in such a way as to allow her to reduce her production of munitions while increasing her production of civilian goods, a key factor in the recovery of both her domestic and export industries.[51] In the Treasury secretary's discussions with Roosevelt over Germany after his return from London, Morgenthau had made a point of informing the president about the dire state of the British economy, including Churchill's observation that England was "broke." Roosevelt found this very disconcerting. Morgenthau then suggested that the destruction of German industry might be one way to improve Britain's postwar economic standing. It would open up new markets for the British and eliminate their chief competitor in the export trade on the continent. In this way, the deindustrialization of Germany, which was called for in the Morgenthau Plan, would serve a dual purpose: it would eliminate Germany's war-making capabilities and improve Britain's postwar economy.[52]

In addition to using the issue of the recovery of the British economy as an indirect means to convince Roosevelt that his call for the destruction of German industry was a good idea, Morgenthau also sought out Hull and Stimson, the two other key members of the Cabinet Committee on Germany, in the hope that he might be able to convince both men of the validity of his plan, thus avoiding a showdown with the president over the future of Germany. Here, however, he was less successful. On the evening of September 4, for example, Morgenthau unveiled the main aspects of his plan to the secretary of war. Not mincing words, Stimson immediately attacked its economic provisions, which, he said, would "force thirty million people into starvation."[53] On the following day, in the first meeting of the Cabinet Committee on Germany, with Hull, Morgenthau, and Hopkins present, Stimson returned to the charge by insisting that the Treasury's plan reduced the Allies to "fighting brutality with brutality."[54] It would, he went on, permanently impoverish the German people, ruin the European economy, and ultimately breed the sort of hatred and tension that would obscure the guilt of the Nazis and sow the seeds of a future war.[55] In spite of a large measure of agreement on such issues as disarmament and denazification, the three Cabinet secretaries were unable to settle on a unified policy, particularly over the issue of deindustrialization. As a consequence, they decided to submit separate memoranda on this question to the president and to ask him to meet with the committee as soon as possible. Two meetings with the president followed, the first on September 6, and the second on the 9th.

In these discussions, Hull seems to have given both Stimson and Morgenthau the impression that he had come around to their respective sides. This may have been deliberate. Hull disliked face-to-face confrontations; he was also ill and tired, and perhaps preferred to let the memoranda issued by his subordinates at the State Department speak for him.[56] These went some way toward meeting the demands for a harsh peace as stipulated by Morgenthau, but in essence, the State Department remained opposed to the forcible partition of Germany and the destruction of her industry.[57] There were a number of reasons for this. In the first place, neither Hull nor his advisers had given up on the idea of creating a new world economic order following the war. This would require a strong

Europe with a healthy economy, and while the State Department agreed
that the German economy should be controlled and should not be allowed
to dominate the continent, it nevertheless insisted that the ultimate aim
of American economic policy must be to reintegrate Germany into the
new interdependent world system. The total ruination of German
industry was incompatible with this goal.[58]

The State Department also had concerns about the effects of the
Morgenthau Plan on postwar Soviet-American relations. On the one hand,
Hull and a number of other senior advisers insisted that it was imperative
that the U.S. and USSR must maintain a close working relationship
following the war. This was vital to the successful establishment of the
postwar peace and security organization that Hull and Roosevelt so ardently
desired.[59] Indeed, from this perspective, Morgenthau's call for a harsh peace
had much to recommend it. Certainly, the Russians would have no
objection to its call for the severe punishment of war criminals, the
destruction of German industry, and the breakup of the Reich. Yet there
remained a number of officials within the State Department who harbored
latent fears about Soviet intentions vis-à-vis Europe.[60] There were concerns
that a weakened and dismembered Germany might fall under the sway of
Moscow or lead to competition for "spheres of influence" among the various
occupying powers. Taken together, these concerns were enough to lead most
State Department officials to continue to insist that dismemberment and
deindustrialization should be opposed.[61] This placed Hull in somewhat of
a dilemma, for he obviously did not want to antagonize the Soviets by
appearing to advocate a "soft peace," nor go against the president's desire—
clearly expressed at Teheran and elsewhere—to see Germany broken up
after the war. As a consequence, the final memorandum that the State
Department issued to the president prior to his departure for Quebec
represented a compromise between the department's position and that of
the Treasury's. It fully endorsed the demilitarization and denazification of
German society, and recommended harsh treatment for war criminals. It
also insisted that the "primary objectives" of Allied economic policy should
be to hold down the German standard of living to "subsistence levels" and
prevent any reconversion to war production. But it refused to endorse
Morgenthau's call for the destruction of the Ruhr and suggested that the
issues of dismemberment, deindustrialization, and reparations (the latter
being intimately linked to the former) should not be decided until the
"internal situation" in Germany was clear and until the views of the British
and the Russians on these questions were known.[62]

Given Roosevelt's inclination for putting off difficult decisions, one
would have thought that the State Department's recommendation for

postponing a decision on dismemberment, deindustrialization, and reparations would have pleased the president. But in meetings held on September 6 and 9, Roosevelt expressed strong support for Morgenthau's hard-line policy, noting that he believed in the idea of returning the German people to the land and fully supported the Treasury's view that it was "a fallacy that Europe needs a strong industrial Germany."[63] In his memoirs, Stimson notes that at this point he remained convinced that the president, in spite of these comments, had not as yet made up his mind about the treatment of postwar Germany. Nor was there any reason to suspect that Roosevelt intended to settle the matter during the course of his conversations with Churchill at the Second Quebec Conference. Hull, for example, had been informed that the conference would deal primarily with military matters (particularly the prosecution of the war against Japan) and that as such there was no reason why he should attend.[64] But this belied the truth, for Roosevelt went to Quebec convinced of the need to accomplish two goals: first, to secure the Morgenthau Plan for the harsh treatment of Germany, and second, to ensure that the United Kingdom received all the economic help she needed via the provisions of Lend-Lease Stage II. Moreover, in spite of the wishes of Stimson and Hull to the contrary, there is no doubt that Roosevelt had never really deviated from his long-held view that the Germans deserved harsh treatment, and when the crush of events forced him to choose between the more moderate proposals put forward by Stimson and Hull, as opposed to the stern policies advocated by Morgenthau, he chose the latter.

Convinced that he had established enough of a consensus at home— by the airing of various points of view among his senior advisers—Roosevelt proceeded to Quebec to meet with Churchill. The subject of postwar Germany soon came up, as well as the difficult question of continued U.S. Lend-Lease aid to Britain, and within two days of his departure, FDR had decided not only to summon Morgenthau to Quebec, but also to ask Churchill to call in Eden.[65] Morgenthau arrived on September 13, and in their first conversation, Roosevelt indicated to his Treasury secretary that he fully intended to pursue the question of the future treatment of Germany with the British. He also suggested that Morgenthau meet with "the Prof.," Lord Cherwell, the British paymaster-general and close adviser to Churchill, to discuss the deindustrialization of the Ruhr and its potential effect on British export markets following the war.[66] Shortly after this conversation, Morgenthau dined with Roosevelt, Churchill, Admiral Leahy, Lord Moran, Lord Cherwell, and a number of other officials at the Citadel. It was Morgenthau's first top-level Anglo-American conference, and one suspects from reading his diary that the secretary looked forward eagerly to the possibility that he might be able to influence the great course of events.[67] But these hopes were soon brought down to earth by Churchill, who responded to Morgenthau's exposition on Germany—which turned out to be the main topic of conversation—with "the full flood of his rhetoric." Indeed, after listening to Morgenthau explain that he wanted to close down the Ruhr in part to help the British postwar economy, Churchill lashed out, saying he was "all for disarming Germany," but this would be like "chaining himself to a dead German."[68] The British people, moreover, would never stand for such a policy, and, in any case, he did not believe Morgenthau's plan would do much to aid the British after the war. After three hours of what Lord Moran termed, "wild talk," in which neither side made any progress, Roosevelt suggested that Morgenthau and Cherwell meet separately to discuss the issue further.[69]

After a sleepless night spent worrying about the future of his program for Germany, Morgenthau met with Cherwell. The latter was clearly sympathetic to Morgenthau's ideas and expressed surprise at Churchill's reaction of the previous evening. Even more encouraging, however, was the fact that Cherwell fully concurred that the destruction of the Ruhr would be good for the British postwar economy. Cherwell soon agreed to "dress up" the proposal in a way that would be more attractive to the prime minister.[70] This was critical, for Cherwell—much like Morgenthau with FDR—was a close confidant of Churchill's who possessed considerable powers of persuasion and had a knack for reducing complex arguments to their bare essentials. Within 24 hours, he had talked Churchill into an abrupt about-face—in part by insisting that Germany would not starve under the Plan, and in part by insisting that Great Britain would reap enormous economic benefits from the shutdown of German industry.[71]

There has been considerable historical debate as to why Churchill suddenly reversed his decision and opted to support the plan. Most historians have interpreted this move as a quid pro quo for the continuation of Lend-Lease during the post-European phase of the war. Certainly, as Brian McKercher has pointed out, there is no question that the British regarded such aid as critical to their efforts to wage a successful war against Japan and to revitalize their economy after the long struggle against fascism.[72] But there may have been other factors as well. Anti-German sentiment was then running strong, and given the possibility that the destruction of German industry might in fact assist the recovery of British exports, it seemed reasonable to allow Germany to assume the burden of postwar suffering.[73] It also appeared, to Churchill at least, that support for a "hard peace" was fairly broad-based. Stalin and the Russians undoubtedly favored it, as did FDR, and during the course of their initial conversations, Morgenthau insisted (erroneously) that both Eden and Hull also supported this policy.[74] Preoccupied with the war, Churchill remained largely unaware that there was considerable dissension within the American government over the merits of the proposal, and in a critical miscalculation, he probably assumed that he would have little difficulty persuading the Foreign Office as well as his colleagues in the War Cabinet that there was little point in opposing the Americans (and particularly Roosevelt) on this issue.[75]

As a consequence, Churchill instructed Cherwell and Morgenthau to come up with a memorandum encompassing their ideas, which he and the president could then endorse.[76] But this turned out to be a difficult task, and after considerable discussion, the two men discovered that they were unable to come up with a document that was acceptable to both. Morgenthau then suggested that they refer the matter again to the president and prime minister for further discussion. On September 15, in a meeting with the two leaders, as well as Eden, who had just arrived from London, Morgenthau did his best to explain these difficulties to Churchill, noting that all the drafts written thus far presented "too weak a case." Churchill, in a buoyant mood after having just signed the joint memorandum that called for the continuation of Lend-Lease, then took matters into his own hands. His stenographer was summoned, and within a few minutes, the prime minister had dictated a memorandum, later known as the Quebec memorandum, which indicated that both he and Roosevelt supported the broad thrust of the Morgenthau Plan.[77]

In concise terms, the Quebec memorandum took note of the need to prevent the renewed rearmament of Germany. Of critical importance, was "the future disposition of the Ruhr and the Saar." The memorandum then stated that: "The ease with which the metallurgical, chemical and electrical industries in Germany can be converted from peace to war has already been impressed upon us by bitter experience. It must also be remembered that the Germans have devastated a large portion of the industries of Russia and of other neighboring Allies, and it is only in accordance with justice that these injured countries should be entitled to remove the machinery they require in order to repair the losses they have suffered. The industries referred to in the Ruhr and the Saar would therefore be necessarily put out of action and closed down . . . [and] the two districts . . . put under some body [of] the world organization. . . ."

"This programme for eliminating the war-making industries in the Ruhr and the Saar is looking forward to converting Germany into a country primarily agricultural and pastoral in its character."[78] Roosevelt's sole contribution to the memorandum was the insertion of the words "in Germany" following the mention of those industries that were listed as being easily convertible from peacetime to wartime production. It was Churchill who chose the controversial term *pastoral.*[79] Somewhat to Morgenthau's surprise, the only objections to the document came from Eden, who appeared "quite shocked at what he had heard." Eden insisted, in fact, that the memorandum contradicted the work of the Foreign Office and stood in sharp contrast to what both he and the prime minister had said publicly on the postwar treatment of Germany. Moreover, Hull's opinion should be sought. "You simply can't do this," he exclaimed.[80] But Churchill, unmoved, replied angrily that it was a matter of economic survival, Britain must have the German export trade. He also warned Eden not to bring the matter up before the Cabinet, as, he went on, "the future of my people is at stake and when I have to choose between my people and the German people, I am going to choose my people."[81]

In his memoirs, Eden notes that this exchange represented the first time that the two men had disagreed sharply in front of foreign representatives. Eden's reaction, and the argument that ensued, no doubt stemmed in part from the arbitrary manner in which Churchill decided to adopt an important line of policy without bothering to consult either his foreign secretary or the Cabinet. Eden disagreed with this type of policy making, and his reference to Hull indicates that he assumed that the U.S. secretary of State would as well. Eden was also aware—through communication with Lord Halifax in Washington—that both Hull and Stimson had strong objections to the Morgenthau Plan, as did the Foreign Office and Cabinet in London.[82] Indeed, unbeknownst to Morgenthau, much of the same debate that had raged in Washington during the summer of 1944 over the postwar treatment of Germany had also gone on in London. In mid-July 1944, for example, Deputy Prime Minister Clement Attlee submitted a report to the Cabinet that posed a number of questions concerning the future of defeated Germany. Attlee wanted to know whether his colleagues, after seeing to it that Germany was disarmed and demilitarized, favored the restoration of normal conditions in Germany as quickly as possible, including providing her with food and facilities for economic revival, or did they think that Nazi influence and the German cult of war must be rooted out, even if the result were, at first, political and economic confusion?[83] Attlee acknowledged that hitherto, it had always been assumed that His Majesty's Government would follow the first alternative—in part to enable Germany to pay reparations and to lighten the burden of the occupying forces, and in part because it was assumed that the economic revival of Germany was essential to the general welfare of Europe. But the deputy prime minister was not so sure that this represented the best policy. He now thought that it might be necessary to destroy the German military machine and Nazi system "even if our policy produced an internal crisis and great hardship."[84] Commenting on this paper, Eden noted that although he agreed with Atlee's aims, he thought that Britain was unlikely to achieve her political and economic ends in Germany if she were to reduce her to chaos. After all, the economic depression of the 1930s had been one of the main factors in the growth of the Nazi party, and it would do no one any good if the Allies were to destroy the Nazis "only to put something equally evil and dangerous in their place."[85]

Most officials in the Foreign Office concurred with this view. It was imperative that the mistakes inherent in the Treaty of Versailles, which had led to the destruction of the Weimar Republic and the rise of Nazism be avoided. This meant that any settlement of the German problem must be acceptable to the German people if it was to have any chance of success. In light of this, both Eden and his advisers, much like Hull and his colleagues at the State Department, remained skeptical about the wisdom of seeking the enforced partition of Germany. The Foreign Office was willing to go along with the amputation of certain border areas, such as East Prussia, and it favored a return to the status quo ante with respect to all of the territory seized by the Nazis through violence or the threat of violence, such as Austria and the Sudetenland, but it was less sure about the further breakup of "the rump state of Germany." It had to be borne in mind that "for the past 100 years" there had been a constant urge among the German people to attain the political unity that their neighbours had already achieved. Moreover, this urge "would at once reappear if German unity were to be destroyed by foreign action . . . [and] disunity imposed by foreign dictation." Indeed, in such circumstances, "the recreation of a united Germany would become the focus for all German discontents, aspirations and activities."[86] Enforced partition, therefore, might very well result in the reestablishment of the conditions that had helped propel Hitler to power. It would also require a long-term commitment of British and American troops, which neither the British nor American public were likely to support. As an alternative, the Foreign Office favored encouraging any particularist movements that might crop up at the end of the war, the separation of East Prussia and other border regions from the rest of the country, and the decentralization of the German government, perhaps through the establishment of a loose confederation or federation. This would render Germany militarily less potent, and achieve many of the same results sought through dismemberment without the concomitant troubles associated with the enforced breakup of the country.[87]

Eden concurred with this analysis. He also agreed with the Foreign Office assertion that it would be in His Majesty's Government's best interest to press for the postwar rehabilitation of the German economy, subject, of course, to certain stringent controls over her heavy industry. This would lighten the burden of the occupation forces, and make it possible for Germany to pay reparations, which the Foreign Office supported. Eden also believed that the economic revival of Germany was essential to the general welfare of Europe, and, like Hull, favored her ultimate reincorporation into the world and European commercial communities.[88]

Thus, when word arrived at the beginning of September that the Americans, under pressure from Secretary Morgenthau, were talking about the necessity for a very severe treatment of Germany following the war, including provisions for the partition and deindustrialization of the country,[89] Eden recommended that the Cabinet oppose such a move. Furthermore, he also insisted that the prime minister (who had already left London for Quebec) be advised immediately that he should do his utmost to convince President Roosevelt that "Mr. Morgenthau's views were wrong."[90] The Cabinet agreed, and on September 14 a message was sent to Churchill recommending that he not commit himself or his govern-ment to the Morgenthau Plan. Such a policy, the message insisted, "would be wholly against our interests," as it would make the occupation difficult, lead to the establishment of a black market, and render all hope of deriving some sort of contribution out of Germany for the economic reconstruction of Europe impossible. It might even necessitate the dispatch of relief goods from Britain to Germany "if only at the insistence of our own forces who would inevitably be effected by the sight of starving children." In short, "[a] policy which condones or favours chaos is not hard; it is simply inefficient," and the Cabinet therefore cautioned the prime minister that he must not arrive at "a snap decision" on a matter "which everyone agreed demands very full and careful study."[91] This telegram arrived too late to effect Churchill's "snap decision" to initial the Quebec memorandum, but it confirmed Eden's objections, and indicated in no uncertain terms that Churchill's acceptance of the Morgenthau Plan would stir up strong opposition in London.

Upon his return to Washington, Morgenthau told his staff that his experience at the Quebec Conference, including the successful promotion of his plan, represented the high point of his career in government. But even before the president and the prime minister had initialed their endorsement of it, the forces of opposition were mustering in Washington to engineer its defeat. Stimson, after learning that Morgenthau had been summoned to the conference—and fearing the worst—immediately dispatched a message to FDR and Churchill imploring the two leaders not to come to any hasty decisions about Germany but rather to defer the matter to a small ad hoc committee. At the same time, Hull tried unsuccessfully to prevent Anthony Eden and his Permanent Under-Secretary, Sir Alexander Cadogan, from joining Churchill at the conference in an effort to ensure that "political matters," such as the postwar treatment of Germany, not be discussed.[92] On the afternoon of September 15, however, an astonished Hull received a telegram from Roosevelt that indicated that "he and Churchill had largely embraced Morgenthau's ideas."[93] Hull was outraged—not so much by the Quebec memorandum itself (which was included in Roosevelt's cable)—but rather by the fact that the president had once again elected to make foreign policy without consulting the State Department. Hull also resented Morgenthau's conduct. He had long been jealous of the latter's close relationship with Roosevelt, and suspected that the Treasury secretary had used his friendship with the president as an underhanded means to secure his objectives without the involvement of the State and War departments.[94] Hull also felt that Morgenthau and the president had committed a grave error by signing the Lend-Lease Stage II agreement extending economic aid to Great Britain for the remainder of the war. Hull would have made this aid conditional upon further British economic concessions, including the outright abandonment of Imperial preference, and he was deeply upset that such a golden opportunity had been lost.[95]

Angered by all of these factors, Hull resolved to fight the matter. So too did Stimson, though for different reasons. Stimson was morally outraged by the means with which Morgenthau hoped to achieve his goals. He continued to insist that in "spirit and in emphasis" Morgenthau's plan was "punitive, not . . . corrective or constructive." Moreover, it was simply not possible "to force seventy million people, . . . who through their efficiency and energy have attained one of the highest industrial levels in Europe . . . to abandon all their previous methods of life" so as to be reduced to "a peasant level." A "subordinate question," Stimson later wrote, is whether, even if you could do this, it would be good for the world either economically or spiritually: "Sound thinking teaches that prosperity in one part of the world helps create prosperity in other parts of the world. It also teaches that poverty in one part of the world usually induces poverty in other parts. Enforced poverty is even worse, for it destroys the spirit not only of the victim but debases the victor."[96]

Morgenthau disagreed strongly with Stimson's interpretation of his plan. He insisted, for example, that its purpose was not punitive, but rather "highly humanitarian." It would render it impossible for Germany to start another war, a noble goal in itself, and contrary to the views of Hull and Stimson, "would not arrest . . . [her] economic development . . . [but] would channel that development along lines fruitful for peaceful pursuits."[97] As

Morgenthau later put it, the road to peace in Germany led to the farm. This would not only absorb her surplus labor, but would make it possible for the German people to feed themselves without the need for imports—and they would never starve.[98] Moreover, in such a milieu, the German people "would not only lack the means to embark again on a mission of conquest; they would also find the means to reconstruct themselves."[99]

Roosevelt, who had assumed that the matter of postwar policy toward Germany had been safely settled at Quebec, returned to Hyde Park following the conference to discover just the opposite. Within a matter of days, in fact, word began to arrive from Washington that both Stimson and Hull were upset by what had occurred at the conference, and that neither of them considered the matter closed. Then on September 21, an article written by Drew Pearson appeared in the *Washington Post* that indicated dissension in the government over the Army handbook, and hinted at a rift in the Cabinet over postwar policy toward Germany generally. Further indications of a split in the Cabinet followed the next day when Arthur Krock wrote a column critical of the fact that neither Hull nor Stimson had been invited to Quebec, in spite of the fact that Eden and Cadogan were present and the treatment of postwar Germany had been discussed. This was unacceptable. The State and War departments, Krock insisted, were "central figures in this problem," and even if these discussions were limited to the difficulties associated with the military occupation, it was still necessary to integrate them with the policies that would eventually be adopted by the civilian authorities, since the latter would ultimately set postwar German policy. The fact that the British had called Eden to Quebec made this blatantly obvious, but unfortunately, it seemed that in the Roosevelt administration personality counted more than position, and hence Secretary Hull had not been invited to confer with his opposite number.[100]

Hull frequently used Krock as a vehicle to air his grievances with the White House, and it is likely that he had a hand in the writing of this column as well. But whatever the case, it was now clear that not everyone within the FDR administration was happy with the way postwar policy toward Germany was being handled. This piqued the interest of the press and for the next ten days a relentless stream of articles appeared speculating on how the administration was going to handle the German problem. These included a fairly accurate summary of the Morgenthau Plan, published by the *Wall Street Journal*, and another published in the *New York Times* that reported that the Cabinet committee on German policy made up of Hull, Stimson, and Morgenthau was "split wide open" in a bitter dispute over Morgenthau's call to convert Germany "into an agricultural country of small farms."[101]

Roosevelt was not happy with these reports. 1944 was an election year, and in spite of his confidence in his ability to win an unprecedented fourth term, he did not wish to tempt fate.[102] The last thing he wanted was a public display of a divided Cabinet, particularly when the dispute involved key members of his administration, such as Hull, who commanded great respect among the American electorate. Roosevelt was also concerned about the public's reaction to Morgenthau's plan. Somewhat to his surprise, the terms of the proposal had sparked a good deal of criticism. On September 28, for example, a letter appeared on the editorial pages of the *New York Times* that stated that "Mr. Morgenthau would destroy the economic utility of a continent to gain revenge upon a few hooligans."[103] The same letter also advised that the best policy for Germany—after her disarmament and denazification—was one based on rehabilitation and reconciliation. It was also widely reported that the announcement of the Morgenthau Plan had stiffened German resistance. Taken together, press reports such as these, coupled with the dissension over the issue within his own government, led Roosevelt to conclude that he should back away from the plan and distance himself from Morgenthau. Accordingly, Roosevelt refused to see his old friend when the latter came to call at the White House near the end of September. He also publicly denied that there was a split over German policy in his Cabinet, and in a move designed to silence the press and end all further speculation that the White House intended "to pastoralize Germany," he released a letter written to Leo Crowley, the head of the Foreign Economic Administration, which called for the FEA to develop policies regarding Germany's postwar foreign trade.[104]

By the beginning of October, then, it was clear that Roosevelt had to decided to withdraw his support for the Morgenthau Plan, and drop all discussion of the German problem—at least for the time being. Hence, the Cabinet Committee on Germany was abolished, and in two separate discussions with Stimson and Hull Roosevelt insisted that his intent in initialing the Quebec memorandum had not been to rid Germany of her entire industrial capacity, but rather to reduce her ability to compete with Great Britain in the world's export market.[105] Badgered by the unexpected controversy that the postwar treatment of Germany aroused, and fearing domestic repercussions, FDR reverted to the much more comfortable and safe policy of procrastination. As he told Hull some weeks later, "it is all very well for us to make all kinds of preparations for the treatment of Germany . . . but speed . . . is not essential at the present moment," and in any case, the president did not like "making plans for a country which we do not yet occupy."[106]

In London, meanwhile, the publication of the Morgenthau Plan did not stir up as much public controversy as it did in Washington, perhaps because it was widely assumed in the United Kingdom that Churchill's endorsement of the Quebec memorandum committed the government only to a general statement of principle—not to the specifics of the Treasury program. Nevertheless, opposition to the plan remained firm and shortly after the close of the Quebec Conference, the Armistice and Post-War Committee (established by the War Cabinet in April 1944 to give the former body advice about questions effecting armistice terms and their execution) expressed grave doubts about the merits of the proposal, particularly from an economic standpoint. In light of this, the committee asked the Economic and Industrial Planning Staff[107] to examine the economic aspects of the plan, and to report its findings to the government as soon as possible. In the meantime, the debate over issues such as the partition of Germany continued, and became further complicated by the release of a report issued by the British Chiefs of Staff (COS) in mid-September. Here, in sharp contrast to the line taken by the Foreign Office, the COS argued that the dismemberment of Germany would be advantageous to British security. It would reduce Germany's capability to rearm, and hence lessen the chance of renewed aggression. It would also provide "insurance" against the possibility of a hostile USSR. Indeed, the Chiefs of Staff insisted that a weakened but united Germany would be an extremely tempting target for Soviet domination. Moreover, if this effort were successful, and the subsequent Russo-German combination was fully armed, the British would face an almost insuperable foe on the continent. By dividing Germany into three zones of occupation (which had just been agreed to at the Quebec Conference[108]), two of which would be controlled by the Western powers, His Majesty's Government would be guarding itself against this possibility, and if necessary might be able to enlist the help of northwest and possibly southern Germany in an effort to contain Soviet aggression.[109]

Eden, who favored a policy of postwar cooperation with the Soviets, sharply disagreed with the Chiefs of Staff report and, fearing that one of Stalin's operatives might get word of it, quickly issued a directive restricting its circulation. He also submitted a further Foreign Office report on the issue of partition to the Cabinet, which argued against dismemberment and in favor of decentralization as a more workable alternative.[110] But the Cabinet came to no decision on the matter. Shortly thereafter Churchill and Eden traveled to Moscow to meet with Stalin, where Churchill's comments appeared to indicate that he still regarded the Morgenthau Plan with favor. The prime minister insisted, for example, that it was imperative "to put the Ruhr and the Saar out of action" as Mr. Morgenthau had suggested. In the process, the machinery and machine tools that Russia, Belgium, Holland, and France needed would be taken away and distributed among these states. Britain, which Churchill claimed would emerge from the war as the "only great debtor nation," would then take up the export markets formerly dominated by Germany. "This was only justice."[111] The two leaders—with Eden looking on, but saying very little—also discussed various schemes for the partition of Germany, including the possibility of creating the so-called Danubian Federation that Churchill had long favored.[112]

It may have been that Churchill, somewhat like Eden in his conversations with Morgenthau in August, stressed all of these measures as a means to impress Stalin, who had consistently favored a harsh peace. Churchill probably also assumed the Roosevelt still supported the plan—he told Stalin at one point that "Roosevelt liked what Morgenthau had said"—and with a Cabinet largely undecided on the specifics of what to do with Germany following the war there was no apparent reason why he need back away from it. Upon his return to London, however, this situation began to change. In late October, the Foreign Office received a report from Washington indicating that Roosevelt had distanced himself from the Treasury proposals. Shortly thereafter, the Armistice and Post-War Planning Committee issued a detailed directive on Allied occupation policy that reflected the prevailing attitudes of the Foreign Office.[113] Morgenthau, aware of what was going on in London and still fighting for the adoption of his ideas in Washington, tried to counter these developments by once again enlisting the support of Cherwell, who took the Treasury secretary's concerns straight to the prime minister. But this move backfired. In an angry minute issued to Churchill, Eden—with the full support of the Foreign Office and the War Office—argued that "it was not the concern of the Secretary of the United States Treasury . . . to comment to the Prime Minister on British Policy towards Germany."[114] Eden also insisted that Morgenthau's suggestions should be rejected.[115] At roughly the same time, it was becoming more and more evident that the Foreign Office would not support a policy based on dismemberment and drastic deindustrialization. There was no indication in the latter's view that turning Germany into an agrarian state would do more to enhance British security than straightforward disarmament, and little evidence to support the American Treasury secretary's claim that such a move would benefit Britain economically. Indeed, in a report issued at the beginning of December, the Foreign Office concluded (much like the State Department) that the destruction of the Ruhr "would tend to impoverish not only Germany but the world as a whole," and hence, must be avoided.[116]

By late fall, then, it was clear that there was little support for Morgenthau's harsh peace within the British government. It was also widely understood that the plan had been severely criticized in "high quarters" in the United States.[117] On November 23, in fact, a War Office paper on the

subject concluded that "the Morgenthau policy was probably dead."[118] In
light of this, Churchill's support for the plan fell off in much the same way
as Roosevelt's, and by the beginning of 1945, with the Allied forces still
reeling from the German counteroffensive in the Ardennes, he had decided
to follow the president's lead and simply put off the matter. The decisions
taken at the Second Quebec Conference would have to be cast aside for
another day.

Morgenthau's attempt to solve the German problem through the imposition
of a detailed plan aimed at the deindustrialization of the Ruhr and the
breakup of Germany had thus failed. In an immediate sense, this failure had
much to do with domestic American politics and the desire of the president
to avoid a public controversy during an election year. But it was also a
reflection of the inability of the Roosevelt administration to bring about a
consensus between the two main reforming impulses of the New Deal: one
that sought to create a new interdependent world order through the
multilateral application of U.S. capitalism and another that sought to bring
about the reform of the German character by returning the German people
to the land. Each had the same goal—the creation of a peaceful democratic
Germany (or Germanies)—but chose radically different means to achieve
that goal. In the absence of a long-term plan for the treatment of defeated
Germany, the initiative passed to the military and the immediate needs of
the occupation forces. Hence, following the withdrawal of the handbook,
the Joint Chiefs of Staff issued an "interim directive on Germany"—the so-
called Joint Chiefs of Staff (JCS) 1067—which in essence granted the
military authorities on the ground in Germany the primary responsibility
for the German economy and what provisions, if any, were to be taken with
respect to her industrial disarmament. The directive also insisted that war
criminals were to be apprehended and that the military should carry out a
thorough program of disarmament and denazification. Some of the less
controversial aspects of the Morgenthau Plan, then, did survive as policy, at
least temporarily. Moreover, in a concession to the Treasury secretary, the
War Department agreed that JCS 1067 should include a statement that
specified that the military authorities should take "no steps looking toward
the economic rehabilitation of Germany."[119] But the autonomy granted the
American military commander was broad enough to ensure that he had the
authority to maintain essential goods and services—for the maintenance of
order, for the prevention of disease, and if necessary to assist in the
prosecution of the war against Japan. The State Department (at Hull's
insistence) also issued a statement declaring that the Supreme Commander
was authorized to interpret the economic provisions of JCS 1067 "as

enabling him to retain or impose such economic controls as he may deem essential to the safety and health of the occupying forces."[120] As Morgenthau feared, these provisions provided enough of a loophole to make it possible for the military governor to establish a program aimed at restoring the German economy. This is exactly what happened with the onset of the Cold War and the introduction of the Marshall Plan, both of which paved the way for the eventual reindustrialization and reunification of Germany, as well as her complete acceptance into the European and world communities—resolving the German problem once and for all.

But in late 1944 and early 1945, the Cold War had not yet begun, and in spite of the growing arguments in favor of establishing some sort of *cordon sanitaire* in Central Europe as a means to check Soviet expansionism, Roosevelt refused to be drawn in by the idea that the West should use Germany as a bulwark against the Russians. Cooperation with Moscow was far more important and Germany was a separate problem. As had so often been the case then, political and military considerations, in conjunction with a clear preference for procrastination, led Roosevelt and Churchill to avoid confronting the major issues at hand and instead to let short-term needs take precedence over long-term policy. The German problem would have to wait. Perhaps this was just as well, for as Churchill wrote in January 1945, coming to terms with Germany was difficult, especially when the heat of the battle still raged. After reconsidering the question in the wake of the rejection of the Morgenthau Plan, Churchill concluded that it was simply "too soon to try to decide such large questions as the treatment of Germany after the war." Indeed, it may be a mistake, he thought "to try to write out on little pieces of paper what the vast emotions of an outraged and quivering world will be, either immediately after the struggle is over, or when the inevitable cold fit follows the hot. These awe-inspiring tides of feeling dominate most people's minds, and independent figures tend to become not only lonely but futile. Guidance in these mundane matters is granted to us only step by step, or at the utmost a step or two ahead. There is therefore wisdom in reserving one's decision as long as possible and until all the facts and forces that will be potent at the moment are revealed."[121]

Notes

1. The author would like to thank Warren F. Kimball, John F. Sears, Richard Kurial, and B. J. C. McKercher for their invaluable assistance in the preparation of this article; my appreciation also goes out to Joseph Maiolo for providing additional British archival material.

2. Quoted from H. Morgenthau, Jr., *Germany is Our Problem* (New York, 1945), pp. xi-xiii.

3. Stimson to Roosevelt, Sept. 5, 1944, President's Secretary's File [hereafter PSF] Box 31, FDR Library [hereafter FDRL].

4. *New York Times,* Sept. 24, 1944, p. 1.

5. The Morgenthau Plan has been the subject of a number of articles and studies. See F. Smith, "The Rise and Fall of the Morgenthau Plan," *United Nations World,* 1 (March, 1947): 32-37; F. H. Gareau, "Morgenthau's Plan for Industrial Disarmament in Germany," *Western Political Quarterly,* 14 (1961): 517-34; J. L. Chase, "The Development of the Morgenthau Plan through the Quebec Conference," *Journal of Politics,* 16 (1954): 324-59; W. F. Kimball, *Swords or Ploughshares? The Morgenthau Plan for Defeated Nazi Germany, 1943-1946* (Philadelphia, 1976) and "US Planning for Postwar Germany: Or Germany is Our Problem, Russia is Our Problem, the Economy is Our Problem," Deutsches Institut für Japanstudien (DIJ) (Berlin, 1995), pp. 21-36; and B. F. Smith, *Road to Nuremberg* (New York, 1981). The Morgenthau Plan is also discussed in J. Blum, *From the Morgenthau Diaries: Years of War,* vol. III; C. Hull, *The Memoirs of Cordell Hull,* vol. II (New York, 1948); H. L. Stimson and M. Bundy, *On Active Service in Peace and War,* (New York, 1947); and briefly in K. Sainsbury, "Central and Eastern Europe at the Second Quebec Conference," in W. Deakin, E. Barker, and J. Chadwick, eds., *British Political and Military Strategy in Central, Eastern and Southern Europe in 1944* (New York, 1988).

6. Morgenthau, *Germany is Our Problem,* pp. v-viii.

7. As professor Kimball has noted, Morgenthau suggested to Roosevelt that Germany should end up like Denmark, "where the people, through small scale farming, were in intimate association with the land and were peace-loving and without aggressive designs upon others" (see "The Two-Sided Octagon," p. 9, and Kimball, *Swords or Ploughshares,* p. 26). It is interesting that Churchill expressed similar sentiments about Austria, Bavaria, and Hungary to Stalin at the Teheran Conference in 1943—noting that these three states should be joined in a "broad, peaceful, cow-like confederation." (L. Woodward, *British Foreign Policy in the Second World War,* vol. V [London, 1962], p. 447).

8. Reports on German atrocities and the mass executions of Jews began to reach the West as early as 1941, but became more widespread in the summer and fall of 1942. In July 1942, for example, the British Minister of Information, Brendan Bracken, reported that the Nazis had begun "the wholesale extermination of the Jews" and that up to 400,000 Jews and Poles had already been murdered in Poland. (*London Times,* July 10, 1942, p. 3) For more on this, and the Allied reaction, see J. P. Fox, "The Jewish Factor in British War Crimes Policy in 1942," *English Historical Review* 92 (1977): 82-106; M. Gilbert, *Auschwitz and the Allies* (London, 1985); and V. Newton, ed., *FDR and the Holocaust* (New York, 1995).

9. On the question of Allied treatment of German war criminals and the possibility that the victors might engage in a fairly widespread campaign of

military justice, including the execution of a large number of Nazi and SS officers, see A. J. Kochavi, "The Roosevelt Administration and War Criminals," *Diplomatic History*, 19 (Fall 1995): 617-639; T. Bower, *Blind Eye to Murder: Britain, America, and the Purging of Nazi Germany—A Pledge Betrayed* (London, 1983); and Smith, *Road to Nuremberg*. Both Churchill and Roosevelt supported the swift punishment of war criminals. Throughout the summer of 1944, for example, Churchill, under pressure from various exiled governments and Jewish representatives in London, sought Cabinet approval for the idea that Nazi war criminals should be disposed of by summary execution, without a trial. Churchill also tried to persuade the Cabinet to issue a declaration stating that anyone who assisted Hitler in the prosecution of mass murder would be handled in the same way as the führer. But the Cabinet refused, fearing that such a declaration might result in reprisals against British POWs on the continent. (Smith, *Road to Nuremberg*, pp. 45-6).

10. Minutes of Tripartite Political Meeting, Dec. 1, 1943, U.S. Dept. of State, *Foreign Relations of the United States* [hereafter *FRUS* plus volume title] *Teheran, 1943* (Washington, 1862-) pp. 600, 602-604.

11. Ibid. For more on the Teheran meetings, see R. Edmonds, *The Big Three: Churchill, Roosevelt and Stalin in Peace and War* (London, 1991), pp. 341-58; K. Sainsbury, *The Turning Point* (Oxford, 1985), chapter VIII; and K. Eubank, *Summit at Teheran* (New York, 1985). The creation of the EAC was largely the work of Anthony Eden and the British Foreign Office. For more on the EAC see Sainsbury, *The Turning Point*, pp. 69-79.

12. D. B. Woolner, "The Frustrated Idealists: Cordell Hull, Anthony Eden and the Search for Anglo-American Cooperation, 1933-1938" (Ph. D. diss., McGill University, 1996), chapters 1-3.

13. B. Kuklick, *American Policy and the Division of Germany. The Clash with Russia over Reparations* (London, 1972), p. 5.

14. As Hull's ranking Far Eastern adviser, Stanley K. Hornbeck put it at the time: "If we wish to achieve in the coming peace settlement . . . [the] economic arrangements along the lines which you have over the years consistently advocated, the more we can do toward getting the British Government committed before the fighting is finished . . . the better. There are many of our ideas to which the British might be induced to give assent while they are still fighting for their national life and are dependent upon us for support of all kinds, but to which, once the enemy has been defeated and the British national life is ensured, it might be exceedingly difficult—if possible at all— to get them to agree." Hornbeck to Hull, July 16, 1942, Hornbeck Papers, Box 181, Great Britain Relations with the USA, Hoover Institution Archives, Stanford, CA. The protracted negotiations over Article VII of the "Consideration Agreement" are not the only example of the U.S. effort to alter British economic practices after the war. Others include: the attempt to insert a provision calling on both powers to support "equal access" to trade and raw materials in the Atlantic Charter; the negotiation of the so-called "Export White Paper" in September 1941; the extension of Lend-Lease Aid for the war

against Japan in 1944-45; and the difficult negotiations over such questions as wheat exports, air routes, oil, and a number of other economic matters. For more on these issues see A. P. Dobson, *U.S. Wartime Aid to Britain, 1941-1946* (London, 1986); *Peaceful Air Warfare: The United States, Britain and the Politics of International Aviation* (Oxford, 1991); and "Economic Diplomacy at the Atlantic Conference," *Review of International Studies,* 10 (April, 1984): 143-146. See also K. Burke, "American Foreign Economic Policy and Lend-Lease" in A. Lane and H. Temperly, eds., *The Rise and Fall of the Grand Alliance,* (Saskatoon, 1994); and W. F. Kimball, "U.S. Economic Strategy in World War II: Wartime Goals, Peacetime Plans," in W. F. Kimball, ed., *America Unbound: World War II and the Making of a Superpower* (New York, 1992) pp. 139-58.

15.   Part of this effort included "decartelization" or the removal and/or restriction of German competitors for reasons of profit and politics. (Kimball, "U.S. Planning for Postwar Germany," p. 22.) For more on the important new work being done in this area see: R. U. Gramer, "Reconstructing Germany, 1938-1949: United States Foreign Policy and the Cartel Question," (Ph. D. diss. Rutgers University, 1996); and Bernd Greiner, *Die Morgenthau-Legend* (Hamburg, 1995).

16.   State Department Memorandum: "The Political Reorganization of Germany,'" Sept. 23, 1943, in *Postwar Plans and Preparations 1939-1945,* ed. H. A. Notter (Washington, 1949), pp. 558-59.

17.   Ibid.

18.   Ibid; and Kuklick, *Division of Germany,* pp. 25-26.

19.   Memorandum of the Executive Committee on Foreign Economic Policy, Aug. 14, 1944, *FRUS, 1944* vol. 1, pp. 279-85. Hull's State Department had consistently advanced the belief that economic change was a precursor to political change and that the best means to encourage the expansion of democracy was through the promotion of an interdependent world economy based on American capitalism. See Kimball, "Wartime Goals, Peacetime Plans," pp. 139-52.

20.   Memorandum of the Executive Committee on Foreign Economic Policy, Aug. 14, 1944, *FRUS, 1944* vol. 1, pp. 279-85.

21.   Blum, *Years of War,* p. 336.

22.   Ibid, pp. 337-38.

23.   See, for example, Eden's conversations with Hull at the 1943 Quebec Conference. Here, Eden informed Hull that "he himself, and . . . the Cabinet in general were not in favour of imposing a dismemberment on Germany largely because of the impracticality of carrying it out." *(FRUS, Quebec, 1943,* pp. 927-28.)

24.   "Handbook of Military Government for Germany," Aug. 15, 1944, PSF Box 82, FDRL.

25.   Ibid., and Memorandum for the President, Aug. 25, 1944, Presidential Diaries, Morgenthau Papers, pp. 1394-96, FDRL.

26. Eisenhower to Craig Cannon, Sept. 19, 1947, Eisenhower Library [hereafter EL], as quoted in S. Ambrose, "Eisenhower and the Germans," in G. Bischof and S. E. Ambrose, eds., *Eisenhower and the German POWs: Facts Against Falsehood* (Baton Rouge, 1992), p. 33. For more on the Morgenthau-Eisenhower talks, see Smith, *Road to Nuremberg*, p. 21; Blum, *Years of War*, p. 335; and D. D. Eisenhower, *Crusade in Europe* (New York, 1948), p. 287.

27. Blum, *Years of War*, p.335.

28. Ambrose, "Eisenhower and the Germans," pp. 29-38.

29. H. C. Butcher, *My Three Years With Eisenhower* (New York, 1946), p. 518; and Record of Conversation between Truman and Eisenhower, July 1945, as quoted in Ambrose, "Eisenhower and the Germans," p. 36.

30. Irwin Gellman, *Secret Affairs: Franklin Roosevelt, Cordell Hull, and Sumner Welles* (Baltimore, 1995), pp. 152-53.

31. R. E. Herzstein, *Roosevelt and Hitler: Prelude to War* (New York, 1989), pp. 3-4, 45-48, 68-70.

32. Morgenthau Diary [hereafter HMD] Aug. 25, 1944, Reel 223, FDRL.

33. The WPA (Works Progress Administration), PWA (Public Works Administration) and the CCC (Civilian Conservation Corps) were all part of the New Deal effort to aid the poor and unemployed.

34. Roosevelt to Stimson, Aug. 26, 1944, PSF Box 82, FDRL.

35. Conversation between Morgenthau and White, Aug. 28, 1944, HMD, Reel 222, FDRL.

36. Ibid.

37. Conversation between Stimson and Morgenthau, Sept. 4, 1944, HMD, Reel 223, FDRL.

38. Telephone transcript, Morgenthau and H. D. White, Aug. 31, 1944, HMD, Reel 223, FDRL.

39. Telephone transcript, Morgenthau, White and Pehle, Sept. 4, 1944, HMD, Reel 223, FDRL.

40. Treasury Department, "Program to Prevent Germany from Starting a World War III," Sept. 9, 1944, *FRUS, The Conference at Quebec, 1944*, [hereafter *FRUS, Quebec, 1944*], pp. 131-40.

41. It was also anticipated that the occupation of Germany by troops from small countries such as the Netherlands or Belgium would humiliate the German people and serve as a constant reminder that they had lost the war (Ibid., and Kimball, *Swords or Ploughshares?*, p. 31).

42. Ibid. These consisted on a south German state composed of Bavaria, Wurttemberg, Baden, and some other smaller areas, and a northern state, comprising a large part of the old state of Prussia, Saxony, Thuringia, and several smaller states. Austria and Czechoslovakia were to have their independence restored.

43. Ibid.

44. Smith, *Road to Nuremberg*, p. 45-46.

45. "Program to Prevent Germany from Starting a World War III, Appendix B: Punishment of Certain War Crimes and Treatment of Certain Groups," Sept. 9, 1944, *FRUS, Quebec, 1944,* pp. 105-07.

46. Ibid. As emigration was prohibited, the population of the Ruhr, particularly those with special skills and training, were expected to settle elsewhere in Germany.

47. Morgenthau, *Germany is Our Problem,* p.144.

48. A. Schlesinger, Jr., *The Age of Roosevelt: The Coming of the New Deal,* vol. 2. (Boston, 1958), pp. 366-67.

49. Morgenthau Diary entries from Aug. 19 to Sept. 9, 1944, HMD, pp. 1386-1432, FDRL. During the same period and in a further effort to convince the president to go along with his ideas, Morgenthau also met with Eleanor Roosevelt, whom he concluded was in basic agreement with his ideas (Morgenthau Diary, Sept. 2, 1944, HMD, pp. 1428-29, FDRL).

50. Blum, *Years of War,* p. 337; and Morgenthau Diary, Aug. 19, 1944, HMD, pp. 1386-87, FDRL.

51. For more on these discussions see Dobson, *U.S. Wartime Aid to Britain,* chapter 7.

52. Morgenthau Diary, Aug. 19, 1944, HMD, pp. 1386-87, FDRL.

53. Conversation "at the Secretary's home," Sept. 4, 1944, HMD, Reel 223, FDRL.

54. Blum, *Years of War,* pp. 359-60.

55. Stimson and McBundy, *On Active Service,* p. 570.

56. H. Feis, *Churchill, Roosevelt, Stalin: The War They Waged and the Peace They Sought* (Princeton, 1970), p. 369.

57. Kimball, *Swords and Ploughshares?,* p. 32; and State Department Memorandum on the Treatment of Germany, Sept. 4, 1944, *FRUS, Quebec, 1944,* p. 94.

58. Ibid.

59. K. Sainsbury, *The Turning Point,* p. 12.

60. The chief proponent of the anti-Soviet forces within the State Department was George Kennan, who rejected the "pipe dreams of collaboration with the Russians" and on frequent occasions warned his colleagues about Soviet designs on Western Europe and the need for a stable and prosperous Germany. See G. Kennan, *The Memoirs of George Kennan* (Boston, 1967), pp. 174-78.

61. Kuklick, *Division of Germany,* pp. 22-23, 40; Kimball, *Swords or Ploughshares?,* pp. 10-11, 14-15, 32; State Department Memorandum on the Treatment of Germany, Sept. 4, 1944, *FRUS, Quebec, 1944,* p. 94

62. State Department Memorandum entitled "Suggested Recommendations on the Treatment of Germany from the Cabinet Committee for the President," issued to Roosevelt, Sept. 6, 1944, *FRUS, Quebec, 1944*, pp. 95-97.

63. Blum, *Years of War,* p. 367.

64. Hull, *Memoirs,* p. 1602.

65. Roosevelt and Morgenthau Conversation at the Citadel in Quebec, Sept. 13, 1944, *FRUS, Quebec, 1944,* pp. 323-24.

66. Ibid.
67. HMD, Sept. 11, 1944, Reel 23, FDRL.
68. Blum, *Years of War*, p.369; and *FRUS, Quebec, 1944*, pp. 325-26.
69. Lord Moran, *Churchill: Taken from the Diaries of Lord Moran* (Boston, 1966), pp. 190-91.
70. Morgenthau and Cherwell Conversation, Sept. 14, 1944, *FRUS, Quebec, 1944*, pp. 329-30.
71. Cherwell and Churchill Conversation, Sept. 14, 1944, Cherwell Papers, H 279/1-4, Nuffield College, Oxford.
72. See B. J. C. McKercher, "Toward a Postwar Settlement: Winston Churchill and the Second Quebec Conference," in D. B. Woolner ed., *The Second Quebec Conference Revisited* (New York, 1998), p. 42. At one point in his discussions with Roosevelt over the question of further economic aid, Churchill, frustrated at his inability to make progress on the matter prior to the understanding reached on September 15, asked the president whether he must get on his knees and "beg" like the president's dog, Fala (*FRUS, Quebec, 1944*, p. 348).
73. Kimball, *Swords or Ploughshares*, p. 38.
74. As noted, Eden gave Morgenthau the impression that he favored a harsh peace in his conversations with the latter in London. See D. B. Woolner, "Coming to Grips with the 'German Problem,'" in *The Second Quebec Conference Revisited*, (New York, 1998), pp. 65-101.
75. Kimball, *Swords or Ploughshares*, p. 38.
76. Conversation between Churchill and Cherwell, Sept. 14, 1944, Cherwell Papers, H 279/1.
77. Morgenthau Diary, Sept. 15, 1944, HMD, pp. 1444-45, FDRL.
78. Memorandum initialed by Churchill and Roosevelt, Sept. 15, 1944, *FRUS, Quebec, 1944*, pp. 466-67.
79. Morgenthau Diary, Sept. 15, 1944, HMD, pp. 1444-45, FDRL.
80. Blum, *Years of War*, p. 371; Lord Avon, *The Memoirs of Anthony Eden: The Reckoning*, vol. 2 (London, 1965), p. 476.
81. Blum, *Years of War*, p. 371.
82. Avon, *The Reckoning*, pp. 475-76; Halifax to Eden, Sept. 6, 1944, FO/954/22, Public Records Office, Kew [hereafter PRO].
83. Woodward, *British Foreign Policy*, vol. V, pp. 466-67.
84. Ibid.
85. Ibid.
86. Foreign Office Memorandum entitled "Confederation, Federation and Decentralization of the German State and the Dismemberment of Prussia," Nov. 27, 1944, FO 371/ 39080, PRO.
87. "War Cabinet Memorandum by the Secretary of State for Foreign Affairs," (Eden), Sept. 20, 1944, FO 371/39080, PRO.
88. Ibid., and Woodward, *British Foreign Policy*, vol. V, p. 466.
89. Halifax to Eden, Sept. 2, 1944, FO 371/ 39080/C11865/146/G18, PRO.
90. War Cabinet Conclusions, Sept. 11, 1944, WM (44) 122, PRO.

91. War Cabinet to Eden, Sept. 14, 1944, Prime Minister's Operational Files [hereafter PREM] 3, File 192/1 PRO.

92. Halifax to Churchill, Sept. 13, 1944, PREM 3/192/1; Kimball, *Swords and Ploughshares,* p. 41; Conversations between Stettinius and Hull, Sept. 12 and 14, *FRUS, Quebec, 1944,* pp. 44-46.

93. Hull, *Memoirs,* p. 1610.

94. J. Pratt, *Cordell Hull,* vol. 2 (New York, 1964) p. 769; Gellman, *Secret Affairs,* pp. 152-53, 355.

95. Pratt, *Cordell Hull,* p. 760. See also Dobson, *U.S. Wartime Aid to Britain,* chapter 7.

96. Stimson to FDR, Sept. 17, 1944, PSF Box 31, Germany, 1941-1944, FDRL.

97. Blum, *Years of War,* p. 376.

98. Morgenthau, *Germany is Our Problem,* pp. 48-63.

99. Blum, *Years of War,* p. 377.

100. Article by Arthur Krock entitled "Why Secretary Morgenthau went to Quebec," *New York Times,* Sept. 22, 1944, p. 18.

101. *Wall Street Journal,* Sept. 23, 1944, p.10; *New York Times,* Sept. 24, 1944, p. 1.

102. Kimball, *Swords or Ploughshares,* pp. 42-43.

103. *New York Times,* Sept. 28, 1944, p. 18.

104. *New York Times,* Sept. 30, 1944, pp. 1 and 18.

105. Stimson and McBundy, *On Active Service,* pp. 580-82; Hull, *Memoirs,* p. 1620.

106. Hull, *Memoirs,* p. 1621.

107. The Economic and Industrial Planning Staff had been established in February 1944 to consider the economic aspects of a German armistice. (Woodward, *British Foreign Policy,* vol. V, p. 203).

108. Shortly after Churchill and Roosevelt had initialed the Quebec memorandum an agreement was reached on which zones of occupation the British and the American armies should occupy. Prior to the conference, Roosevelt had been anxious for the United States to move into the northwestern zone of occupation, primarily because he wished to avoid having U.S. supplies trucked in through France. But after the Quebec memorandum was signed, Roosevelt changed his mind and agreed to the southwestern zone on the condition that the United States be given two German ports on the Baltic Sea (Bremen and Bremerhaven), and the right to ship goods through the British zone. There is speculation that Roosevelt came to this decision in part out of a desire to avoid the difficult job of policing the Ruhr while Morgenthau's program of deindustrialization was taking place. (Kimball, *Swords and Ploughshares?,* p. 46). For more on this see J. H. Backer, *The Decision to Divide Germany* (Durham, 1978), chapters 1-3; and T. Sharp, *The Wartime Alliance and the Zonal Division of Germany* (London, 1975), chapters 1-4.

109. Woodward, *British Foreign Policy,* vol. VI, p. 469.

110. Woodward, *British Foreign Policy,* vol. V., p. 204.

111. Conversation among Churchill, Eden, and Stalin, Oct. 17, 1944, PREM 3/434/2, PRO.

112. Ibid.

113. Foreign Office Memorandum entitled "Confederation, Federation and Decentralization of the German State and the Dismemberment of Prussia," Nov. 27, 1944, FO 371/ 39080, PRO.

114. Minute by Cherwell, Nov. 19, 1944, Cherwell Papers, H 279/1-4; Eden to Churchill, Nov. 21, 1944, PREM 3/195/2, PRO; and idem, Eden Papers, FO 954/22, PRO.

115. Ibid.

116. Armistice and Post-War Committee, Dec. 1944, FO371/46720/4010, PRO.

117. Foreign Office Minute, Nov. 23, 1944, FO 371/C15888/1074/18, PRO.

118. Ibid.

119. Directive to Supreme Commander Allied Expeditionary Forces [SCAEF] Regarding the Military Government in Germany, Sept. 22, 1944, *FRUS, Yalta,* p. 153.

120. Hull to Stimson, Sept. 28, 1944, HMD, Reel 223, FDRL.

121. Minute by Churchill, Jan. 4, 1945, PREM 3/195/2, PRO.

PART TWO

CANADA'S ROLE IN THE LATTER STAGES OF WORLD WAR II

FIVE

ATLANTICISM AT HIGH TIDE

THE QUEBEC CONFERENCE 1944

JOHN ENGLISH

FOUR YEARS AFTER THE SECOND QUEBEC CONFERENCE, Lester Pearson, Canada's newly appointed Secretary of State for External Affairs, presented a brief to the Cabinet calling for its support for an international institution, one "which will have within itself possibilities of growth and of adaptation to changing conditions. The North Atlantic Community is today a real commonwealth of nations which share the same democratic and cultural traditions. If a movement towards its political and economic unification can be started this year, no one can forecast the extent of unity which may exist five, ten or fifteen years from now."[1] Canada's Cabinet approved the document and, apparently, the sentiments and prophesies it expressed.

Such hopes and feelings seemed to come naturally for Lester Pearson and his generation of Canadian politicians and diplomats. Pearson, then 51, reflected that particular North Atlantic experience that gave intellectual and personal understanding to the meaning of an Atlantic community. An adolescence steeped in the lore of Henty, Kipling, and the King James Bible took him inevitably to Britain and World War I in his late teens. His two brothers went with him, and their experience of war marked them for life. After the war, the strength of the continental economy drew both Lester and his brother Duke to the United States, where Duke and his family remained. Lester's business career in Chicago was brief; he did not return

to Canada at this point but rather went to Oxford in the early 1920s. When
he came back to Canada he joined the History Department at the
University of Toronto and began a research project on the United Empire
Loyalists, the dissenters in the first American civil war. He left academic life
at the age of 31; and in the 20 years between his entry into the Department
of External Affairs in 1928 and his election to Canada's House of
Commons in 1948 he spent most of his time outside of Canada. Certainly
those times in London between 1935 and 1941, Washington between
1941 and 1946, and New York so frequently thereafter, were the ones he
recalled with most nostalgia and warmth. In London, he claimed that he
felt North American; in the United States, more British. In both places he
kept a diary, which he never did in Ontario. What mattered most seemed
to have happened elsewhere. "In those civilized days," John Kenneth
Galbraith recalls, "it was felt by some that responsible citizenship did not
involve an exclusive commitment to the political life of Canada." Indeed,
in Mr. Galbraith's experience, which began in southern Ontario, the
question of why "one's affections must be confined, as once with women,
to a single country, was paramount." For Professor Galbraith, as with so
many others in southern Ontario in those times, "Canada might be a
mother, but Michigan was a mistress."[2] The duty to mother abided, but,
for Pearson, Galbraith, and many others, the mistress tempted.[3] And it was
she who gave much of the verve and the passion to the declarations of the
North Atlantic community that filled the air in the 1940s.

In fact, the air Canadians breathed had not always been so salubrious.
Canada in the 1930s was a nation much divided on the problem of its
national identity and, therefore, its national security. Having achieved
autonomy in its external relations in the 1920s—an autonomy symbolized
by the Statute of Westminster in 1931—Canadian politicians and the
informed public spent the 1930s deciding upon and disagreeing about what
autonomy meant and what new responsibility Canada had in the troubled
international system of the depression years.

The major contemporary study of prewar Canadian foreign policy, R.
A. MacKay and E. B. Roger's *Canada Looks Abroad* (1938) described three
principal schools of thought: "isolation," "a British front," and "collective
security." It added that there were other points of view, such as "pacifism"
and, most interestingly, "an Anglo-American front."[4] Although public
opinion polling was fairly common in the United States, it had not yet
reached Canada in the 1930s. Hence judgments about the relative size of
each group had to be subjective. The "collective security" viewpoint was
vigorously promoted by the League of Nations Society, which had a large

membership and access to the leading political figures. Some could imagine that this view had the most adherents—certainly League of Nations Society officials argued that it did—but, in reality, its influence in Ottawa was limited.[5] The Department of External Affairs thought the society's fury during the Italo-Ethiopian crisis of 1935 actually signified very little. Canadians, the new prime minister Mackenzie King was advised, "are not expecting or demanding intervention. The public have been mildly interested in the dispute—from the sidelines. Newspaper comment throughout Canada shows frequent condemnation of Italian aggression, little knowledge of the details of the issue or the Covenant provisions, and still less for active participation by Canada. People are immensely more interested in Alberta than Abyssinia. The League of Nations Society contains many fine members, but the attitude of a few of its leaders or officers does not reflect any widespread and informed public opinion."[6] The same could have been said of the "isolationists," who were numerous in leftist and academic circles, or the "British front" adherents, who were prominent in veterans' groups and in the business class. In truth, as MacKay and Rogers noted, public opinion in Canada was both confused and inchoate, with Canadians not yet agreeing even "on the fundamental objectives of policy, and the principal means whereby these objectives may be attained."[7] When, therefore, the political leaders began to realize in 1938 that a war was possible, perhaps even likely, they knew that their task was large. King's leading Quebec minister, Ernest Lapointe, warned the prime minister that public opinion "will have to be prepared, not aroused by irrevocable steps."[8]

The public, in short, was divided, confused, and uninformed on the details of international political change. That is not to suggest that public opinion, such as it was, avoided the careful scrutiny of Canada's political leaders. But making sense of it was frustrating. Canada's most articulate prime minister, Sir Wilfrid Laurier, complained when the Boer War broke out that there was no opinion, only sentiment. The same might be said of Canadians in the 1930s: the political debate on Canada's national security interests was awash in sentiment. The events of 1939-40, however, soon shaped sentiments into opinion.

Unlike the United States, where public opinion in 1939 strongly favored staying clear of European entanglements, Canadians generally came to an agreement that they should go to war. Dissent came from some Quebec nationalists, some academics who favored American-style neutrality, Canadian Communists who declared the war an imperialist war, and from pacifists such as J. S. Woodsworth, leader of the Socialist Cooperative Commonwealth Confederation. Woodsworth, however, had to resign as leader because he and his party saw that its political future was doomed if it opposed the war. Sentiment had led Canada into war; the task was to turn sentiment into informed discussion.

Prime Minister Mackenzie King fretted about this task. He disliked "the publicity aspect of the business in connection with anything so grave as the war—a sort of self-advertising."[9] The summer of 1940 removed these doubts as Canada moved onto the front lines with the fall of France. English Canadian opinion demanded a more intense war effort, and most dissenters kept quiet or, in some cases, joined the pro-war side. The monstrosity of Hitler, the reality of the German threat, and the sense that Canada and Britain's fundamental values were threatened, all gave new meaning to the war and to the conception of national security. Canadian resentment of American neutrality abounded, but, paradoxically, there was a recognition that Canada's national security depended upon cooperation with the Americans for the defense of North America. It is this context that explains the warm Canadian reception of the Ogdensburg Agreement of August 1940, which created the Permanent Joint Board of Defence between the two countries. As the U.S. Minister in Ottawa reported to Washington, "[t]he old fear that cooperation with the Unites States would tend to weaken Canada's ties with Great Britain has almost entirely disappeared. Instead, Canada believes that such cooperation would tend to bring Britain and the United States closer together, rather than to force Britain and Canada apart."[10] That was indeed what Canada believed—with the exception of a few old-fashioned British imperialists; the Communists, many of whom were interned; the extreme Quebec nationalists; and, of course, the few Canadian Fascists.

The Anglo-American-Canadian alliance quickly became the North Atlantic Triangle, a triangle that enclosed a community united by common language, history, and liberal democratic practice. For Canadians, this alliance required little promotion on the part of the government. It was built upon the mingling of the Canadian and American peoples, which Mike Pearson, John Kenneth Galbraith, and the American-born C. D. Howe, who emerged as King's strongest Cabinet minister during the war years, so well represented. Moreover, it removed the vestigial Canadian fear of the United States while it simultaneously provided a common cause that united sentiment and reason. The two major political parties, the Liberals and the Conservatives, regarded the Anglo-American comity as the ideal solution to their major foreign policy concerns: in the case of the Liberals, the fear of a too close link with Britain; in the case of the Conservatives, the fear of absorption by the United States. The Socialist CCF, which, like many Liberals, greatly admired Roosevelt's New Deal, applauded Canada's closer link with the United States. Ironically, there was some dissent from some of the main Canadian bureaucrats who had served in the wedding party at Ogdensburg, but who had come to find the American spouse somewhat less attentive than they had hoped. For the public, however, the romance was pure Ginger Rogers and Fred Astaire, with the Mountie Nelson Eddy saluting as they swept by.[11]

The triangle became a lens through which war events gained clarity. When, for example, Germany attacked the Soviet Union, Mackenzie King welcomed the Soviet entry into the war: "Every day in which Russian resistance holds German aggression, is a day contributed to the cause of freedom and the growing power of the British Commonwealth and the United States." Those American officials who were troubled by the "cheerfulness" with which the Canadians and the British greeted their Soviet ally were reassured privately by Canadian diplomats. The alliance with the Soviet Union was not an affair of the heart but rather a mariage de convenance. Department of External Affairs official Hugh Keenleyside pointed out that "both Mr. Churchill and Mr. King had prefaced their collaboration with Russia by repeated statements of their dislike of Communism."[12] Such public statements disappeared as the Red Army hurled back the Germans, but there was no doubt that the Soviets remained outside the triangle.

When Franklin Roosevelt and Winston Churchill came to Quebec in September 1944, the Soviets were most definitely outside, as Professor Kimball's collection of the Roosevelt-Churchill correspondence makes clear.[13] The Canadians, we now know, played little direct part in the conference, and Mackenzie King's major efforts were ceremonial. Press reports at the time clearly recognized that Canada played no important part in the deliberations. Indeed, Mackenzie King did not bother to conceal that fact from *Le Devoir*, openly admitting when asked what he had done at the conference: "Le meme rôle que j'ai joué l'an dernier, c'est-à-dire que je me contenterai d'être l'hôte."[14] But unlike the Soviets, the Canadians felt "on the inside." For King, Quebec was a family gathering. At a private dinner on the final night "Churchill sat and talked like one who was father of a family." At the dinner's end, when Churchill rose to go, King "lifted [his] glass and said God bless, guide and guard you." Churchill's eyes filled with tears, he went across to King's side of the table, put his arm in King's, and "spoke about the years we have had together," and, quite inaccurately, "how faithful a friend" King had been. Perhaps it was the sense, at Quebec, that Churchill and Britain had become the junior partner that made King somewhat wary of Roosevelt's familial ways. Upon Roosevelt's arrival, King wrote in his diary, the president "said at once: I wanted to see you first; also to be ahead of Winston, so I gave orders to have the [railway car] moved in."

TABLE 5.1

	YES	NO	UNDECIDED
National	78 %	15 %	7 %
Quebec	56 %	34 %	10 %
All Others	85 %	9 %	6 %

It seemed, King wrote, "that the President was rather assuming that he was in his own country."[15]

Small slights aside, the meeting and its mood reveal how public opinion had formed out of sentiments, and how convincing and congenial the North Atlantic idea was for Canadians in those times. The war brought a consensus that had eluded Canadians in the prewar days. Although the new premier of Quebec, Maurice Duplessis, was a recognized Nationalist whose election reflected francophone Quebec's annoyance with the federal government's plebiscite on conscription, Duplessis issued no dissent in September 1944. Indeed, when he brought Churchill and King to the legislature, they were wildly cheered as they entered, and in private discussions with the Quebec Cabinet Duplessis assured Churchill, according to King's account, that "nowhere was there greater loyalty than in Quebec."[16]

Within a few weeks Canada faced its second conscription crisis and consensus seemed to be dissolving through rancorous exchanges between francophone and anglophone Canadians. A closer examination, however, suggests that fundamentally the consensus held. Just as the Quebec Conference began, the newly founded Canadian Institute of Public Opinion asked whether after the war, "some sort of League of Nations would work" or whether it was "impossible for the nations of the world to work together to keep the peace." Fully 55 percent thought the league would work and only 21 percent said it would not. Almost the same question asked a year earlier had produced results of 62 percent yes and 20 percent no. More important, when asked whether they would "like to see Canada take an active part in maintaining world peace after the war even if that meant sending Canadian soldiers, sailors, or airmen to help keep peace in other parts of the world," Canadians responded affirmatively (see Table 5.1).[17]

When asked if the British Empire should be given one vote in such a league or whether each dominion should have a separate vote, the difference among anglophones and francophones disappeared (see Tables 5.2 and 5.3):

King told his British and American guests that he had to be very careful because of differences between Canadians, but his diary makes it clear that his instinctive caution and even isolationism were no longer

TABLE 5.2

Separate vote	84 %
One vote for empire	8 %
Undecided	8 %

TABLE 5.3

	Ontario	Quebec
Separate	92 %	90 %
One vote	8 %	10 %[18]

shrewd political stances. Far from the fearful and uncertain people emerging from economic depression and terrified of war that Rogers and MacKay had described in 1938, Canadians had become more open to change, more generous, and more willing to see themselves as part of a broader democratic movement that was embodied in the wartime leadership represented at Quebec. They were, for example, more willing to believe than were Americans that Russia could be trusted to cooperate after the war. They were also far more generous in their attitude toward Germans than were Churchill and Roosevelt who, at Quebec, approved the Morgenthau Plan to reduce Germany to pastoral country despite Churchill's own first reaction that the plan was "unnatural, unchristian and unnecessary."[19]

Traditional caution was gone. One of the first Gallup polls taken in Canada, the United States, and Britain had revealed that Canada was considerably more willing "to see many changes or reforms" than were the two larger countries. And polls consistently showed that Canadians no longer worried about competing with American factories as they had before. When asked whether there should be "free trade with the United States—that is, that all products and merchandise crossing the border either way should be free of all tariff and customs duties," 67 percent said yes and only 17 percent said no. Sixty-four percent in both Ontario and Quebec said yes. Although the Ontario response to a later similar question was more guarded, the national approval of free trade continued throughout the war.[20] But on one question apart from military conscription a deep divide remained: immigration. When asked in January 1943 and a year later whether after the war Canada should "open its doors and permit people from all parts of the world to settle there," the answers differed according to national origin (see Tables 5.4 and 5.5).[21]

Canada, it must be stressed, in the 1940s was not a nation of immigrants, as it had been before 1914. World War I choked off the great migration from Europe, and in the 1920s nativism and economic uncertainties meant that politicians barely opened the gates. They were slammed shut in the depression years, and, as critics have often noted, they remained closed to the refugees fleeing fascism in the early 1940s. There had been much movement of Canadians, from east to west, west to east, and, above all, across the American border. But these movements were very different from the great migrations of the pre–World War I or post–World War II periods.

Although King never failed to mention to Roosevelt and Churchill the difficulties he faced in pursuing a stronger war policy because of the presence in Canada of a significant francophone minority, the differences among Canadians may well have been less severe than those among the various ethnic groups in the United States. The deep divisions that arose over American participation in the war, for example, that had divided American opinion largely along ethnic lines until December 7, 1941, led to great fears among King and his colleagues that the United States might revert to isolationism after the war. At the Second Quebec Conference, King even cautioned that Roosevelt should delay the promotion of an international conference dealing with the structure of the postwar world until after the 1944 American election, since U.S. participation might rekindle ethnic divisions and lead to renewed calls for the withdrawal of American influence on the world stage. This was a theme that had been raised in earlier conversations between King and Roosevelt, and it was commonplace at the Canadian embassy in Washington, where Lester Pearson and others worried that the ethnic diversity of the United States would prevent it from assuming the leadership role that postwar circumstances required.[22] Such "domestic difficulties" made the Canadians more patient with, and admiring of, Roosevelt's wartime diplomacy.

In Canada, there were, as in the title of Hugh MacLennan's 1945 novel, two solitudes but not many others. The public opinion polls testify to the strength of the differences between francophone and anglophone Canadians, as do the results of the conscription plebiscite of 1942. But there were, in English Canada, very few of the "domestic difficulties" that Roosevelt confronted, and few of the upheavals that had marked Canada's participation in World War I. In the language of a later time, the dominant discourse in defining national meaning was the Anglo-Canadian tradition. Again, in the language of a later day, it was a tradition that firmly rejected multiculturalism. In his 1945 essay, "The Canadian People," the United Church's leading intellectual Lorne Pierce was openly assimilationist and bitterly critical of "the state of moral coma, spiritual

TABLE 5.4

	Attitude Nationwide	
	Jan. 1943	Jan. 1944
	%	%
Open doors	14	13
Allow some in	59	50
Keep all out	21	29

TABLE 5.5

Breakdown of opinion of those a favoring a closed door policy by national origin		
	Jan. 1943	Jan. 1944
British origin	13	18
French origin	46	56
Other origin	14	15

fibrillation and political paralysis" that had marked prewar Canada. The prewar Canadian educators and writers who had boasted of their "cosmopolitanism, forgetting that it is easier to be anything in the world except oneself" drew Pierce's scorn. The war, and the revival of Britain and Canada, had shown Canadians that "[l]ife is all of a piece, and we enter it when and where we must. Our racial inheritance, the soil upon which we live, our climate and basic industries, landscape and atmosphere, all qualify our way of looking at life and our manner of living it." To Pierce, "[a]n infinite amount of rubbish has been written about the cosmopolitan outlook, the international mind and so on. No one ever shook off his inheritance, and the greatest never tried to."[23]

The early Canadian Institute of Public Opinion polls as well as the plebiscite of 1942 point to a remarkable coherence of opinion in anglophone Canada. To be sure, there were differences in support among political parties, but, as numerous observers have pointed out, the three major parties moved toward a center that became vital with the social and economic legislation of 1944-45.[24] What gave strength to that coherence was the astonishing homogeneity of anglophone Canada, particularly in its cities. Its largest city, Toronto, had approximately 900,000 residents in 1941, of which 81 percent told the census takers that they were British in origin. No other group exceeded 6 percent except those of Jewish origin who comprised roughly 6.2 percent of the population. Italians may appear often in Michael Ondaatje's novel about the interwar years, but in fact there were only 17,000, less than 2 percent of the population and of that 17,000, 11,000 were born in Canada. Indeed, all but 83,000 of Toronto residents were born in either Canada or in Britain, and of that 83,000 more than 18,000 were born in the United States. Vancouver was more diverse, but there too 75 percent were of "British background," 87 percent were born either in Canada or Britain (with 25 percent being born in Great Britain), and no single group exceeded 2.5 percent except Scandinavians (3.9 percent) and the Japanese (2.8), who within a year would be forcibly reduced to almost zero. Winnipeg, where J. S. Woodsworth had worried in pre–World War I days about the strangers at "our gates who brought diverse traditions and tongues," had surprisingly few immigrants in 1941. Eighty-three percent of its residents were born in Britain or Canada. Almost 9 percent of the population was of Ukrainian extraction, with more than 60 percent of them born in Canada. The next largest group was Jewish (6 percent), and it offered strong support for the war.[25]

In fact, the only city over 25,000 with a majority population not of British origin was Mackenzie King's birthplace of Kitchener where 48 percent of residents declared themselves to be German origin. But Kitchener was no longer the Berlin of World War I when riots between the English and the Germans marred civic life, young German Canadians refused to enlist, and war bonds found few buyers. In 1915, L. J. Breithaupt, a leading businessperson and former member of the provincial legislature, bitterly and publicly protested when German instruction in the public schools was banned. In 1939, his son, who was soon to be elected a member of Parliament, called for a ban on the speaking of German in public places. War bonds sold in record quantities and recruiting offices were crowded. Kitchener was a different city in more than its name, but so too was Canada a different country.[26]

A recent discussion of culture and identity in American foreign policy argues that "a nation is constructed in relation to how a group of people imagines itself as a community." The author, Susan Jeffords, further argues that "national identity—the narratives and symbols through which the people of a nation see themselves as a nation and in terms of which they elaborate how they want the people of other nations to see them—is the crucial aspect of that activity. Understanding how national identity is constructed is an essential part of understanding foreign policy."[27] Without accepting all of the tenets of a cultural approach to an understanding of foreign policy, one can suggest that the evidence of World War II suggests that Canadians did develop narratives and symbols, among both anglo-phones and francophones, which allowed them to see themselves, albeit sometimes differently, as a nation. Those narratives and symbols were understood by Churchill and Roosevelt because in so many ways they were so familiar in the North Atlantic world. They lingered long after until the high tide of a later day finally swept them away.

NOTES

1. Cabinet Document 754, Oct. 4, 1948. RG2 B-2, v. 245, National Archives of Canada [hereafter NAC].
2. J. K. Galbraith, *A Life In Our Times* (Boston, 1981), p. 5. Mr. Galbraith states that "[w]e were, of all the peoples of the world, the most nearly emancipated from the burdens of national passion."
3. "Accordingly, a man could vote in Canada in the summer and, by courtesy of the Detroit Democratic organization that assigned registered names, possible from the local funeral directors, [vote] in Michigan in the autumn. No thought of corruption was involved. Men wished to have the best people in office in both countries." Ibid.
4. R. A. MacKay and E. B. Rogers, *Canada Looks Abroad* (Toronto, 1938), pp. 249-50.
5. See especially, D. Page, "The Institutes's Popular Arm: The League of Nations Society in Canada", *International Journal,* XXXIII (Winter 1977-78): 28-65.
6. "Memorandum on the Italo-Ethiopian Question," Oct. 24, 1935, King Papers, vol. 164, File 1507, NAC.
7. MacKay and Rogers, *Canada Looks Abroad,* p. 248.
8. Quoted in H. B. Neatby, *William Lyon Mackenzie King: The Prism of Unity* (Toronto, 1976), p. 296.
9. King Diary, Jan. 17, 1940, NAC.
10. J. P. Moffat to Sumner Welles, Aug. 14, 1940, in *Foreign Relations of the United States 1940,* vol. 3, pp. 144-45.
11. See J. L. Granatstein, *A Man of Influence: Norman A. Robertson and Canadian Statecraft 1929-1958* (Ottawa, 1981), p. 119ff. The impact of Roosevelt upon young Liberals is seen in the memoirs of Paul Martin, who was first elected in 1935: "My ideas about the necessity and direction of reform had been greatly influenced by Franklin Delano Roosevelt. No political leader, with the single exception of Laurier, has ever impressed me as much as Roosevelt did." Mackenzie King, Martin thought, "lacked Roosevelt's drive and modernity." P. Martin, *A Very Public Life: Far From Home,* vol. 1 (Ottawa, 1983), p. 119, 127.
12. Hugh Keenleyside to Norman Robertson, July 2, 1941, *Documents on Canadian External Relations 1939-41,* vol. 8, part II, pp. 1103-105. Keenleyside was the author of the most commonly used textbook on Canada and the United States and wrote that "[t]he basic unity of outlook and interest in the two nations made it inevitable that, faced with a critical threat to their common inheritance, they should find themselves united on every vital issue;

that the war should bring them more closely than ever before to a course of mutual action based on mutual ideals and resulting in an enhanced mutual esteem." *Canada and the United States: Some Aspects of Their Historical Relations,* second ed. (New York, 1952), p. 385.

13. W. F. Kimball, ed., *Churchill and Roosevelt: The Complete Correspondence: Alliance Declining: February 1944-April 1945,* vol. III (Princeton, 1984), pp. 310ff. The Russian attitude toward the Warsaw rising was a significant factor at this time.

14. *Le Devoir,* Sept. 15, 1944.

15. J. W. Pickersgill and D. Forster, eds., *The Mackenzie King Record: 1944-1945* vol. III (Toronto, 1968), pp. 65, 89. The race between Roosevelt and Churchill to reach Quebec first is described in Kimball, *Churchill and Roosevelt,* 313-14. King had been strongly critical of Churchill before the war, fearing his "imperialist" tendencies.

16. Pickersgill and Forster, *The Mackenzie King Record,* vol. III, p. 79. Duplessis was allowed to keep his room at the Château Frontenac from which he had been forced out during the 1943 conference. He was the only person not participating in the conference who was permitted beyond the security at the château. *Le Devoir,* Sept. 13, 1944, p. 1.

17. *Public Opinion Quarterly* (Spring 1944): 160; and *Public Opinion Quarterly* (Winter 1944-45): 602. These early polls have been criticized for their lack of scientific rigor. Although the samples were large, there was no attempt to work with the raw data to deal with irregularities. Nevertheless, the polls did manage to predict wartime elections fairly accurately, which is not always the case today. Moreover, citizens may have been more willing to speak with pollsters then.

18. *Public Opinion Quarterly* (Winter 1944-45): 602.

19. On Russia, see *Public Opinion Quarterly* (Fall 1943), in which the U.S. figures are 44 percent for trusting Russia and the Canadian figure 51 percent, even though the figure in Quebec was only 30 percent. On Germany, a Nov. 4, 1944, poll revealed that 57 percent of Canadians blamed the German leaders, 25 percent the German people, and 11 percent blamed some of the German people. Women were more forgiving than men. *Public Opinion Quarterly* (Winter 1944-45): 602. On the Morgenthau Plan, see W. F. Kimball, *Swords or Ploughshares? The Morgenthau Plan for Defeated Nazi Germany* (Philadelphia, 1976).

20. On reform, see *Public Opinion Quarterly* (Winter 1943): 748. On free trade, see *Public Opinion Quarterly* (Fall 1943): 504; and *Public Opinion Quarterly* (Spring 1944): 160.

21. *Public Opinion Quarterly* (Spring 1944): 160. An interesting related question was asked in May 1944: "A great many Canadian soldiers are marrying girls in Britain. Do you approve of this or not?" Sixty percent of the men approved, but only 47 percent of the women. In Quebec, however, 61 percent disapproved with 27 percent in favor. *Public Opinion Quarterly* (Summer 1944): 300.

22. Pickersgill and Forster, *Mackenzie King Diary*, vol. III, pp. 65 and 86. On Pearson, see Pearson Diary, March-April 1945, Pearson Papers, NAC; J. G. Parsons, "Canadian Views on Dumbarton Oaks," Jan. 11, 1945, State Department Papers, 500-CC/2-345, National Archives of the United States; and my *Shadow of Heaven: The Life of Lester Pearson, 1897-1948*, vol. 1 (Toronto, 1989), pp. 252ff.

23. L. Pierce, *A Canadian People* (Toronto, 1945) pp. 5-6,11.

24. See, for example, M. J. Brodie and J. Jenson, *Crisis, Challenge and Change: Party and Class in Canada* (Toronto, 1980), ch. 7, in which the authors describe the Liberals' successful wooing of the labor vote and the CCF's move toward reformism.

25. These figures are taken from *Census of Canada, 1941* (Ottawa, 1942), pp. 444-54.

26. *Kitchener Daily Record*, Sept. 20, 1939.

27. S. Jeffords, "Commentary: Culture and National Identity in U.S. Foreign Policy," *Diplomatic History* (Winter 1994): 93.

SIX

THE QUEBEC CONFERENCES AND THE ANGLO-CANADIAN MONTREAL LABORATORY, 1942-46

DONALD AVERY

> More than four hundred scientists and engineers are now
> engaged on research and development of atomic energy
> in the project and in addition, there are more than five
> hundred mechanics, electricians and other workers of
> various kinds engaged in supplying the industrial and
> auxiliary services. The 10,000 acres of sparsely populated
> land expropriated by the Government as a site for the
> Project . . . has become the centre of a great scientific
> activity in the most exciting and promising field of the
> moment, and Canada for the first time in its history has
> the privilege of being an effective pioneer in a great world
> development.
> —C. J. Mackenzie's radio broadcast of June 3, 1947,
> on the status of Canada's
> nuclear operation at Chalk River.[1]

INTRODUCTION

CANADA'S INVOLVEMENT IN THE DEVELOPMENT OF NUCLEAR WEAPONS
was an important aspect of how the country was influenced by its wartime
alliance with Great Britain and the United States. It was also testimony of
the enormous changes that occurred in the nuclear field during these years.
Under the pressures of war, there was an amazing transition from the self-
sustained laboratory fission experiments of Otto Hahn's German scientific
team in December 1938 to the first atomic bomb tests in New Mexico on
July 16, 1945. While innovative research was carried out by scientists in
Great Britain, aided by the Free French contingent under Hans von Halban,
only the United States had the technological and industrial resources to
actually manufacture the bomb. In the end the Manhattan Project would
spend more than two billion dollars, and employ thousands of scientists at
the Metallurgical Research Laboratory in Chicago; the Oak Ridge and
Hanford production facilities; and the weapons assembly laboratory at Los
Alamos.[2] Canada became an aspiring member of the nuclear club in 1942
with the establishment of the Anglo-Canadian Montreal Laboratory, and
the subsequent Chalk River Nuclear Laboratory in the autumn of 1945.
During the next 30 years Canadian nuclear technology would continue to
evolve with the NRX (National Research X-perimental), which became
operational in 1947, and ultimately the acclaimed CANDU (Canadian-
Deuterium-Uranium) system, which emerged in 1966.[3] Canada would also
assume an important role in the tortuous international discussions about
the postwar future of atomic energy and nuclear weapons.[4]

In this process of atomic cooperation the two Quebec conferences
assumed great importance. During the 1943 deliberations the emphasis was
on how the British and their Canadian partners could be brought into the fold
of the Manhattan Project, essentially on terms set down by American scientific
advisers, and with the approval of President Roosevelt. The results of the
second Quebec Conference are more complex. By this stage the Montreal
Laboratory was able to share some of the U.S. atomic secrets, and would
gradually expand its activities despite some apprehension in Washington.

This chapter deals with a number of important questions about the
Anglo-American-Canadian atomic partnership between 1942 and 1946.
First, how did scientists of the three countries, and especially the key
scientific administrators, view cooperation and the exchange of information
prior to the Quebec Conference of August 1943? Why did U.S. scientific
and military administrators such as James Conant and General Leslie
Groves continue to have misgivings about the Montreal operation, especially on security grounds? In what ways did the Montreal Laboratory assist

in the work of the Manhattan Project after the technical agreement of June 1944 and the Quebec Conference of September 1944? And how did these arrangements influence the direction of Canada's postwar nuclear development, as well as Canada's response to the 1946-47 Anglo-American controversy over the sharing of atomic secrets?

EARLY DEVELOPMENT OF THE ATOMIC BOMB

The genesis of the Montreal Laboratory really began in August 1941 when the British MAUD Committee submitted its final report to the special sub-Committee of the British War Cabinet.[5] After 18 months of deliberations,[6] this elite group of British scientists had arrived at three major conclusions about the viability of an atomic bomb: it could be built within five years; its explosive power would dwarf all existing chemical explosives; and massive casualties would be caused by the blast and by radiation.[7] The report also included a variety of recommendations about the technical problems of creating a uranium 235-bomb. The most important of these involved the immediate establishment of a U-235 gaseous diffusion separation plant that, it was predicted, should be able to have "material for the first bomb . . . ready by the end of 1943," unless there was "a major difficulty of an entirely unforseen character."[8]

Yet by August 1942 the British atomic effort, so boldly proclaimed in the MAUD report and in the creation of the Tube Alloys project, was in serious trouble. Supplies of essential raw materials and instruments were scarce, while the gaseous diffusion separation process remained an exotic Oxford experiment rather than a full-scale plant. Even more alarming was the fact that American atomic scientists, effectively organized and assisted by Office of Scientific Research and Development (OSRD) and the U.S. Army, had now become the dominant partner within the Anglo-American exchange system.[9] In June 1942 Brigadier General Leslie Groves, of the newly formed Manhattan Engineering District, replaced Vannevar Bush as the chief executive officer; and the U.S. atomic project was in full flight. This was reflected by scientific euphoria when on December 2 the chain-reacting pile at the Chicago Metallurgical Research Laboratory became operational. This was enough to convince President Roosevelt, who authorized $400 million dollars for uranium separation plants and a plutonium-producing pile. This was followed by Groves's decision to construct a gaseous diffusion and electromagnetic facility in Oak Ridge, Tennessee, and to order the construction of a massive plutonium pile complex in Hanford, Washington.[10]

CREATING THE ANGLO-CANADIAN
NUCLEAR LABORATORY, 1942

The establishment of the Montreal Laboratory was based almost exclusively on British priorities—or more accurately, on their belated recognition that a wartime atomic partnership with the United States was impossible without having direct access to the resources of the Manhattan Project.[11] On July 30, 1942, an agitated Sir John Anderson informed Prime Minister Churchill that the British pioneering work on atomic bomb research was "a dwindling asset and that, unless we capitalize it quickly, we shall be out stepped. We now have a real contribution to make to a 'merger.' Soon we shall have little or none."[12] With Churchill's endorsement, Anderson took the next step of trying to convince the King government that a joint Anglo-Canadian nuclear laboratory was essential for the war effort. On August 6, 1942 Anderson instructed British High Commissioner Malcolm Mac-Donald to pursue the matter immediately with Canadian officials since the British atomic project was "in danger, owing to our comparative lack of resources, of being outstripped by the Americans who are working on four alternative methods." In order to remain competitive, Anderson noted, it would be necessary to shift the British U-235 fast neutron team to the United States," where it would be incorporated in the U.S. program on equal terms." On the other hand, he argued, the Cambridge slow neutron team of Dr. Hans von Halban should be moved to Canada, not the United States, since their primary task was to concentrate on "the production of the element (plutonium) by using 'heavy water' or even ordinary water, if uranium enriched with U 235 can be obtained."[13]

While Anderson acknowledged that Halban's team were involved with the longer term project, he expressed confidence that it would "in the end prove the more efficient method and the one which will eventually hold the field for the purpose of power production." The key question was whether Canadian authorities would agree that the slow neutron project was a vital wartime undertaking. Anderson, shrewdly assessing the scientific "booster-ism" of his Canadian allies, concluded that they would come on board, especially since the project meant "the development of the use of a raw material indigenous to Canada."[14]

In fact, being "hewers and drawers" of uranium was of only minimal importance in convincing Canadian authorities to endorse Anderson's proposal. A more important reason for their ready acceptance was that by August 1942 there was already a whole series of collaborative arrangements in place, most notably in the areas of radar and sonar, explosives and propellants, and chemical and biological warfare. For C. J. Mackenzie and his NRC associates the Montreal Laboratory was, therefore, another important Canadian contribution to the British war effort.[15] On the other hand, Mackenzie quickly recognized the advantages of getting in "on the ground floor of a great technological process." And he made great efforts to convince Cabinet strongman C. D. Howe, minister of Munitions and Supply, and Prime Minister King, that this venture would have many long-term benefits for Canadian science, technology, and industry.[16]

The final agreement of October 1942 was based on a shared cost and responsibility formula. The two national research agencies, DSIR and NRC, would jointly supervise the operation; with High Commissioner MacDonald and C. D. Howe mutually responsible for general policy matters.[17] Administratively, the role of William Akers, director of Tube Alloys, was of central importance both in coordinating the activities of the Montreal Laboratory with the British fast neutron team, and in establishing a viable relationship with the newly established Manhattan Project.[18] Laboratory research would be coordinated by the NRC and a scientific committee chaired by the Austrian-born scientist, Hans von Halban.[19]

At first the prospects of the Montreal Laboratory appeared most favorable.[20] Despite initial concerns about site location, equipment, and supplies, the local logistical requirements were effectively handled by the NRC. Equally important for British officials were reports that Vannevar Bush welcomed the arrival of the British nuclear team and that they could count on OSRD "for American supplies."[21] Considerable headway had also been made in recruiting high-quality atomic scientists both abroad and in Canada. On November 10, 1942 a list of 26 British Tube Alloy scientists and technicians destined for Montreal was submitted to Canadian immigration officials. Eighteen were British citizens;[22] the remainder were refugee scientists from a variety of backgrounds including four Free French atomic physicists and chemists.[23]

At this stage, Mackenzie was quite impressed with the Tube Alloy scientific vanguard.[24] Of somewhat greater concern was the difficulty of recruiting high-quality Canadian nuclear scientists.[25] But Mackenzie persevered and by April 1943 he was able to place a number of Canadian scientists in key positions within the Montreal Laboratory scientific hierarchy.[26] Unfortunately this new sense of purpose was complicated by the competing visions of Hans von Halban and C. J. Mackenzie, and by the subsequent deterioration in their relationship.[27] And this tension would intensify as relations with the U.S. atomic venture abruptly changed in January 1943.

TOWARD THE 1943 QUEBEC AGREEMENT

The new basis of Anglo-Canadian-American atomic relations was defined in James Conant's letter to C. J. Mackenzie on January 2.[28] Its message was clear. The United States was now committed to a new atomic exchange policy based on the principle "that we are to have complete interchange on design and construction of new weapons and equipment only if the recipient of the information is in a position to take advantage of it in this war." Security considerations, he added, also made these changes imperative.[29]

But why was Mackenzie the first to receive this bad news? The answer was obvious, the Montreal Laboratory had a limited future. Conant did not mince words: "Since it is clear that neither your [Canadian] Government nor the English can produce elements of '94' or '25' on a time schedule which will permit of their use in this conflict, we have been directed to limit the interchange accordingly."[30] Conant then set forth the specific exchange guidelines. First, all efforts would be made "for the development, construction and operation of the Chicago Plant, the erection of our own heavy water plants and the design of a plant making element '49' and using heavy water." In this endeavor the OSRD envisaged a support role for the Montreal scientists in carrying out "the fundamental scientific work for the use of heavy water so that duPont Company could base their designs on this experience." Montreal would not, however, be given access to "the methods of extraction of element '49,' nor the design of the plant for the use of heavy water for this purpose, nor the methods for preparing heavy water."[31] In closing, Conant expressed confidence that his good friend C. J. Mackenzie would soon recognize that these Manhattan Project guidelines were a good thing, which would, in the future, greatly enhance the Anglo-American-Canadian goal, "namely, the production of a weapon to be used against our common enemy in the shortest time under the conditions of maximum secrecy."[32]

Neither Mackenzie nor Howe derived much solace from Conant's gratuitous exhortation. They were confused and angry that the Montreal Laboratory was now redundant, especially since Bush had assured them three days earlier that "the programme for co-operative work as between Canada, the United Kingdom, and the United States, had been finally approved and he was very pleased about it."[33] On the other hand, Mackenzie recognized that both the Americans and the British, as they had done on other occasions, were prepared to use Canada as a pawn in their scientific chess game. He was particularly concerned that Akers and Anderson favored the "big stick" approach in dealing with the Americans. This was evident in Akers's January 7 memorandum that bluntly reminded Conant and Bush that by refusing "to co-operate one hundred percent" the Americans had violated "the original spirit" of the agreement.[34]

Mackenzie, however, decided not to rubber-stamp the Akers missive on the grounds that the arguments were redundant and pointless.[35] In his opinion the real problem was not U.S. injustice, but British naiveté: "I can't help feeling that the United Kingdom group emphasizes the importance of their contribution as compared with the Americans and this attitude has been one of their real shortcomings."[36] He also empathized with U.S. apprehension over "discussing all the details and know how with the Montreal group which is really not an Anglo-Saxon group," but a potpourri of various nationalities whose loyalties could not "be guaranteed for any length of time."[37]

Mackenzie was determined not to be caught between the British and U.S. scientific establishments; at the same time, he did attempt to resolve the differences between his two allies throughout the winter and spring of 1943.[38] On July 26, for instance, he and C. D. Howe entertained General Leslie Groves, head of the Manhattan Engineering District (MED) in Ottawa. According to Mackenzie, Groves appeared "very favourably disposed" toward the Laboratory. "I told him he was crazy that he did not have the Montreal group working with his people and he said he would like that very much as he realized that the workers are in a comparatively unknown field, that there are no experts really, and he is not anxious to lose any bets."[39]

Although the Free French scientist Bertrand Goldschmidt had managed to obtain samples of plutonium from his former colleagues at the Chicago Metallurgical Laboratory prior to his joining the Anglo-Canadian team, this was only a minor asset. Without the assistance of the Manhattan Project, especially for heavy water and uranium oxide, the Anglo-Canadian nuclear project was dead in the water. In August 1943, Akers and Anderson acknowledged this reality and conceded defeat.[40] The British would accept junior partner status on terms dictated by the United States.[41] Mackenzie had a preview of this capitulation when he met Anderson in Washington, just three days prior to the Quebec Conference. "Sir John," he noted, "has a real negotiating job on his hands, but is not as rigid as he was in London, and I think he will be willing to compromise." On this occasion, Mackenzie also met with Conant who assured him that "things were going to break . . . although . . . cooperation won't be wide open."[42] What Mackenzie didn't see was Conant's private moment of triumph,[43] as he relished Anderson's acceptance of terms "tantamount to . . . our original offer."[44] Conant was especially pleased that the British now recognized that the partnership was based exclusively on military principles: "on that basis . . . we can now proceed with an interchange which will be in the best interests of the United States and the war effort."[45]

DEFINING THE ROLE OF THE MONTREAL LABORATORY 1943-44

The major features of the 1943 Quebec Agreement are well known: the commitment to develop atomic bombs at the earliest possible moment; the importance of pooling British and American scientific talent and resources; and an agreement not to duplicate large-scale plants. The two countries also agreed never to use atomic weapons against each other, or against third parties "without each other's consent." The protection of atomic secrets was to be rigorously enforced, and both agreed not to communicate "any information about Tube Alloys to third parties except by mutual consent." In the sensitive area of postwar commercial utilization of atomic energy, British authorities deferred to the authority of the United States.[46]

Although the Quebec Agreement was of decisive importance in restoring Anglo-American atomic cooperation, it did not create an equal partnership.[47] Full interchange of information between Allied scientists was confined to those "engaged in the same section of the field," and "between members of the Combined Policy Committee and their intermediate technical advisers."[48] Responsibility for coordinating the Anglo-American partnership was entrusted to the newly created Combined Policy Committee (CPC). The U.S. members were Henry Stimson, Bush, and Conant; Field Marshall Sir John Dill and Colonel J. J. Llewellin represented Britain, and C. D. Howe spoke for Canada. The three scientific advisers were Groves, Chadwick, and Mackenzie. Further refinements were soon forthcoming. During the first meeting of the CPC on September 7, 1943, Groves made it perfectly clear that the agreement would not include operational collaboration "since the heads of the American sections were not allowed to know anything outside their own sections."[49] Whether they liked it or not, British and Canadian scientists would have to accept Manhattan Project rules. And one of these rules was the removal of Willim Akers as scientific director of the Tube Alloys project; and the appointment of nobel laureate Dr. James Chadwick as his successor. Fortunately for Anglo-American-Canadian atomic cooperation Chadwick understood the name of the game. His shrewd assessment not only of the problems that plagued the Montreal Laboratory, but also of the dynamics of the Manhattan Project were revealed in a letter he sent to C. J. Mackenzie on December 31, 1943:[50] "I do not think that Groves is aware of all the troubles in his own organisation, and while I cannot tell him about them, I think I can at least help him to avoid some of the rocks in our path. . . . I want to assure you that I am going to work with Groves, and not against him."[51] Mackenzie was delighted that Chadwick recognized that compromise, not confrontation, was the only viable approach in dealing with the Americans since the Manhattan Project was "one hundred times greater than any possible United Kingdom effort, that the Americans can get along if necessary without the U.K., while the U.K. can do nothing without the U.S."[52]

Chadwick's pragmatism and quiet diplomacy soon produced results.[53] He was particularly successful in providing British atomic scientists with maximum exposure to the Manhattan Project so that they could acquire knowledge and experience of as many aspects of the project as possible. Between September 1943 and August 1945 more than 150 British scientists would serve in the North American theater of war.[54] The first to come were Rudolph Peierls, Fritz Simon, Klaus Fuchs, and other members of the gaseous diffusion team who arrived in New York City in early December.[55] Another group, led by Mark Oliphant, became deeply involved with the electromagnetic project at Berkeley and Oak Ridge.[56] But the scientists who contributed most to the development of the atomic bomb were those who went to Los Alamos, the most secret part of the U.S. atomic operation.[57]

To Montreal scientists it seemed paradoxical that while Oliphant, Peierls, and Placzek were given access to the innermost secrets of the Manhattan Project, they continued to operate under severe security restrictions. The explanation, however, was simple. In the eyes of Bush, Conant, and Groves, the Montreal Laboratory was a symbol of all of the problems that bedeviled Allied atomic collaboration: It would not advance the making the bomb; it was an attempt to exploit American research and development for postwar military and commercial advantage; and the loyalty of its scientific community was suspect. Although the situation improved considerably when John Cockcroft replaced Hans von Halban as research director in April, 1944, the status of the Montreal Laboratory remained uncertain as long as Manhattan Project officials continued to view it as an atomic Trojan horse.[58]

The only hope for the Montreal Laboratory was to convince the U.S. members of the Combined Policy Committee (CPC) that it could assist the Manhattan Project. Chadwick and Mackenzie had begun this campaign on September 18, 1943, when they invited Groves and his scientific entourage to visit the Montreal facilities, and to discuss the merits of constructing a much larger heavy water boiler, which would have a heterogeneous rather than homogeneous pile. Although MED officials remained noncommittal, the meeting was a social success and reinforced the good communication that had developed among Groves, Chadwick, and Mackenzie.[59] A more profitable joint session was held at the Chicago Metallurgical Laboratory on January 8, 1944, which included ten members of the Montreal team. On this occasion, Dr. Samuel Allison gave a detailed talk on the relative merits of homogeneous and heterogeneous piles, and he endorsed the Montreal proposal, much to the relief of its scientists.[60] Chadwick was particularly pleased that Groves took the opportunity to promise that future collaboration between Chicago and Montreal would include "engineering research and development as well as physics and chemistry,"[61] and that Montreal scientists would be given information about the technical process for the extraction of U-233.[62]

What was now required was for John Cockcroft to replace Halban as the scientific director of the Montreal Laboratory. This was finalized in April 1944.[63] Shortly afterwards, heavy water experts Lew Kowarski and A. E. Kempton brought their badly needed talent to the Montreal team.[64] Relations with the NRC were also greatly improved, especially after Ned Steacie, a highly regarded NRC chemist, became Cockcroft's personal assistant. They soon became an effective administrative team; and there was much to be done.[65]

While there was growing evidence that Groves was becoming more amenable to an expansion of the Montreal operation under joint British-American-Canadian auspices, the project still faced formidable obstacles. Key U.S. scientific administrators, notably James Conant, continued to view the Anglo-Canadian project as a postwar project. And he openly scoffed at Chadwick's claim that the Montreal pile could "produce approximately two hundred grams of '49' a day," and that the plant could be constructed within 20 months.[66] While Groves shared many of Conant's reservations, his primary concern was in developing an atomic bomb, not winning a scientific argument. He was, therefore, not prepared to alienate Chadwick and thereby lose badly needed British scientific assistance at Berkeley, Oak Ridge, and, above all, at Los Alamos. Both Groves and Chadwick also had to consider the serious political difficulties that would arise if the Montreal group ceased to exist.[67]

The battle shifted to Washington and the meeting of the CPC committee. From his vantage point as Howe's scientific adviser, Mackenzie was able to assess the respective arguments of Conant and Chadwick.[68] On one hand, he could appreciate the American position and why "they would not wish to be in the position of providing all of the material, heavy water etc., and having our group at a small fraction of the cost . . . produce in quicker time . . . results which they had got at such greater effort."[69] On the other hand, he was determined that Canada's investment in the Montreal

Laboratory should be rewarded. Mackenzie had an opportunity to push the Canadian point of view when he was appointed as a member of a special CPC subcommittee, along with Groves and Chadwick, to try and break the Anglo-American deadlock.[70] On April 11, 1944, he addressed the Combined Policy Committee: "The present proposal is to build the pilot plant ... as a joint United States, United Kingdom and Canadian effort. Our ownership of uranium ores, our early interest in the production of heavy water at Trail, and the presence of a highly expert group of workers in Canada gives us a special interest and facility for this work."

"In my opinion Canada has a unique opportunity to become intimately associated in a project which is not only of the greatest immediate military importance, but which may revolutionize the future world in the same degree as did the invention of the steam engine and the discovery of electricity. It is an opportunity Canada as a nation cannot afford to turn down."[71] Mackenzie's passionate appeal soon produced positive results.

SUCCESSFUL PARTNERSHIP, 1944-46

On June 8, 1944, the arrangements for the Anglo-American-Canadian heavy water project were negotiated at Chicago.[72] The agreement consisted of six major points: (1) to maintain existing levels of production for heavy water; (2) to continue programs at both Chicago and Montreal "for the development of fundamental information on heavy water piles"; (3) to undertake the design and construction of a heterogeneous heavy water pile "of about 50,000 K. W." at Montreal as a joint project; (4) to review the status of the Montreal plant "when the performance of the first large scale graphite pile at Hanford could be assessed"; (5) to create the necessary administrative machinery to properly supervise the Montreal pilot pile project; and (6) to strengthen the manpower resources at Montreal "by the inclusion of American scientists as well as British and Canadian scientists."[73] The joint project would follow clearly defined guidelines, largely determined by Groves. On the positive side, there was provision for the interchange of all information "essential to the construction and operation of the Canadian Pilot Plant," from both the Oak Ridge graphite pile and the Argonne heavy water pile. Equally promising was the assurance that *all* information "connected with the transformation of thorium to element '23' [U-233] and the separation and the measurement of the physical and chemical properties of thorium and 23," would be freely exchanged. On the negative side, plutonium information and supplies were totally excluded from the agreement; this included health research into "the toxic effects of either '49' or fission products."[74]

To ensure that these conditions were rigorously followed, Groves assigned two American scientists, physicist H. W. Watson and chemist John Huffman, to the staff of the Montreal Laboratory with the understanding "that they would have access to all Metallurgical Project information and they would keep themselves informed by means of reports and . . . would have the responsibility of recommending visits required by the Montreal Group to Chicago."[75] They were joined by Major Horace Benbow, a member of Groves's special security team, whose primary mission was to prevent Montreal from becoming too dependent on U.S. resources and expertise, and to protect American plutonium secrets.[76]

But in many ways the June 8, 1944, tripartite agreement rendered these tasks impossible. Not only had Montreal been given full access to U-233 research, it had also been promised "a limited amount of irradiated tube alloy in the form of Clinton (Oak Ridge) slugs . . . in order . . . to work out independently the extraction and chemical properties of 49."[77] This meant, according to H. W. Watson, that there was no way that Manhattan Project officials could "prevent the U.K.-Canadian chemists from obtaining ideas about possible 49 extraction processes from our discussion about a 23 extraction process."[78] And he was right. In July 1944, with the arrival of the irradiated ingots, Goldschmidt's team began their "radioactive alchemy"; by November they were ready to discuss their plutonium research results with Chicago experts.[79]

Meanwhile, at the diplomatic level British and American officials appeared on the verge of expanding the scope of atomic cooperation. This was confirmed and reinforced during the high-level meetings between Churchill and Roosevelt at Quebec City in September 1944, and by their subsequent negotiations at Hyde Park.[80] On September 19 the two leaders signed an aide-mémoire that stipulated that "[f]ull collaboration between the United States and the British Government in developing Tube Alloys for military and commercial purposes should continue after the defeat of Japan unless and until terminated by joint agreement."[81] That Churchill believed that he had finally convinced Roosevelt to support Britain's postwar atomic research and development was evident in his September 21 communiqué to his scientific adviser Lord Cherwell: "The President and I exchanged satisfactory initially notes about the future of T.A. [Tube Alloys] on the basis of indefinite collaboration in the postwar."[82] Unfortunate for the British, Roosevelt did not inform either Bush or Conant about this arrangement. Nor was the aide-mémoire part of the atomic briefing package that Harry Truman received when he became president in April 1945.[83]

While Mackenzie was not aware of the Hyde Park negotiations, he did notice an improvement in the attitude that MED officials adopted toward the Montreal Laboratory. In part, this was related to the encouraging progress report that he had received from Cockcroft and Ned Steacie in September 1944 on the future of the N.R.X. heavy water pile, which contained an outline for an ambitious program: "The Pilot Plant should operate before mid-1945. It should have a production of 300 grams per month of 49 and about 25 grams per month of 23. Provided that separation plants for 49 and 23 are built this output should enable us to build up stocks of two of the three fissionable elements, stocks which would form a useful starting point for the next stage of experimental work." The report went on to describe how the Pilot Plant would provide "an extremely intense source of slow and fast neutrons," which could be used in future technical experiments in nuclear physics, in radiation chemistry, and for tracer techniques. This project would also give the Montreal team the necessary skills and experience "to design and build a higher power plant for large scale production of 23 [U-233]."[84] Mackenzie was delighted with these prospects. At the same time, however, he was becoming increasingly concerned about Canada's postwar nuclear development once he learned that the British government intended to concentrate their research and development operation at Harwell not Chalk River. Cockcroft summarized Mackenzie's concerns in a May 1945 letter to Chadwick:

> First, he fears the U.S. may withdraw their heavy water at the end of the war and leave Canada with a derelict plant.
>
> Second, he feels that he would be unable to justify the expenditure of the order of $2,000,000 a year . . . if the expenditure were for scientific and technical purposes only.
>
> Third, he is in some doubt as to whether Canada can afford the number of scientists required to carry on the work.[85]

In his usual diplomatic fashion, Cockcroft sought to reassure Mackenzie that the existing complement of 500 could be reduced to 150 once the war was over, and that Canada could easily provide "70 -80 scientific and engineering staff, of whom only 20-25 need be scientists." Mackenzie was, however, not reassured and grumbled that the British were once again ready to take "all the cream off the last two or three years with very little expense."[86]

Chadwick had little time to reassure his Canadian ally. Germany's defeat and the imminent use of the atomic bomb against Japan had created a variety of new challenges for Britain's atomic ambassador. What, for instance, was the future status of the British scientists at Los Alamos? Would they, as some were suggesting, be transferred to the Montreal Laboratory in order to accelerate

the construction of the pilot plant?[87] And what should these scientists take
with them when they left Los Alamos?[88] On this final point, Chadwick's
message was clear: "We cannot leave all our information behind and go with
empty hands. Either British workers must take their notebooks with them or
they must copy out the important abstracts. Further, they should collect
copies of all technical memoranda and reports in which they have been
concerned. In addition, I think all our people should be asked to give you [Dr.
P. B. Moon] a note about the reports which they consider important for our
future work in England. You could then give me a full list and I would try and
clear these reports through General Groves."[89]

HIROSHIMA AND NAGASAKI

C. J. Mackenzie was one of the few Canadian wartime administrators to be
informed about the forthcoming use of the atomic bomb. On July 5, for
instance, he recorded an important conversation with C. D. Howe, who had
just returned from a meeting of the Combined Policy Committee, where the
decision to use the bomb had been announced: "the main event [the Trinity
tests] will take place in the immediate future. The Americans have all their
press releases ready and it is going to be a most dramatic disclosure. They
are going to tell a great deal about the project in general terms, all the money
spent, where they are working, etc. Mr. Howe said we must get busy
immediately and get our press releases ready as it is the biggest opportunity
Canada will ever have to participate in a scientific announcement."[90]

By July 30, Mackenzie was anticipating the Hiroshima attack: "Doctors
Steacie, Cockcroft and Lawrence" he wrote, "were working on the release in
connection with the atomic bomb which is to be dropped in the near future.
Cockcroft has been down to Washington several times and there is a great deal
of work to be done in getting all three releases—U.S., U.K., and Canada
harmonized."[91] One week later Mackenzie reflected on his own actions during
the momentous week when atomic bombs were used against Japan: "On
Monday, August 6 the President of the United States announced that the first
atomic bomb had been dropped on Hiroshima. The day before I telephoned
to Dr. Cockcroft and Mr. Howe asking if he wanted me to come in but Howe
said he had given out the first announcement. . . . It was an eventful week. The
Russians declared war on Japan, the second bomb was dropped on Nagasaki,
which was where the first bomb was to be dropped, and then the rumours
regarding Japanese surrender started flying thick and fast."[92]

As the Manhattan Project began to wind up its operation, there was
much concern in Ottawa that wartime exchange commitments would be

terminated. That was, however, not the position adopted by General Groves who continued to be generous in meeting reasonable requests from the Montreal Laboratory. This benevolence was enhanced when he received favorable reports about the potential of the forthcoming NRX pilot plant at Chalk River, and the operation of the Zero Energy Experimental Pile (ZEEP), which went critical in September 1945.[93] The most glowing reports came from Dr. Weil, the new MED liaison officer, who in November 1945 recommended a free exchange of scientific information between Chalk River and U.S. nuclear research centers: "It is well recognized that the effect of such free interchange will be to stimulate and advance the activities of all laboratories, rather than, as has been sometimes suggested, to discourage original work. This is especially true in the present situation, not only because of the unique facilities which will be available at Chalk River, but even more because of the high quality of the NRC scientific personnel. It would be an extremely unfortunate circumstance if the research activities at the Chalk River laboratory were to be deprived of the experience and knowledge outlined in the U.S. laboratories, and the latter, in turn, deprived of information developed at Chalk River."[94]

Groves was interested, but his price was high. In order to improve collaboration, the remaining Free French scientists—Gueron, Kowarski, and Goldschmidt—would have to leave the Montreal project on the grounds that their "double loyalties" posed a serious security threat.[95] Nor was Groves swayed by an angry appeal from C. J. Mackenzie about the devastating impact these expulsions would have on the Montreal Laboratory and on Canada's postwar nuclear policies.[96]

Years later Bertrand Goldschmidt reflected on his four years with the Montreal Laboratory, and the complexities of alliance cooperation in the development of atomic energy: "Reading this correspondence today, in which I am but a pawn of strong personalities wanting to assert the primacy of their own theses, I find myself filled with amazement and a certain admiration for the manner in which each of them conducted his battle. Groves fought for U.S. isolationism and an atomic monopoly, Chadwick for the survival of the Anglo-American collaboration, Cockcroft for his independence as project manager, and Mackenzie for a fair shake for Canada in this tripartite association."[97] It is a fitting summary.

CONCLUSION

On August 14, 1945 C. J. Mackenzie wrote James Conant, congratulating him on his wartime contributions, and his obvious "great relief and satisfaction . . . when the first atomic bomb was dropped and the results of months and years of extraordinary activity were known to be successful."[98] In reply, Conant acknowledged that his years as OSRD atomic liaison had "been a very interesting and rather strange journey through 'Alice in Wonderland,'" especially in 1942 and 1943 "when the responsibilities were heavy and the decisions difficult." He expressed satisfaction that, in the end, the atomic relationships among Canada, the United States, and Great Britain had "worked out so smoothly," and he praised Mackenzie for his "understanding spirit in the difficult days and . . . diplomatic help in handling international complications."[99]

While their words were guarded, there is little doubt that both men believed that they, and their governments, had acted correctly; that it was British naiveté and inflexibility that had caused the 1943 alliance crisis. Throughout the war, American and Canadian scientific administrators often had difficulty understanding fluctuations in British defense policies in general, and atomic policies in particular. But for the Americans the task was much easier. After 1943, Conant and Bush realized they held the winning cards, and they played them well. While they were not enthusiastic about the 1943 Quebec Agreement, they were prepared to live with it. They also became reconciled to the gradual emergence of the Montreal Laboratory/Chalk River project as a promising slow neutron research center. But what they were not prepared to accept was a permanent Anglo-American atomic partnership.

Yet the Quebec City meetings of September 1944 and the even more significant sessions at Hyde Park the following month had established the basis of long-term cooperation. While Bush, Conant, and Groves suspected that Roosevelt had moved away from the America First policy, they were not sure how much their president had compromised the United States's atomic monopoly. Not being informed, they preferred to believe that the British had no substantial postwar claims on American nuclear expertise or materials. Nor did the Washington Agreement of November 1945, with its apparent endorsement of a revival of the wartime "special relationship," translate into meaningful U.S. cooperation despite constant pressure from British Prime Minister Clement Attlee. And with the passage of the McMahon Act during the summer of 1946, a strict interpretation of scientific interchange was imposed that virtually outlawed the sharing of U.S. atomic technology. It was as if the two Quebec City conferences had never occurred.[100]

NOTES

1. Cited in R. Eggleston, *National Research in Canada* (Toronto, 1978), p. 314.

2. D. Kevles, *The Physicists* (New York, 1974), p. 326; S. Weart, *Nuclear Fear: A History of Images* (Cambridge, MA, 1988).

3. R. Bothwell, *Nucleus: The History of Atomic Energy of Canada Limited* (Toronto, 1988), pp. 107, 127, 286, 414.

4. M. Gowing, *Britain and Atomic Energy, 1939-1945* (London, 1965); B. Goldschmidt, *Atomic Rivals* (New Brunswick, 1990); S. Weart, *Scientists in Power* (Cambridge, 1979).

5. Code-named MAUD, this small uranium subcommittee, under the jurisdiction of the Ministry of Aircraft Production, had an impressive array of scientific talent: Professors George Thomson (Chairman); James Chadwick; John Cockcroft; Mark Oliphant; and Dr. P. B. Moon; while Professors Patrick Blackett; Charles Ellis; Fritz Simon; and William Haworth were later added. Membership was further expanded by the creation of a MAUD Technical Sub-Committee that included refugee scientists Ruduloph Peierls and Hans von Halban and a number of Britain's leading physicists. Gowing, *Britain and Atomic Energy*, pp. 46-49.

6. The MAUD Committee began its deliberations in April 1940. While Tizard was skeptical about the viability of the project, he supported its work, and his Mission discussed atomic matters with the Americans. In fact, Cockcroft carried out an extensive survey of U.S. activity during the fall of 1940. Ibid., pp. 45-55.

7. MAUD Committee, "The Use of Uranium for a Bomb," cited in Gowing, *Britain and Atomic Energy*, pp. 394-436.

8. The estimated cost for having a plant that could produce 1 kg. of U-235 a day, "or 3 bombs per month," was estimated at $5,000,000. Ibid.

9. Ibid., pp. 122-23.

10. Kevles, *Physicists*, pp. 326-27.

11. Gowing, *Britain and Atomic Energy*, pp. 185-189; Bothwell, *Nucleus*, pp. 20-43.

12. Cited in F. Szasz, *British Scientists and the Manhattan Project: The Los Alamos Years* (New York, 1990), p. 9.

13. Lord Anderson to Malcolm MacDonald, Aug. 6, 1942, AB1/379, Public Record Office [hereafter PRO].

14. Anderson was also convinced that if Halban's team remained at Cambridge not only would they be isolated from the British U-235 research team, but also from the plutonium work being carried on at the Metallurgical Laboratory in Chicago. Ibid.; Gowing, *Britain and Atomic Energy*, pp. 188-89; J. Wheeler-Bennett, *John Anderson, Viscount Waverley* (New York, 1962).

15. While a member of the Tizard Mission, John Cockcroft had shown great interest "and friendly concern" for Canadian work in the nuclear field, especially the uranium-graphite research of Dr. George Lawrence of the NRC

McGill-owned building on Simpson Street, Montreal, until the University of Montreal location was ready. Lesslie Thomson memo, Nov. 18, 1942 vol. 173, NAC; Mackenzie to Conant, Dec. 12, 1942, vol. 173, NAC.

28. This subject has been extensively discussed in Gowing, *Britain and Atomic Energy;* J. Conant, *My Several Lives: Memoirs of a Social Inventor* (New York, 1970), pp. 286-304; J. Hershberg, *James Conant: Harvard to Hiroshima and the Making of the Nuclear Age* (New York, 1993), pp. 154-194; and M. Sherwin, *A World Destroyed: The Atomic Bomb and the Grand Alliance* (New York, 1977), pp. 77-79.

29. Sherwin, *A World Destroyed,* pp. 77-79; Hershberg, *Conant,* pp. 183-85.

30. Since the British fast neutron team was "well along" in the development of a gaseous diffusion process they would obtain "full interchange on this phase of the work." Conant to Mackenzie, Jan. 2, 1943, vol. 284, NRC; Conant, *My Several Lives,* pp. 286-95.

31. Goldschmidt, *Atomic Rivals,* p. 180.

32. This offer did not extend to British and Canadian engineers who were excluded from contact with the Chicago research teams. On the other hand, Conant did offer to release all of the Trail heavy water for the use of Montreal Laboratory scientists. Ibid.; Bothwell, *Nucleus,* pp. 31-33.

33. Mackenzie Diary, Dec. 29, 1942, NAC.

34. Gowing, *Britain and Atomic Energy,* pp. 154-164.

35. Mackenzie Diary, Jan. 7, 1943, NAC.

36. Nor was Mackenzie's assessment of Sir John Anderson as an obstinate and naive politician altered after their short and nasty meeting in London in 1943. Ibid., May 11, 1943.

37. Ibid., Jan. 18, 1943.

38. On Jan. 18, 1943, Mackenzie had an amicable meeting with Conant and Bush; they emphasized that the restrictions that had been imposed on the Montreal Laboratory "were no greater than the restrictions they were putting on their own (scientific) groups." Ibid., Jan. 18, 1943.

39. Ibid., Aug. 3, 1943; July 26, 1943.

40. Prior to the Quebec Conference, Akers was contemptuous of NRC claims that they were quite effective in dealing with U.S. scientific administrators. This, he snorted, usually meant that Canada was "in the position of the 'have not.'" Akers to Perrin, July 29, 1943, AB1/379, PRO.

41. In April 1943, Cherwell had requested a thorough study of the problems associated with constructing a British separation plant for U-235, a heavy water plant and a large plutonium- producing reactor. The message was discouraging. For Britain to produce an atomic weapon in five years the British government would have to increase its commitment to the Tube Alloys project tenfold. This was obviously impossible. Goldschmidt, *Atomic Rivals,* 192.

42. Mackenzie Diary, Aug. 3, 1943, July 26, 1943, NAC.

43. Ironically, just prior to the Quebec Agreement, Conant's position had come under assault from quite an unexpected source—Nobel laureate Harold Urey. On June 2, 1943, the Columbia University scientist launched a lengthy attack

on American policies that, he claimed, had caused "a delay of a year or more, in establishing the feasibility of a homogeneous heavy water pile." This policy, he continued, had "no justification on scientific grounds," since it meant that American plutonium research was deprived of both the technical expertise of Halban's team and their 150 kilograms of heavy water. In closing, he warned against any attempt to exclude "our principal ally . . . on nationalistic grounds." Urey to Conant, June 21, 1943, vol. 201, Urey File, Records Manhattan Engineering District [hereafter MED], National Archives, Washington [hereafter NAW].

44. Conant and Bush had, however, been concerned that Roosevelt might reverse American policy because of Churchill's sustained pressure for a renewal of cooperation. Conant, *My Several Lives*, pp. 298-300; Goldschmidt, *Atomic Rivals*, p. 193.

45. Conant to Bush, Aug. 6, 1943, Bush-Conant File Relating to the Development of the Atomic Bomb, 1940-1945, microfilm, Roll 1, NAW.

46. The negotiations leading up to the Quebec Agreement are extremely complex and have been extensively analyzed by Martin Sherwin, Margaret Gowing, Bertrand Goldschmidt and others.

47. Bush to Conant, Sept. 2, 1943, OSRD (Sherwin file), NAW.

48. Ibid.

49. Bush to Anderson, Aug. 6, 1943, OSRD (Sherwin file), NAW; Akers Report, Sept. 13, 1943, vol. 273, NRC.

50. After the Quebec Conference, Mackenzie had little doubt that Groves dominated the American atomic program for one fundamental reason: "he is the man who is actually entrusted with the spending of hundreds of millions of dollars. . . . I do not believe that it will be possible to go farther than Groves is willing to do." Mackenzie Diary, Sept. 10, 1943, NAC.

51. Chadwick to Mackenzie, Dec. 31, 1943, vol. 284, NRC.

52. Chadwick to Mackenzie, Dec. 31, 1943, vol. 284 NRC; Mackenzie Diary, Sept. 17, 1943; L. Groves, *Now It Can Be Told: The Story of the Manhattan Project* (New York, 1962); W. Lawren, *The General and the Bomb: A Biography of General Leslie R. Groves, Director of the Manhattan Project* (New York, 1988).

53. Chadwick to Mackenzie, Dec. 31, 1943, vol. 284, NRC.

54. The gaseous diffusion team at Columbia numbered 15; at Berkeley and Oak Ridge there were 35; at Los Alamos there were 20; while at Montreal, there were more than 80 British scientists. Gowing, *Britain and Atomic Energy*, pp. 241-60. Szasz, *British Scientists*, pp. 3-49.

55. Under this arrangement the Montreal team would "carry on research on chemistry of Heavy Water Pile on a program to be agreed upon in full collaboration with those doing similar work in the United States." Howe Papers, "Memorandum By Brigadier General L. R. Groves," Dec. 10, 1943, vol. 14, File 32, NAC.

56. Cockburn and Ellyard, *Oliphant*, pp. 47-93.

57. Gowing, *Britain and Atomic Energy*, pp. 261-62; Szasz, *British Scientists*, xix, pp. 16-31.

58. Gowing, *Britain and Atomic Energy,* pp. 270-71.

59. Mackenzie Diary, Sept. 18-20, 1943, NAC.

60. Minutes of Meeting in Chicago on Jan. 8, 1944 to Discuss Future Collaboration Between the Chicago and Montreal Laboratories Engaged In Tube Alloy Research, vol. 284, NRC.

61. Goldschmidt, *Atomic Rivals,* pp. 210-11.

62. By February 1944, Chadwick felt that he had established good personal relations with Groves. Chadwick to Appleton, Feb. 5, 1944, AB1/58, PRO.

63. Halban had already accepted the fact "that the titular head of the organization should be Anglo-Saxon; and that Cockcroft would be his successor." Akers shared this opinion. Akers to Perrin, Dec. 8, 1943, AB1/379, PRO.

64. Chadwick to Appleton, April 17, 1944, AB1/58, PRO.

65. According to Christine King, "Steacie found in Cockcroft a kindred spirit of manner of doing things which meant brief and to the point." King, *Steacie,* p. 86.

66. Conant also questioned whether American scientists could rely on Montreal Laboratory experiments "since there has been so many difficulties in the past in interpreting the data obtained by Dr. von Halban." Conant to Groves, Feb. 18, 1944, Conant/Bush File, #33A, NAW.

67. Webster to Chadwick, Mar. 23, 1944, AB1/485, PRO.

68. Mackenzie was not particularly impressed with Henry Stimson, the U.S. secretary of War, who he described as being "a well preserved man but not particularly acute mentally." He found Field Marshall Sir John Dill, chairman of the British CPC, "more alert than Stimson but not terribly impressive." Mackenzie Diary, Feb. 17, 1944.

69. During the discussions Chadwick became increasingly annoyed with Conant, and his anti-British arguments; and according to Mackenzie, he even "talked about withdrawing and going back to England if they [the CPC] did not agree to the Montreal proposals." Mackenzie Diary, Feb. 17, 1944 NAC; Chadwick to Mackenzie, Feb. 24, 1944, vol. 284, NRC.

70. Mackenzie Diary, Feb. 17, 1944; Chadwick to Mackenzie, Feb. 24, 1944, vol. 284, NRC.

71. While these delicate negotiations were being conducted, the Canadian government nationalized the Eldorado Mining Company, a major supplier of uranium for both the Montreal Laboratory and the Manhattan Project. For a complete account of the ongoing dispute over Canadian uranium, see Gowing, *Britain and Atomic Energy,* pp. 269-319; R. Bothwell, *Eldorado: Canada's National Uranium Company* (Toronto, 1984), pp. 107-54.

72. After signing the agreement, Groves, in a spirit of cooperation, gave Chadwick and Mackenzie a tour of the Argonne pile. Both were greatly impressed with both its potential and its problems "in connection with radiation, corrosion, sheaths for the (uranium) rods." Mackenzie also met the Argonne director, Walter Zinn, "a Canadian from Kitchener." Mackenzie Diary, June 9, 1944.

73. "Resume of Report of Subcommittee on Joint Development of a heavy water pile to the Combined Policy Committee," Apr. 10, 1944, Howe Papers, vol. 14, File 32, NAC.

74. Canadian Liaison File, Minutes of meeting June 8, 1944 of the CPC subcommittee, MED, NAW. "Canadian Liaison, A Review of Liaison Activities Between the Canadian and the United States Atomic Energy Projects," Feb. 20, 1947, OSRD, Box 63, NAW.

75. Cockcroft actually welcomed the arrival of American scientists, suggesting that he could use ten good American physicists. Ibid.; Cockcroft to Appleton, May 8, 1944, AB1/278, PRO; "Canadian Liaison File," minutes of June 8, 1944 meeting of the CPC sub-committee, MED, NAW.

76. As one of his first duties, Benbow had made arrangements for the RCMP to assign a permanent security officer to the Montreal Laboratory. "Liaison with the Canadians," Memorandum, Benbow to Groves, July 13, 1944, Box 21, MED, NAW.

77. Goldschmidt, *Atomic Rivals,* p. 209.

78. There had been extensive collaborative work on U-233 since June 1944, with the exchange of monthly reports and reciprocal visits. Ibid., Report, Oct. 23, 1944, Box 21, MED, NAW.

79. Watson and Benbow were given special instructions to monitor communications between Goldschmidt and Seaborg to ensure that no plutonium information was exchanged. As an associate member of Goldschmidt's team, Watson also had the responsibility of keeping Groves informed about their progress. Ibid., Report, Aug. 5, 1944, Nov. 18, 1944, Box 21, MED, NAW.

80. Sherwin, *World Destroyed,* pp. 108-111.

81. Ibid., p. 284.

82. Ibid., p. 285.

83. Ibid., pp. 143-50.

84. Cockcroft and Steacie to Mackenzie, Sept. 27, 1944, AB1/278, PRO.

85. Cockcroft felt that Mackenzie was overreacting, in part, at least by the possibility that the King government would be defeated in the election of June 11, "and the necessity of explaining and justifying the project to a new Administration." Cockcroft to Chadwick, May 22, 1945; Mackenzie Diary, May 17, 1945, NAC.

86. Cockcroft also proposed that Britain would supply about ten high quality scientists "and that other Dominions might welcome the opportunity of contributing staff." Ibid.

87. Although none of the British Los Alamos team were transferred to Chalk River, Rudolph Peierls and Otto Frisch visited the site on their way back to England. Chadwick to Peierls, Apr. 6, 1945 AB1/485, PRO; O. Frisch, *What Little I Remember* (Cambridge, 1969), pp. 192-96.

88. See Peierls's interesting account of his last few days at Los Alamos, Sir R. E. Peierls, *Bird of Passage: Recollections of a Physicist* (Princeton, NJ, 1985), pp. 205-9.

89. Chadwick to Moon, Sept. 10, 1945, AB1/485, PRO.

90. Mackenzie Diary, July 5, 1945.

91. Ibid., July 30, 1945.

92. Howe's statement emphasized the role of "Canadian scientists and engineers in cooperation with distinguished workers from Britain and America . . . that guarantees us a front line position in the scientific advance that lies ahead." Ibid., Aug. 1-12, 1945; Press Release By Honourable C. D. Howe, Howe Papers, vol. 13, File 30, NAC.

93. Groves had previously been quite critical of the serious delay in building the NRX plant, and felt it was a waste of precious heavy water and scientific manpower to construct the ZEEP. By the fall of 1945 he was, however, encouraging American nuclear scientists to visit Chalk River. These included Glenn Seaborg (Nov. 1945); Walter Zinn (Sept. 1945); Eugene Wigner (Oct. 1945); and J. A. Wheeler and Edward Teller (Sept. 1946). Ibid., Groves to Chadwick, Nov. 6, 1944; OSRD, Reports May 1945-July 1946 in passim; Mackenzie Diary, July 16, 1945.

94. In 1945, the Americans sent Chalk River ten tons of uranium rods, a number of radioisotopes, additional irradiated slugs, radiation detecting devices, and various instruments. Canadian Liaison, Report, Nov. 17, 1945, OSRD.

95. In his memoirs, Goldschmidt indicates that he and Auger had briefed General de Gaulle about the atomic bomb project when he came to Canada in 1944. Goldschmidt, *Atomic Rivals*, pp. 213-217.

96. Cockcroft also fought hard to keep Goldschmidt, arguing that he had helped make "the Chalk River laboratory . . . a live scientific unit." Cited in Goldschmidt, *Atomic Rivals*, p. 280.

97. Ibid., p. 282.

98. Mackenzie File, Mackenzie to Conant, Aug. 14, 1945, Bush-Conant Files, NAW.

99. Ibid., Conant to Mackenzie, Aug. 24, 1945.

100. G. Herken, *The Winning Weapon: The Atomic Bomb in the Cold War, 1945-1959* (New York, 1982), pp. 63-78.

SEVEN

THE GHOSTS OF FISHER AND JELLICOE

THE ROYAL CANADIAN NAVY AND THE QUEBEC CONFERENCES [1]

ROGER SARTY

CANADA'S NAVAL LEADERS BELIEVED that the destiny of their service hinged on the outcome of Quadrant and Octagon, the Anglo-American conferences at Quebec City in 1943 and 1944. For these senior officers and their minister, the Royal Canadian Navy's struggle during the Second World War was as much to overcome the service's unhappy history as to defeat the Axis powers. The Quebec conferences offered both heady opportunity and, Octagon especially, the menace of renewed setback. The navy was keenly aware of both possibilities, for the circumstances echoed earlier experiences of hopes dashed. Two of the past players, British admirals Sir John Fisher and Earl Jellicoe of Scapa, had long since died, but Canadian sailors and politicians keenly felt their presence in 1943 and 1944 when the course of the war in the Pacific seemed to promise that the Royal Canadian Navy could finally procure large warships. [2]

Fisher, in 1909, had hatched the idea that the self-governing dominions of the British Empire could have their own high-seas navies by acquiring modern cruisers. This vision had triggered the founding of the Royal Canadian Navy in 1910, the Royal Australian Navy in the following year, and, ultimately, the Royal New Zealand Navy. Yet his justification for the scheme, that the dominions fleets were needed in the Pacific to

counter Japan's growing navy and thereby would free Britain to concentrate against Germany, in no way convinced the Canadian government.
This gulf in strategic outlook, and Fisher's subsequent political machina-
tions conceived narrowly in Royal Navy self-interest, helped fuel a
political division in Canada that nearly killed the newborn service.[3]

Earl Jellicoe, who visited the dominions in 1919 to advise on naval
policy in the wake World War I, revived the Fisher's vision. He was certain,
as were Canadian naval officers, that Japan had maintained its alliance with
Britain only as a convenient cover for territorial and military expansion that
would inevitably lead to war with the Western powers. He therefore urged
the dominions to acquire major warships as components of an Imperial
Pacific fleet. Convinced of the importance of both land-based aircraft and
the still-experimental aircraft carrier in future maritime warfare, Jellicoe also
encouraged the dominions to develop naval aviation.[4]

For a brief period it seemed that things might work out for the
Canadian navy this time. In 1919-20 the Royal Navy made a gift to the
dominion of a modern 6-inch gun cruiser, two destroyers, and two
submarines. Soon after, however, William Lyon Mackenzie King's new
Liberal government so slashed the naval budget that all the ships save the
two destroyers had to be paid off.

Although King had imposed the defense cuts to capitalize politically
on postwar antimilitary and isolationist sentiment, he had some strategic
justification. In 1914-18 Britain (and later the United States) had provided
ample heavy ship coverage off Canada's coasts. This had not been charity,
but self-interest driven by the geographical fact that the Canadian Atlantic
seaboard dominates the most direct ocean routes between North America
and Great Britain. Canadian waters had to be protected if vital supplies were
to reach Britain and if the enemy were to be prevented from making attacks
in strength in U.S. waters. What neither Britain nor the United States had
been able to supply was the smallest class of warships that were needed in
large numbers to screen the Canadian coastal area against a new threat that
had caught the Allies by surprise: submarines that the Germans had used in
an aggressive campaign against merchant shipping. The U-boats, which
could sight approaching warships and dive long before Allied lookouts
could discern the low profile of the surfaced submarine, had no difficulty
evading detection and counterattack. German submarines in fact operated
within a few miles of the mouth of Halifax harbor. The Royal Canadian
Navy found itself rushing into service more than a hundred converted
civilian craft and small emergency-built antisubmarine craft manned by
crusty old merchant mariners and inexperienced youths, many of whom
had no affinity for naval discipline and training.[5]

Disaster had been avoided, but the naval staff reminded the government that the war had ended before the Germans had been able to follow up their initial reconnaissance into Canadian waters with a fully organized assault. Even if the only future need was coastal patrols, the sailors warned the government, minor craft would have to be supported by at least destroyers, the smallest of the major warships types, but fast, well-armed vessels that could fill a variety roles. The sailors made the case with particular reference to the west coast. The increasing dominance of the Pacific by the large Japanese and U.S. fleets, and the shrinkage of British power on that ocean, meant that in the event of a Far Eastern conflict Canada could no longer depend on the big-ship protection of the mother country. There would be nearly complete dependence upon the United States. If Canada could not defend at least the waters immediately off British Columbia's shores, the Americans might occupy the area to secure their communications with Alaska and ensure that the many isolated bays along the Canadian coast were not used by the Japanese to stage raids against U.S. ports. King had long worried about the menace excessive reliance on American assistance might pose to Canadian sovereignty. Although he did not relent in his opposition to cruisers, which he believed would inevitably drag the country into Empire-wide military commitments, in the late 1920s and 1930s he supported the navy in acquiring a total of seven large, modern destroyers, ships that could be represented as coast defense types. The value of these vessels was that they would be equally useful against enemy cruisers that seemed to be the major threat until the late 1930s, and, with some re-equipment, against submarines as well.[6]

In 1938 the Munich crisis and German expansion of its U-boat fleet made it clear that war might come with Germany before Japan, and that there would likely be a new submarine campaign against Allied shipping. Although King allowed important joint naval planning with the British, he would not support the base construction and warship building programs needed to create adequate antisubmarine forces.[7]

When war broke out in 1939, the chief of the naval staff, Rear-Admiral P. W. Nelles, had no illusions about the capabilities of his tiny service. There were only 1,596 regular and 1,879 reserve personnel,[8] six destroyers (the seventh would arrive shortly), a handful of minor craft, and two small dockyards, one on each coast. Nelles, who had spent a good proportion of his 31-year career in Ottawa, did not delude himself that the politicians would suddenly be converted to a big-navy policy.[9]

He therefore proposed a modest expansion primarily for duties in North American waters. His immediate object was to do properly what had been forced upon Canada in 1914-18: to relieve the Royal Navy in the western hemisphere so that it could concentrate on the main combat theaters. The British had made no secret of the fact that their diminished navy could do much less in the western hemisphere than had been possible during World War I, and looked to Canada for more self-sufficiency and to supply light patrol forces for the local security of Newfoundland and British possessions in the Caribbean.

King was delighted with the naval proposals. Alone among the three services, the navy emphasized North American operations, made modest demands on manpower, and gave a leading role to industry, especially for the production of the coastal types of warships that were within its limited capacity. This matched King's priorities of primarily economic support for Britain, and the commitment of only minimal forces overseas in order to avoid the enormous battle casualties of World War I, which had divided the country. King, after all, had built his political career on a pledge of never again.[10]

Nelles soon found that he was dealing with a government he scarcely recognized. A total of 92 corvette and Bangor escorts, patrol vessels that were much larger and more seaworthy than the antisubmarine craft built in Canada during World War I, were ordered in Canadian shipyards. The prime minister also agreed to place orders for Tribal-class destroyers in Britain. These ships were half again bigger and carried a gun armament fully twice as heavy as previous destroyers. In some respects the ships were really small cruisers, which was precisely why the Canadian naval staff wanted them.

Although the Canadian navy of 1939 could not carry out much more than the coastal type of operations it had performed in 1914-18, Nelles was determined to avoid a repetition of that experience. The government, he believed, had had no difficulty in quickly disposing of the inglorious little antisubmarine craft and then turning back the modern warships Britain had given as gifts in 1919-20 because the navy had not had any opportunity to distinguish itself during the war.[11] From the first months of World War II the naval staff quickly responded to the Royal Navy's calls for the loan of certain categories of personnel, such as those with a knowledge of electronics or experienced yachtsmen. These men could gain a fighting reputation and the skills that would later be needed for the Canadian fleet. Officers fervently hoped as well that the best of the Canadian warships—the destroyers—would carry out tours in the most active theaters. The naval staff's intention was that those high-profile missions would ultimately be performed by the big new Tribal destroyers. These ships, unlike the humble corvettes and Bangors, could form the backbone of a strong postwar navy. The government would not dare pay off impressive vessels that had roared into battle with the maple leaf on their funnels.

The navy was helped by the presence of Angus L. Macdonald, the former premier of Nova Scotia, whom King brought into the federal government for the new portfolio, minister of National Defence for Naval Services, in the summer of 1940. Macdonald, although he disliked the social elitism he detected in the attitudes of the regular force officer corps,[12] fully supported the shaping of wartime policies to create a larger and more capable service for the future. "The policy of 1910," he informed his Cabinet colleagues, "remained a sound one."[13] He was referring to the scheme for a cruiser squadron capable of independent high seas operations that had grown out of Admiral Fisher's proposals but had never been carried out because of political controversy. In November 1940, he elaborated on the need for a big-ship navy in the House of Commons: "The dignity of Canada demands that we should have a navy worthy of our importance in the world of nations, adequate to the needs of the great trading nation which Canada now is, and which she is bound to become in greater measure after the war; a navy sufficient to meet the obligations which rest upon us as members of the British commonwealth, and as a country in close association with the United States in the matter of the joint defence of this continent."[14]

By the time Macdonald came into office, Canadian warships had had an opportunity to prove themselves in combat earlier than anyone had anticipated. With the fall of France in the spring of 1940, Britain had appealed for help, and four Canadian destroyers, all the ones ready for extended operations, rushed to the scene. As the German U-boat fleet, now with direct access to the Atlantic through French ports, began an intensified assault on British shipping in the fall and winter of 1940, Canada increased its commitment in British waters.

The U-boats had meanwhile proved that they could strike effectively not only in coastal waters, as had been the case in World War I, but far out in the central Atlantic. In the late spring of 1941, at Britain's request, the Royal Canadian Navy pulled back all of its ships to Newfoundland for the task of escorting convoys to Iceland (later Northern Ireland) and back. In addition to the destroyers, most of the 64 corvettes built in Canada in 1940-41 were assigned to the Newfoundland Escort Force, making it a largely Royal Canadian Navy organization. King, despite his usual fretting about costs and the possibility Canada might be laden with more than its fair share of the burden, welcomed this commitment.[15] Defense of the Atlantic bridge between the new world and the old was precisely the sort of role he thought Canadians should carry out. Expansion of the Royal Canadian Navy became open-ended, governed only by the rate at which Canadian shipyards could produce still more escorts. By the end of 1941 the service had grown to 27,000 personnel, with more than 100 escorts in service and 30 others in building.[16] This was nearly double the personnel strength and half again as many ships as had been projected for 1943 in the mobilization plans of 1939.[17]

The naval staff's focus on the postwar future faded in the second half of 1941 as the service faced the enormous task of organizing the Newfoundland Escort Force. The strains grew more severe in 1942. With the United States's entry into the war after Pearl Harbor, Hitler unleashed the expanding U-boat fleet for an offensive in North American coastal waters from Newfoundland and Nova Scotia to the Caribbean. At this very time, the U.S. Navy was withdrawing much of its escort fleet from the north Atlantic to meet its own pressing needs in the two-ocean war (the Americans had accepted a large share of convoy escort on the north Atlantic as far east as Iceland in September 1941 to help the beleaguered British). Now the Canadian escort force had to help fill the gap left by the Americans on the transocean routes, while also organizing coastal convoys in Canadian waters, and extending assistance to the U.S. Navy in escorting shipping in American waters. The strain grew greater in September 1942 when Churchill appealed to King to release 17 Royal Canadian Navy corvettes from Canadian waters for the Mediterranean to support the Torch landings in North Africa. These withdrawals came as the U-boat fleet was able to concentrate large "wolf packs" against convoys in the mid-north Atlantic, while still keeping up pressure in North American waters.[18]

The price of the Royal Canadian Navy's rapid expansion and overcommitment became clear in the late fall and winter of 1942. Convoys escorted by understrength Canadian escort groups whose ships were frequently poorly maintained, lacking in the latest sensors and weapons, and manned by inadequately trained crews, suffered some of the most severe losses to the wolf packs.

The all-out Royal Canadian Navy effort in the Atlantic antisubmarine escort role looked like it was having exactly the opposite results intended of building a fighting reputation and a cohesive national force. What some senior officers regarded as the cruelest blow came in December 1942 from the Royal Navy whose pleas for help had been largely responsible for the overextension of the Royal Canadian Navy. Churchill supported Western Approaches, the principal British command in the Battle of the Atlantic, in demanding that the battered Canadian mid-ocean groups be withdrawn to the U.K. - Gibraltar run where they could retrain and reequip under British supervision. Naval Service Headquarters' response was to step up efforts already begun to "consolidate" the Canadian forces. This included successful demands upon the Admiralty for additional escort destroyers, much the best antisubmarine vessels, and the return, by the spring of 1943, of ships that had been dispatched to the Mediterranean and U.K. - Gibraltar run.

Most important, Naval Service Headquarters wanted the Royal Canadian Navy's Atlantic forces removed from the command of the U.S. Navy, which had assumed responsibility for convoy operations in the western part of the ocean in September 1941. The acceptance of that task by the then still neutral United States had been a vital boost to Britain and the Commonwealth in 1941, but it had become an anomaly since the removal of most of the U.S. escorts early in 1942. As it happened, Fleet Admiral Ernest J. King, commander-in-chief of the U.S. Navy, wanted to streamline his organization, in part by escaping the shared, and by now rather tangled, Anglo-American command in the north Atlantic. The Royal Navy reassumed command of convoy operations right across the Atlantic to just east of Newfoundland, but the whole of the Newfoundland and Canadian ocean area, north to the Arctic and south to the Georges Banks below Nova Scotia, was placed under Canadian control for convoy and antisubmarine operations. On April 30, 1943, Royal Canadian Navy Rear-Admiral L. W. Murray, assumed the new appointment as commander-in-chief, Canadian Northwest Atlantic at Halifax; he was the only Canadian to command a theater in World War II.[19] Unexpectedly, at this same time the worst crisis of the Battle of the Atlantic was passing. Heavy losses of U-boats to reinforced British escort groups brought Admiral Karl Dönitz, the commander-in-chief of the German U-boat fleet, to pull back his forces from the north Atlantic, although this by no means ended the menace from this large and still efficient force.

For all the difficulties, Canada's achievements in the Atlantic had been outstanding. A navy that had scarcely existed in 1939 had in 1943 been acknowledged by the Great Powers as a partner, even if a junior one, in the decisive maritime campaign of the war. The very process of consolidating the service's position in the Atlantic, however, brought senior officers to think again about what lay beyond the escort role. Even in the battle against the U-boats it seemed that surface escorts alone, no matter how well equipped and efficient, were no longer enough. Front-rank American and British antisubmarine groups now included small "escort" aircraft carriers (CVEs) that could, with technical ingenuity and highly skilled crews, operate maritime bomber aircraft. This development, together with the dramatic successes of larger carriers in fleet operations in all theaters and especially the Pacific, suggested that no navy of the future would be truly capable without an aviation component. Since December 1942, Naval Service Head Quarters (NSHQ) had been considering the Royal Canadian Navy's entry into the complex and expensive endeavor of naval aviation with the immediate goal of acquiring escort carriers for the Atlantic antisubmarine groups.[20]

For the longer term, with fortunes turning for the Allies on all fronts in the summer of 1943, one could for the first time foresee the defeat of Germany and the massing of fleets for the final seaborne offensive against Japan's island empire. The meeting between Churchill, Roosevelt, and their chiefs of staff scheduled to take place in Quebec City in August 1943 to hone plans for the Allied offensives signaled that the war was at a turning point.

A paper drafted at the end of July 1943 by Lieutenant-Commander Geoffrey Todd, a capable volunteer reserve officer who was serving in the plans division under acting Captain H. G. DeWolf, one of the most talented members of the regular force, highlighted the dangers and opportunities for the Canadian service in the rapidly changing situation.[21] The unique nature of the U-boat offensive, Todd pointed out, had handed Canada the unusual chance to gain recognition through the creation of an unbalanced fleet of small, specialized vessels. None of these special advantages obtained in the Pacific, where Canadian bases and territory had no strategic bearing on the combat theater, and, in the absence of a concerted Japanese submarine offensive, the escort role was an unglamorous one of tertiary importance. If on the defeat of Germany the Royal Canadian Navy merely shifted its escorts to the Pacific, the service would lose its international profile and end the war with a fleet ill-suited to serve as the foundation for further development of the service. Ships much larger than escorts were needed to carry out training programs for the production of professionally well-rounded personnel, to conduct diplomatic missions, to sustain Canada's position within alliances, and to secure Canadian waters against threats other than submarines that could well emerge in another war, one that Todd predicted might be fomented by Russia. The time had come, he concluded, to push for the acquisition of four cruisers and to multiply the fleet-destroyer force from the eight Tribals (four completed, four under construction) to a total of 24. Cruisers, supported by adequate numbers of big fleet destroyers, were the smallest warships that could play a significant role in the front line in the Pacific. Happily, the cruiser-fleet destroyer combination would also provide a good basis for the postwar fleet. Aircraft carriers, Todd allowed more cautiously, were also a "possibility"; he was aware of the difficulties that already surrounded the question of Canadian naval aviation.

There was little that was new in Todd's paper. The fleet he described, and the arguments about capability, status, and sovereignty were the same ones that had emerged from the debates of 1909-14, the Jellicoe mission of 1919, and had been urged by senior Canadian officers ever since. What was significant was Todd's timing and strong language—"It is vital for the maintenance of Canadian prestige that the Canadian Navy takes a direct and important part in the war against Japan"—which reflected the sense at headquarters that the service had again arrived at a crossroads.

In contrast to those earlier occasions the Canadian service now had something to bargain with: a good supply of manpower at precisely the time the Royal Navy faced a grievous shortage of crews. In mid-1943 the British Ministry of Labour warned that it might be possible to find less than half of the 912,000 additional men and women already allocated for expansion of the armed forces and war industry during the latter half of the year.[22] This put the Admiralty in a particularly tight spot. Because of the length of time it takes to build warships, the navy had been slower to expand than the other services, but was at this very moment confronted by the need to man a flood of new construction. Many of these vessels were being built in the United States for the Royal Navy under Lend-Lease, and delays in taking them over would raise doubts in Washington about Britain's ability to back up its claims as co-leader of the Western alliance. These pressures reflected the inescapable strategic fact that the offensive operations planned were almost all amphibious in nature and made particularly heavy demands on the navy for the movement of troops and equipment, security of these military convoys, and the landing craft and fire support required for the actual assault. The improving situation in the Mediterranean promised some relief as forces were released from that theater, but large resources would still be needed there for the assault on Italy, and, of course, massive strength had to be built up for the invasion of northern France planned for 1944. Although the U-boats had been pushed back from the main convoy routes, the German submarine fleet was as large as ever, and several major surface ships were still poised to strike from Norway, meaning that there could be few economies in the Atlantic. It was thus not possible to greatly expand the Royal Navy's presence in the Far East and Pacific, even though it was imperative for reasons of international stature that the Americans should not be left as the sole liberators of the Pacific and Southeast Asia.[23]

There was some excitement at the Admiralty when in the summer of 1943 reports came from officers on duty in North America that the Canadians had a surplus of personnel. Construction in Canada of frigates, the new escort warship that was half again bigger than the corvette, had fallen behind the rate of recruitment. Out of a total strength of nearly 70,000 personnel in the Royal Canadian Navy fewer than 22,000 were assigned to ships when some 35,000 should have been. The Canadian naval staff and the Admiralty quickly recognized the possibility of mutual benefit.[24]

On the evening of August 11, the day after the British delegation for Quadrant arrived at Quebec, Admiral Sir Dudley Pound, first Sea Lord, and Vice-Admiral Lord Louis Mountbatten, chief of Combined Operations, met secretly with Nelles and Captain DeWolf. Pound did not want the other British services, with which he was competing for manpower, to know what was up and Nelles did not want word to get out to his government. Pound quickly declared that he could help the Canadians in their quest for cruisers. Nelles frankly stated that the intention was to build toward a postwar navy of five cruisers, two light fleet aircraft carriers (vessels twice as large and much better built than the emergency-type escort carriers that had previously been discussed), and three flotillas of fleet destroyers. Pound steered discussion toward his immediate problem: to find personnel for combined operations to meet British commitments to Overlord, the invasion of France in 1944. Mountbatten then stepped in. Aware of Canadian anger at the manner in which some of their loaned personnel had been scattered almost irretrievably through the Combined Operations organization, he made it clear that any further drafts of Royal Canadian Navy personnel would be kept together, forming complete crews for the largest landing craft. On the carrier question, there was a fundamental Anglo-Canadian disagreement.[25] The British were only too willing to have the Royal Canadian Navy provide ships' crews for carriers. However, they insisted that the entire flying organization on those carriers should be Royal Navy in order to avoid wasting resources—resources that otherwise might be pooled with Britain—in attempting the large task of organizing a Canadian naval aviation branch.[26]

During the course of the conference, members of the Admiralty delegation fleshed-out arrangements with the Canadian naval staff in the areas where there was agreement. These included the early transfer of two modern fleet destroyers to the Royal Canadian Navy, Canadian manning of a squadron of large infantry landing craft (30 vessels), and the provision of other landing units. The Canadians were also to infiltrate personnel into British cruisers for training, thus giving early relief to the Royal Navy in its shortages and assuring that qualified Canadian crews were ready when ships became available for transfer.

Nelles privately informed the British that the whole scheme should initially be raised with the Canadian government by Churchill himself "for political reasons."[27] Nelles was only too well aware of King's resistance to the acquisition of any ships larger than destroyers. Since the latter part of 1942, moreover, King had made it clear that Canada was doing enough, and that the programs already approved would represent the maximum effort. He was especially worried about manpower and the looming threat of overseas conscription for the army, but also wanted to cut expenditure and give the population tax relief. His political antennae had picked up war-weariness among the public that found expression with the rising popularity of the Socialist Co-operative Commonwealth Federation party and a slump in the polls for King's Liberal party. The navy, at its moment of great opportunity, was feeling the chill wind of domestic politics—as it had so often in the past.[28] There was a new card to play, however. On several occasions during the war King, after casting a cold eye on advice from the Canadian chief of staff, had buried his reservations on receiving the same request in a personal appeal from Churchill.[29] It worked this time too.

At a meeting of the Canadian Cabinet War Committee with Churchill and the British chiefs of staff in Quebec on August 31, the British prime minister and Admiral Pound presented the list of naval undertakings already negotiated with Nelles as a plea for help with the British manpower crisis.[30] When the War Committee discussed these requests, on September 8, Nelles was present and King chided him about the way in which the British had suddenly sprung the naval demands on the government. What had the naval staff known? Nelles, like Macdonald, admitted to "informal" talks with the British officers, but claimed ignorance that the British had had any intention of rushing ahead with specific requests. King warned at length that the manpower ceiling of 84,000 that had been set for the navy for 1943 was the absolute maximum the service could hope for, "that from now on we would have to contract." He then hinted darkly that the Liberal government could well be replaced within the next year by one much less favorable to the military. Nelles and Macdonald reassured the prime minister on the critical question of manpower. There were ample numbers of personnel available to meet the British requests, and also to press forward with the acquisition of two carriers and the organization of a Canadian naval air arm. The War Committee approved Pound's manning proposals, including the cruisers, but held over, as it had already done earlier in the year, a decision on the carrier scheme.[31]

No evidence has come to light as to whether Macdonald was privy to the arrangements with the Admiralty, but at the Canadian War Committee meetings of August 31 and September 8 he was an enthusiastic supporter of the naval staff. After the first meeting he reflected "I am eager to have the cruiser as our training is now purely on convoy escort and in small ships."[32] After the government agreed on September 8 to begin infiltrating Canadians into British cruiser crews, Macdonald crowed: "This step is very significant. The RCN is stepping out of the small ship class—the Laurier plan is being realized after more than 30 years."[33] He was so pleased, that two days later, while at a press conference on the Battle of the Atlantic, he blurted out the news about "the Cruiser programme." "This," he noted with satisfaction, "received the most attention in the papers."[34]

The arrangements made at Quebec proved to be only the beginning of Royal Canadian Navy assistance to the Royal Navy in meeting its most immediate large difficulty: carrying out its part in the invasion of France in June 1944. As British resources continued to fall behind requirements in the fall of 1943 and spring of 1944, the Admiralty continued to call for help, and in virtually every case the Royal Canadian Navy responded.[35] Ultimately some 10,000 Royal Canadian Navy personnel in 100 Canadian ships participated in the landing operations. Nor was that all. The Royal Canadian Navy escort forces took over full responsibility for north Atlantic convoys in order to release British warships for invasion duties.[36]

For King this huge effort was integral to what he saw as Canada's war, the Atlantic battle, the security of Britain, and the liberation of western Europe. By contrast, the prime minister and several of his Cabinet colleagues viewed the carriers, the cruisers, and future offensive operations against Japan with increasing caution. King had never been happy with the manner in which big ships had been thrust upon the government at Quebec in August 1943. His suspicions were heightened during the fall when Macdonald and Nelles tied renewed British requests for help in manning escort carriers to the much more ambitious and costly plans to organize a full-fledged Canadian fleet air arm. On October 21, 1943, Nelles admitted under questioning in a War Committee meeting that the Royal Canadian Navy aviation scheme was really for the postwar navy.[37] The prime minister's suspicions were confirmed when at the end of November Admiral Sir Percy Noble, head of the British Admiralty Delegation in Washington, visited Ottawa to press for the provision of carrier crews by the Royal Canadian Navy. When Admiral Noble explained that the British request was a modest one simply for the use of Canadian manpower, the full scope of the Canadian naval staff's scheme for an aviation branch suddenly became clear to the prime minister. Admiral Noble's easy and well-informed talk about the Royal Canadian Navy's plans for a big postwar navy, as exemplified by the acquisition of cruisers, then caused the pieces to fall into place in King's mind: "it was our department rather than the British that really occasioned the cruisers being forced upon us by Churchill and Dudley Pound." King blamed his defense ministers who had "not . . . played the game with the rest of the Cabinet in the way they have forced the pace for their services."[38]

His resentment burst into the open in January 1944. A. V. Alexander, first lord of the Admiralty, sent a message confirming that two of the most modern cruisers, just then nearing completion, would be transferred to the Canadian government as a "free gift." Alexander, with the encouragement of Vincent Massey, Canada's High Commissioner in the United Kingdom, took the occasion "to welcome the advent of the RCN as a 'big ship' navy able to take an ever greater part both now and after the war in maintaining the naval traditions of the British Commonwealth."[39] Massey was shaken to receive back for transmission to the Admiralty a reply that coldly declared that the ships were no "free gift." Rather, Canada was helping Britain with its manpower shortage. In financial terms, the ships were only a small return to Canada in exchange for the massive economic aid it had already given Britain.

Canada's formal reply to Alexander also noted that the cruisers "will become an integral part of the Canadian Navy . . . at the sole disposal of the Canadian Government." A private note to Massey put it more strongly: "it must be clearly understood, both by the United Kingdom authorities and by the public, that no strings are attached to the transfer of the ships," meaning they would not be considered part of a united Commonwealth navy that could be deployed by the Admiralty.[40] When Massey protested at the mean-spirited message, Hume Wrong, assistant under-secretary of state for external affairs, warned that he had already tried to cool King down, but that it had done no good. The prime minister was on the warpath against what he saw as a new movement to absorb Canada into a scheme for integrated British Empire armed forces.[41]

Angus L. Macdonald left a detailed record of his argument with King in the War Committee over Alexander's cheerful message. The ghosts of Fisher and Jellicoe were raised by both self-proclaimed Laurier Liberals, a fact that reveals how wide disagreement could be over the old master's masterfully ambiguous naval policy.

> Prime Minister said this was old Imperialistic stuff—a unified navy—mention made of Round Table Group, Smuts (whom P.M. said Willingdon described as blue eyed boy of Tory party). I said I felt that from 1910, through Jellicoe report days and this war, Britain had not tried to direct us but was willing to let us run our own naval show. Alexander's words were meant to be complimentary.
>
> P.M. seemed to think that if we accept ships as a gift—we would somehow be falling into line with idea of British direction—also we were committing ourselves to a big ship navy after war. (He had frequently spoken recently on the danger of making commitments now which will extend into post war period.)[42]

Significantly, however, King made no effort to reverse the big ship projects that were already underway. Royal Canadian Navy personnel had been "infiltrated" in large numbers into British cruisers for training, and on October 21, 1944, these crewmen would commission the large six-inch cruiser *Uganda* as Her Majesty's Canadian Ship, followed by a second, HMCS *Ontario,* on April 26, 1945. Meanwhile, in January 1944, King, while grumbling about the Commonwealth navy conspiracies, had allowed the Cabinet to give final approval for the Canadian manning of two British escort carriers, HMS *Nabob* and HMS *Puncher,* which had been built by the Americans under Lend-Lease. Because Canadian policy was not to accept Lend-Lease, and the Americans were unwilling for political reasons to allow transfer of Lend-Lease material to third nations, the ships were commissioned into the Royal Navy. As the Admiralty had urged, the aircraft and aviation crews were from the British Fleet Air Arm.

While the government was tackling the big-ship program in January 1944, the question of Canadian participation in the offensive against Japan after the defeat of Germany surfaced in a substantial way for the first time. The occasion was negotiations with the British Air Ministry concerning the scaling-down of the British Commonwealth Air Training Plan (BCATP) in Canada in light of the impending defeat of Germany and the lesser requirements for the war with Japan. Because of the BCATP, which had fed more than 50 percent of Canadian aircrew into Royal Air Force units, the Royal Canadian Air Force was the least national of the Canadian services. The Canadian government insisted that after the defeat of Germany, Royal Canadian Air Force members would have to be unscrambled from Royal Air Force units, and assembled into a full, balanced Canadian force for service in the Pacific. The Canadians also reminded the Air Ministry that Canada would be fighting in the Pacific not only as a member of the Commonwealth, but also as a North American partner of the United States, with which Canada had already closely cooperated in the development of bases and forces in British Columbia and Alaska. As the negotiations concluded the government declared that the Royal Canadian Air Force or any of the Canadian forces might serve under American rather than British command, if possible on the Alaska - north Pacific route to Japan that reflected Canada's historic ties and interests.[43]

King and C. G. Power, the Canadian air minister, readily agreed that the Pacific effort should be primarily air force and navy, with only token army representation. King did not openly quibble when Power suggested a very large air contingent, "60-70 squadrons," but privately he was reluctant. "While I feel strongly America should and will bear an overwhelming measure [of the final offensives against Japan] as far as North America is concerned, it may be necessary for Canada to participate if she is to maintain her position vis-à-vis the US and Britain, though I am sure she will get little credit from either for what she does."[44]

The government's desire to send air and sea rather than land forces to the Pacific undoubtedly encouraged the naval staff, as did the evident acceptance of the air force's ambitious proposals. Indeed the navy's thinking was not much different from that of the air force. With cruisers and carriers, the Royal Canadian Navy could finally make its mark in the Pacific as a balanced, integrated national service in much the same way that the Royal Canadian Air Force was seeking through its Pacific force to overcome the effects of the BCATP. Moreover, resources for naval expansion were available under the ceiling the government had imposed. Containment of the U-boats allowed the cancellation in late 1943 of the last 41 frigates and 11 corvettes due to be built in Canada, freeing the personnel and funds for these ships that had already been approved. The intention, as the naval staff's planning took shape in the fall and winter of 1943, was to press for acquisition from the Royal Navy in 1945 of two more cruisers, eight additional fleet destroyers, and to trade up from the escort carriers to two light fleet carriers. In addition to the big ships, the naval staff proposed sending to the Pacific 108 of the best antisubmarine escorts, and all of the Royal Canadian Navy amphibious forces.[45]

These goals were not affected by a shake-up among the navy's leadership. Macdonald and Nelles fell out in late 1943 as a result of the aftershocks over the shortcomings in equipment, refit, and training among the Atlantic escorts in the winter of 1942-43. In January 1944 Macdonald reassigned Nelles to the United Kingdom in the new and nebulously defined appointment "Senior Canadian Flag Officer Overseas."[46] He was replaced as chief of the naval staff by Vice-Admiral G. C. Jones, formerly the vice-chief. There is some evidence to suggest that Jones was at the head of a faction of senior officers who joined Macdonald in blaming Nelles's toadying to the British for the overexpansion of the Atlantic escort force, and hence the slow progress toward big ships.[47] Given Mackenzie King's view of cruisers and carriers as the embodiment of Empire commitments, there was some paradox in his reaction to the news that Nelles was going to England: "I hope Nelles," he remarked to Macdonald, "would not lead us into any further effort to have one Navy for the whole British Empire."[48]

Admiral Jones left few records. What traces remain in navy files suggest that he was a careful bureaucrat.[49] The new chief seems to have left Nelles, who had always prized and guarded his personal connections in the Admiralty, to lobby in London for the allocation of big ships to the Royal Canadian Navy. Jones, meanwhile, carefully kept himself and the rest of the staff in Ottawa out of the fray. Among Jones's first actions in his new appointment was to withhold further action on the director of plans' Pacific fleet recommendations until the government laid down its policy.[50]

Nelles, by contrast, wasted no time in letting the Admiralty know what the Royal Canadian Navy wanted. His handpicked assistant was Commander Todd, the officer who as a member of the plans division in Ottawa had drafted most of the basic papers on the Pacific and postwar fleets. Todd, seeking out Admiralty staff officers at his level, ran into a "ban" on any discussion of Pacific strategy. This blackout was the result of bitter disagreements between Churchill, who wanted to make the main effort in Southeast Asia, and the services, who wanted to join the Americans in the Pacific offensive.[51] Todd noted a certain "complacency" in the Admiralty's confidence that Canada would automatically fall into line the instant the British government made its decisions.[52]

On June 14, 1944 the Admiralty finally gave Nelles's office an informal estimate of what help would be wanted from Canada. The estimate, by including the cruisers and escort carriers already allocated or earmarked for the Royal Canadian Navy, all of the Canadian fleet destroyers, 91 of the Royal Canadian Navy's most modern escorts, and the possible transfer of additional modern ships such as fleet destroyers, reflected what the British knew the Canadian service wanted. In a thinly disguised quid pro quo the Admiralty also urged the Canadians to undertake substantial, new commitments among the less glamorous chores, especially the manning of more landing craft and other amphibious warfare vessels whose seemingly endless thirst for manpower was the bane of the Royal Navy. The British proposals gave an estimated total of 40,000 personnel, including immediate reserves in theater for the replacement of casualties.[53] This figure did not come out of thin air. The British forces were planning to remain as fully mobilized for the Japanese phase of the war as the deepening manpower shortage would allow, which was 70 percent of the peak wartime strength. Canada, the Admiralty hoped, would follow suit.

Nelles and Todd were excited about the promise of a big Royal Canadian Navy presence in the Pacific, but the staff in Ottawa was more restrained. Observing that reorganization and partial demobilization after the defeat of Germany would create a manpower "squeeze,"[54] the staff proposed a personnel ceiling for the Pacific of 25,000, put the demand for landing craft crews at the bottom of the list, and suggested that planning should be limited to the escorts and major warships.[55] Nor was that all. The proposal had to be reviewed by the Naval Board, the Royal Canadian Navy's senior administrative authority, on which the minister sat as chairman with the chief of the naval staff and heads of the other staff branches as members. The board concluded that in the absence of an overall plan for Commonwealth participation in the Pacific nothing could be decided, and withheld approval.[56]

There was good reason for caution. In Ottawa, the air and army staffs raised concerns about the British secrecy and delay in planning for the offensive against Japan. Both services feared that they might be embarrassed by sudden demands that Canada pour large contributions into Southeast Asia, a sideshow known for meager gains at the cost of heavy losses to tropical diseases and Japanese skill in jungle fighting. There was no evidence that the British had taken into account the Canadian preference, expressed in the BCATP negotiations of January 1944, to participate in the main assault against Japan in the central or northern Pacific, even if that meant serving with the Americans.[57] King shot off a restatement of this position to London at the end of June.[58]

These issues were of less interest to the navy, which concluded that its British-type warships made operations as an integral part of the American fleet impractical for logistical reasons. Further, the tropical environment that complicated air and land operations in Southeast Asia posed less serious problems for the navy, although the unhealthy climate of coastal areas was one reason why the naval staff shied away from amphibious operations. At Quebec in August 1943, Nelles had readily agreed to the British suggestion that Canadian warships should initially join the existing British Eastern Fleet in the Indian Ocean, wherever the final offensives might be launched. The naval staff did not change that position during 1944, even when in July and August, as the British chiefs of staff broke their impasse with Churchill, important news came from Nelles and Todd: the main Commonwealth fleet would ultimately be based on Australia to join the American forces in the southwest Pacific for the drive north to the Philippines.[59] The Indian Ocean was still the staging route for entry of Commonwealth ships into the theater. Further, because certain Canadian vessels, such as the short-ranged Tribal destroyers, were better suited for Southeast Asian waters than the vast expanses of the Pacific, the Royal Canadian Navy remained receptive to specific British proposals for participation in the Indian Ocean.[60]

There was also a sentimental dimension to the navy's attitude, albeit mixed with self-interest. The navy's experience was different from that of the army, which since the latter part of World War I had been distinctly nationalist in its relations with the British forces, and the Royal Canadian Air Force whose senior officers had been embittered by British foot-dragging over "Canadianization" of the Royal Canadian Air Force in Britain and northwest Europe. By contrast, a key naval staff paper of late June 1944, after declaring Canada's right "as a sovereign state" to choose between the British and American zones of operations, and the need to assure the maximum recognition of the "Canadian identity" of any Pacific force, came down squarely for cooperation with the British. The Royal Navy truly needed Canadian help whereas the U.S. Navy did not. "All precedents that exist," moreover, "are in the form of co-operation with the Royal Navy and our commitment of September 1939 to render full assistance to the Royal Navy is probably applicable to Pacific as well as Atlantic waters." The self-interest derived from the fact the Royal Canadian Navy was already beginning to acquire the big ships it needed by cooperating with the Royal Navy, and prospects were good for completing the balanced fleet program so long as the Royal Canadian Navy continued to respect the partnership.[61]

What worried Nelles and Todd in London was the lukewarm reception the British proposals for a major contribution had received in Ottawa. Although the British chiefs of staff accepted the limit of 25,000 personnel,[62] the Admiralty put pressure on the Canadian naval officers in London. Canadian hopes to get additional modern warships, especially the light fleet carriers and the eight fleet destroyers, might be disappointed if the Royal Canadian Navy could not guarantee that the vessels would be available to serve under British control in the Pacific.[63] Still Nelles's appeal to Jones for a firming up of the Canadian commitment evoked only the response that the government had yet to decide.[64] All that Nelles could give to the First Sea Lord, Admiral Sir Andrew Cunningham, as the latter departed in early September for the second Quebec Conference, was a reiteration of the naval staff's 25,000-man proposal of July with an explanation that it had not received the sanction of either the Naval Board or the Cabinet.[65]

Jones was right to be cautious. On August 31 King had begun to move in the Cabinet War Committee to impose his stamp on the military program for the Pacific War. He now laid it down as a hard rule that the Canadian forces should be committed only north of the equator, and pressed for a reduction of the forces to the bare minimum. He was able to use to good effect intelligence from Washington that the Americans did not want or need substantial British forces in the Pacific. Angus Macdonald was out of town, but King nevertheless grasped the essence of the naval proposals: to send virtually the whole of the Royal Canadian Navy to the Pacific. The prime minister braced himself for the "struggle" to cut back that ambitious scheme.[66] It is clear that King remembered Macdonald and the naval staff's maneuvers at the First Quebec Conference, and was determined to avoid a repetition.

On September 6, when the British delegation was en route to Quebec, King pulled out the heavy artillery, a rare meeting of the full Cabinet to demonstrate to the defense ministers how weak support was for a major effort in the Pacific. Macdonald was present this time, and his account shows that the ghosts of the past were once again in the room: "Mr King then said there was one point that had not been mentioned which he thought was very important. The Tories generally were always talking about an Empire force, while the Liberals should stick to the doctrine of national forces. Dispatches from England were constantly talking about Imperial armies and Imperial forces. We must not lose our identity. He felt that our forces should not fight below the Equator. The climate in those areas was very unsuitable for our men. Consequently, he would favour an approach on the north." It dawned on the naval minister that King was turning the "preference" Canada had expressed for operations in the central and north Pacific into a rigid principle. He could scarcely believe it: "The Equator theory seems to me fantastic. It is true that our troops are not used to hot weather, but certainly in air and naval operations it is impossible to draw lines arbitrarily and say that you will not go beyond them."[67]

At Quebec, on September 13, the War Committee thrashed out the Pacific question for three and a half hours in preparation for a meeting with Churchill and the British chiefs of staff scheduled for the next day. Again King loosed the ghosts:

> Prime Minister then went on to the question of a Canadian election, and said that we must not let it develop into an argument about Imperialism and the use of Canadian forces as part of an Imperialistic Army. We have done a great deal in this war, our taxes are very high. How much more could our people stand? The great financial contributions that we had made should be considered and should be taken to some extent as in lieu of manpower contribution.
>
> We must have a national force and not be swallowed up in an Imperial Army. Otherwise, we would lose the support of Quebec and the West. If Canadians were killed in Burma, people would say "What were they there for?" Even a few casualties there would make a lot of talk. It was all right for Britain to want to recapture lost territory, but is it our job to help in such an effort? In 1926, the question of contributing to the building of the Singapore base came up at an Imperial Conference. Canada would not contribute on the ground that it was not our job.

When the chiefs of staff joined the meeting, Jones said he favored a substantial naval effort, along the lines of 70 percent of peak wartime strength rule that the British were applying. He also argued that the geographical demarcations were meaningless in the naval context, especially because of news from the main conference confirming that the Royal Navy would be mounting a Pacific fleet that would work as an integral part of the main American fleet. Macdonald, for his part, took the prime minister on directly, accusing him of distorting agreed policy by converting the "preference" for the north and central Pacific into a demand.[68]

While mustering his strength against the defense ministers in Cabinet, King also prepared the ground in personal, politician to politician, talks about his difficulties with Churchill. The prime minister was receptive not least because of the earlier decisions that the main British push against the Japanese would be in the Pacific with the Americans, rather than an independent Commonwealth effort in Southeast Asia. As a result, the main Anglo-Canadian meeting of September 14 was notably different from the similar meeting that had taken place during Quadrant a year earlier. Churchill readily agreed that Canadian forces should be engaged north of the equator, and that the hard slogging to recover colonies in Southeast Asia was properly a British job. He chided Air Marshal Sir Charles Portal about the huge demands the Royal Air Force was placing on the RCAF, and agreed to support the Canadian desire to have its army contingent serve with the Americans. On the naval side, he referred to the struggle he had just had in getting the Americans to accept a British Pacific Fleet that would work with the U.S. fleet. He doubted that the Royal Canadian Navy could hope for anything other than "sub-participation" as a part of the new British Pacific Fleet. King found that acceptable, and agreed that the Philippines qualified as a northern theater in terms of his geographical formula.[69]

It reveals much about the strained relations between Nelles on the one hand, and Jones and Macdonald on the other, that the only inkling the London naval staff got of the developments at Quebec was a report on the Anglo-Canadian meeting of September 14 from the British chiefs of staff. Nelles smelt trouble, and was under considerable pressure as the Admiralty, not fully understanding King's hedging, pressed for Canadian action to prepare for the dispatch of ships through the Indian Ocean. Finally on October 5, Nelles signaled a plea directly to Macdonald, urging that he be allowed to return to Ottawa from England immediately to get the full picture. "I now feel that I and my immediate staff are quite out of touch with the views of NSHQ regarding the plans and/or proposals for the war against Japan, and that in effect we are representing Admiralty to NSHQ rather than NSHQ to Admiralty."[70]

Macdonald was at that moment in a struggle with the prime minister. As soon as the Octagon Conference had finished, King, had borne down on the services to slash their proposals for the Pacific. Macdonald fought back: "we were the first to declare war on Japan. We had been summoned to a meeting at eight o'clock on Sunday evening [December 7, 1941] and even before the US had declared war, the Government stated that we should declare war. We did not even wait for Parliament, furthermore, we had consistently talked about an all-out effort, about being in the war until the end, about standing side by side without Allies, and so on. We were quite generous about giving away millions and billions of dollars in Mutual Aid, UNRRA, and so on, but when it came to our own service, we seemed to apply a different rule."[71]

On October 5, the day Nelles cried out for information, the scene in the War Committee was particularly tense. King specifically applied the "north of the equator" rule to the navy, despite Macdonald's protests that although the British Pacific Fleet would indeed fight there, the whole effort would have to be staged through the Indian Ocean. King rejoined, "why not keep our navy on our own coasts . . . and use it when the final thrust was made against Japan." Louis St. Laurent, the minister of Justice, chimed in that "the real point was whether our navy was to be appendage of UK navy or not. He seemed," Macdonald recorded, "to be thinking of the anti Imperialistic sentiment." This interchange put Macdonald into a quiet fury: "More and more it seems to me, the PM is putting the winning of the next election first, and in consequence of playing up to Quebec.

"There is a lack of frankness in him it seems to me that one should not find in a colleague. Thus he said today that keeping our navy on the coasts of Canada was the same as keeping our men in England 4 years. That was part of the Grand Strategy of the war and it worked he says. The fact is that until November 1942 when the Allies landed in North Africa there was no place for our men to fight."[72]

Nelles got the news he had been fearing in a signal on October 13, 1944. The ceiling of 25,000 personnel had been sliced to 13,000 personnel afloat. There were to be no operations whatever in the Indian Ocean; if the British needed specialized Canadian ships for that theater they would be welcome to man them with their own personnel. Plans for the early movement of Canadian frigates to Southeast Asia to gain experience in tropical operations were canceled because of the need to maintain antisubmarine defenses on the Canadian Atlantic coast where schnorkel-equipped U-boats were sinking ships and successfully evading Allied forces.[73]

Nelles had to endure rebukes from the Admiralty that the Canadian government was going back on the Octagon agreements.[74] While struggling to mend fences with the Royal Navy, he finally received permission to come home for consultations. He and Todd arrived in Ottawa at the end of October,[75] but it was Todd alone who returned to London with staff papers and briefing notes.[76] Macdonald had Nelles retired with effect from January 1945, when he was only fifty-three. The minister allowed him the one honor of a promotion from vice-admiral to full admiral, but only to date from after his retirement so as not to increase Nelles's pension.[77]

Macdonald was by then a lame duck himself. The controversies within the Canadian Cabinet over Pacific policy at the time of the Octagon Conference are of particular interest because they had hardened divisions previously created by the issue of overseas conscription. Thus the battle lines were clearly drawn when in late October 1944, within days of the arguments over the Pacific, J. L. Ralston, minister of national defense for the army, announced that conscripts would now have to be sent overseas. Macdonald was one of Ralston's key supporters in the pitched battle in November that nearly saw the government come apart. King narrowly mastered the situation by firing Ralston, and ultimately allowing the dispatch overseas of only the minimum number of infantry-trained conscripts needed for the immediate reinforcement crisis.[78] Macdonald let it be known he would not fight the next election, and in April 1945 King accepted his resignation with relief and pleasure.[79]

The navy's Pacific program meanwhile continued to be buffeted by the familiar crosscurrents of hard British bargaining and the prime minister's deepening concern with domestic politics and the upcoming election. In January 1945 the Admiralty agreed to transfer the light fleet carriers the navy wanted, but attached terms, among them that the ships could be deployed to the Indian Ocean or south Pacific if needed there.[80] King held firm, as he related in his diary: "In reply to Macdonald's questions: what was the difference of fighting there, or anywhere else, I pointed out that central and north Pacific ocean meant the defence of Canada just as the destruction of Hitler in Europe did, whereas fighting in the south Pacific meant Canadians giving their lives for the protection of British Protectorates, Colonies, Crown Dependencies, etc., where only British interests as distinct from our own were at stake." Even so, the prime minister's association of the Pacific effort with the Atlantic campaign he had strongly supported was somewhat encouraging. Further, he declared a few lines later that "I, personally, did not oppose accepting the ships." His difficulties were with the terms.[81]

Within these limits the prime minister remained willing to press on with the reduced but still ambitious program agreed to in October 1944. HMCS *Uganda* arrived in the Pacific in time to join the British Pacific Fleet's operations in the pitched battle for Okinawa in May 1945. Although King's politically motivated new policy that all servicemen would have to revolunteer specifically for the Pacific resulted in the cruiser having to then return to Canada at the end of July to change crews while refitting, the ship would have been back on station within a matter of weeks.[82] The second cruiser, HMCS *Ontario,* and the first fleet destroyer, HMCS *Algonquin,* were en route to the Far East when the dropping of the atom bomb hastened the Japanese surrender. More important for the future, the prime minister allowed the light fleet carrier acquisition to continue, though for one rather than two vessels, despite his repeated declarations that wartime programs should not become a basis for the postwar forces.

After 35 years, the Royal Canadian Navy had finally achieved its big ship ambitions. Although the political forces that had killed the Fisher and Jellicoe schemes had been loosed again during Octagon, their effect this time had been only to reduce the scale of the fleet project launched during Quadrant. Mackenzie King, who had wielded the axe in the final blows against the Jellicoe program in 1921-22, had, however reluctantly, come to realize that a substantial navy could indeed serve Canadian national and not merely British imperial interests.

NOTES

1. More than usual I am indebted to my colleagues, past and present, on the Naval History Team at the Directorate of History and Heritage. I especially thank Shawn Cafferky, W. A. B. Douglas, Donald Graves, Jane Samson, and Michael Whitby, who as always shared their notes, drafts, and insights.

2. The seminal work on the aspirations of the Canadian naval staff during World War II is W. A. B. Douglas, "Conflict and Innovation in the Royal Canadian Navy, 1939-45," in *Naval Warfare in the Twentieth Century: Essays in Honour of Arthur Marder,* ed. Gerald Jordan (London, 1977), pp. 210-32. The basic account of Canadian naval policy to 1945 is G. N. Tucker, *The Naval Service of Canada: Its Official History,* 2 vols. (Ottawa, 1952). This sound piece of scholarship is still the fundamental published source.

3. See M. L. Hadley and R. Sarty, *Tin-Pots and Pirate Ships: Canadian Naval Forces and German Raiders 1880-1918* (Montreal and Kingston, 1991), chaps. 1-3 for a recent account.

4. S. Roskill, *Naval Policy between the Wars: The Period of Anglo-American Antagonism 1919-29* vol. 1 (London, 1968), chap. 7; B. D. Hunt, "The Road to Washington: Canada and Empire Naval Defence, 1918-21," *RCN in Retrospect 1910-1968,* ed. J. A. Boutilier (Vancouver, 1982), pp. 44-61

5. Hadley and Sarty, *Tin-Pots,* chaps. 8-12.

6. R. Sarty, *The Maritime Defence of Canada* (Toronto, 1996), pp. 79-109; B. J. C. McKercher, "Between Two Giants: Canada, the Coolidge Conference, and Anglo-American Relations in 1927," in *Anglo-American Relations in the 1920s: The Struggle for Supremacy,* ed. B. J. C. McKercher (Edmonton, 1990), 81-124; M. Whitby, "In Defence of Home Waters: Doctrine and Training in the Canadian Navy during the 1930s," *The Mariner's Mirror,* 77 (May 1991): 167-76.

7. R. Sarty, "Mr King and the Armed Forces," in *A Country of Limitations: Canada and the World in 1939/Un pays dans la gêne: le Canada et le monde en 1939,* eds. N. Hillmer, R. Bothwell, R. Sarty, and C. Beauregard (Ottawa, 1996), pp. 217-46.

8. "Summary of Naval War Effort," Jan. 18, 1940, p. 5, filed with Naval Staff Minutes, Directorate of History and Heritage [hereafter DHH], National Defence Headquarters, Ottawa.

9. For the most revealing statements of Nelles's policies see Nelles to minister, "Review of the Naval Requirements of Canada and the Existing Situation, 29th September, 1939," DHH, Naval Historical Section files [hereafter NHS] 1650-1 (Policy) pt. 1; Brand to Godfrey, Sept. 25, 1939, NSS [Naval Service Headquarters "secret" file] 1017-10-22 pt. 1, National Archives of Canada, Ottawa [hereafter NAC], RG 24, vol. 3841.

10. Sarty, "Mr. King and the Armed Forces."

11. Dreyer to Secretary of the Admiralty, Jan. 31, 1940, Public Record Office [hereafter PRO], ADM 1/10608; see also M. Whitby, "Instruments of Security: The Royal Canadian Navy's Procurement of the Tribal-Class Destroyers, 1938-1943," *Northern Mariner,* vol. 2 (July 1992): 1-15.

12. Early evidence of this was Macdonald's pressure on the naval staff from his first weeks in Ottawa to find officers by promoting from the lower deck rather than on the existing basis of direct entry from civil life on the basis of assessments of personal qualities by serving officers: first meeting of Naval Council, Sept. 19, 1940, also Minutes for Oct. 30, 1940, NSS 1078-4-3 pt. 1, NAC, RG 24, vol. 4044.

13. Cabinet War Committee [hereafter CWC] Minutes, Sept. 26, 1940; a full original copy of the minutes and supporting memoranda is available in NAC, MG 26 J4, vols. 424 and 425.

14. House of Commons, *Debates,* Nov. 19, 1940, pp. 206-7.

15. See William Lyon Mackenzie King Diary, May 21, June 5, 10, 13, 20, 24, 1941, NAC, MG 26 J13.

16. "Summary of Naval War Effort October 1st to December 31st, 1941," NSS 1000-5-8 pt. 1, DHH.

17. Chief of the Naval Staff to Acting Deputy Minister (Naval and Air), Oct. 30, 1939 and Feb. 16, 1940, HQC 8215 pt 1, NAC, RG 24, vol. 2826.

18. On the Royal Canadian Navy in the Battle of the Atlantic see M. Milner, *North Atlantic Run: The Royal Canadian Navy and the Battle for the Convoys* (Toronto, 1985).

19. W. G. D. Lund, "The Royal Canadian Navy's Quest For Autonomy in the North West Atlantic: 1941-43," in *RCN in Retrospect,* pp. 138-57.

20. J. D. F. Kealy and E. C. Russell, *A History of Canadian Naval Aviation* (Ottawa, 1965), 21-23; I am grateful for insights from Donald Graves and Shawn Cafferky from their recent work on naval aviation.

21. Plans Division, "Appreciation of RCN Ship Requirements for the War Against Japan and for the Post-War Navy," July 29, 1943, NSS 1017-10-34 pt. 1, NAC, RG 24, vol. 3844. DeWolf and Todd had in May 1943 toured the west coast to formulate plans for the expansion of base facilities and forces with a view to increased Royal Canadian Navy participation in the Pacific: DeWolf, "Diary of Visit to West Coast," May 13, 1943, NSS 1037-3-7, NAC, RG 24, vol. 3901; Director of Plans, "Appreciation of A/S Escort Requirements on the West Coast," May 28, 1943, filed with Naval Staff Minutes for May 31, 1943, DHH. I am grateful to Michael Whitby for drawing this material to my attention.

22. J. Ehrman, *Grand Strategy: August 1943-September 1944*, vol. V (History of the Second World War, United Kingdom Military Series) (London, 1956), pp. 41-4.

23. Admiralty to British Admiralty Delegation [Washington], signal 1847A, Nov. 6, 1943, PRO, ADM 1/13009; A. V. Alexander to Stark, Dec. 10, 1943, enclosing "Aide Memoire" on British manpower problems ADM 1/17025; D. E. Graves, "'Fourth Service or Problem?': The British Combined Operations Organization and the Royal Navy's Manpower Crisis, 1942-1944," in *Selected Papers from the 1992 (59th) Meeting of the Society for Military History Hosted by the Command and Staff College of the Marine Corps University*, ed. D. F. Bittner (Marine Corps University Perspectives on Warfighting Number Three) (Washington, 1994), pp. 175-186.

24. See, for example, Director of Personal Services, "Canadian Naval Personnel," Aug. 1, 1943, Hickling to Second Sea Lord, July 1, 1943, Brockman to First Sea Lord, Aug. 9, 1943, PRO, ADM 205/31; "Summary of Naval War Effort," July 1-Sept. 30, 1943, pp. 2-3, NSS 1000-5-8 pt. 4, DHH.

25. "Minutes of a Meeting held in Conference Room B at the Chateau Frontenac on Wednesday, the 11th August 1943," PRO, ADM 205/31; the copy of the minutes given to the Canadians is in NSS 4300-9, NAC, RG 24, Accession 83-4/167, vol. 1481.

26. See, for example, Assistant Chief of the Naval Staff (A) to First Sea Lord, Aug. 3, 1943, Director of Plans to First Sea Lord, "Canada--Naval Aviation," Aug. 7, 1943, PRO, ADM 205/31.

27. Quadrant to Admiralty (personal for First Lord from First Sea Lord), signal 2308Z, Aug. 21, 1943, PRO, ADM 1/13044.

28. See, for example, King Diary May 26 and June 17, 1943; on the beginnings of strains on the supply of manpower see C. P. Stacey, *Arms, Men and Governments: The War Policies of Canada 1939-1945* (Ottawa, 1970), pp. 405-12.

29. For example, on the question of releasing the 17 corvettes from Canadian home waters for service in Torch in the fall of 1942, see W. A. B. Douglas, *The Creation of a National Air Force: The Official History of the Royal Canadian Air Force*, vol. II (Toronto, 1986), p. 503.

30. CWC Minutes and King Diary, Aug. 31, 1943.

31. King Diary (quoted), Sept. 8, 1943; and CWC Minutes, Sept. 8, 1943.

32. L. Macdonald Diary, Aug. 31, 1943, file 391, Angus L. Macdonald Papers, Public Archives of Nova Scotia [hereafter PANS].

33. Macdonald Diary, Sept. 8, 1943.

34. Macdonald Diary, Sept. 10, 1943.

35. Admiralty to BAD and NSHQ, signal 1847A, Nov. 6, 1943, Admiralty to NSHQ and BAD, signal 1840A, Nov. 6, 1943, CNS Canada to Admiralty, signal 2052Z, Nov. 10, 1943, signal 0137A, Nov. 17, 1943, PRO, ADM 1/13009; "Summary of Naval War Effort, 1st October to 31st December 1943," pp. 2-3, NSS 1000-5-8 pt. 4, DHH.

36. On the complex redeployments and reorganization of the Atlantic escort forces see Hodgson, "The First Year of Canadian Operational Control in the Northwest Atlantic," Aug. 18, 1944, DHH 81/520/8280, Box 1, File 8280A, pt. 1.
37. King Diary and CWC Minutes, Oct. 21 and Nov. 10, 1943.
38. King Diary, Nov. 27, 1943 (quoted), see also entry for Dec. 16, 1943.
39. Massey to Secretary of State for External Affairs, Telegram 3254, Dec. 24, 1943, *Documents on Canadian External Relations, 1942-1943,* vol. 9, ed. J. F. Hilliker (Hull, Que., 1980), pp. 365-6.
40. Secretary of State for External Affairs to High Commissioner in Great Britain, Telegrams 58 and 59, Jan. 9, 1944, *Documents on Canadian External Relations: 1944-5, Pt. 1,* vol. 10 [hereafter *DCER, plus volume number*], ed. J. F. Hilliker, (Ottawa: Department of External Affairs, 1987), pp. 316-18.
41. Massey to Secretary of State for External Affairs, Telegram 116, Jan. 12, 1944, Wrong to Massey, Jan. 18, 1944, *DCER,* vol. 10, pp. 319-21.
42. Macdonald Diary, Jan. 5, 1944, file 392, PANS, Macdonald Papers; King Diary, same date, is briefer but confirms the salient points.
43. *DCER,* vol. 10, pp. 276-83; B. Greenhous, S. Harris, W. Johnston and W. G. P. Rawling, *Crucible of War 1939-1945: The Official History of the Royal Canadian Air Force,* vol. 3 (Toronto, 1993), pp. 106-9.
44. King Diary, Jan. 5 and 12, 1944.
45. Miles to ACNS, "Creation of RCN Task Forces," Jan. 14, 1944, NHS 1650-1 (Policy) pt. 1, DHH; see also Director of Plans, "Post-War Canadian Navy," Jan. 21, 1944, ibid., and Todd, "The Post-War Canadian Navy," Nov. 17, 1943, ibid., pt. 2.
46. Milner, *North Atlantic Run,* pp. 245-64; on the haste with which the new overseas post had been created and delays in defining the terms of reference see the Jan. 1944 correspondence in File 376, Macdonald Papers, PANS.
47. For evidence of the anti-Nelles faction in the navy, see King Diary, Mar. 29, 1943; see also Howell, serial 44-46, Jan. 19, 1946, File E-3-e, Register 23371/46, National Archives and Records Administration, Washington, RG 38, CNO Intelligence Division, Confidential Reports of Naval Attaches 1940-46, box 616.
48. King Diary, Jan. 7, 1944.
49. Compared to Nelles, Jones's minutes in files are sparse and brief; similarly, Jones in contrast to Nelles refused to get drawn into general discussion when he was present at Cabinet War Committee meetings. Jones's personnel file comprises only a few thin dossiers that contain few if any documents like efficiency reports; there is little doubt that much of the file was destroyed after his death.
50. Naval Staff Minutes, Jan. 24, 1944, DHH.
51. Ehrman, *Grand Strategy,* vol. V, chap. 11-12; C. Thorne, *Allies of a Kind: The United States, Britain, and the War against Japan, 1941-1945* (London, 1978), pp. 410-14.

52. Todd, "Memorandum to Senior Canadian Flag Officer (Overseas)," Feb. 29, 1944, Naval Assistant, Policy and Plans, [hereafter NA (PP)] file, "Policy and Plans Reports from 14 Jan. 1944 to 7 Sept. 1944," in NHS 1650-1 (Policy) pt. 3, DHH.

53. Higham, Military Branch, Admiralty to Todd, June 14, 1944, Todd to Secretary of the Naval Board, June 14, 1944, Canadian Naval Mission Overseas [hereafter CNMO], File MS 46-1-1 "Far Eastern Policy," NHS 1650-1 (Policy and Plans), DHH.

54. Hodgson to Director of Plans, June 21, 1944, NSS 1655-2 pt. 1, NAC, RG 24, vol. 8150.

55. Naval Staff Minutes 245-9, July 3, 1944, DHH.

56. Naval Board Minutes 158-10, July 12, 1944, DHH.

57. "Extract from minutes of 289th meeting Chiefs of Staff Committee held at 1200 hrs, Wednesday, 7th June, 1944," DHH 112.3M2009 (D79); Heeney, "Re: Canadian Participation in the War against Japan: The Position of the Three Services," June 14, 1944, *DCER*, vol. 10, pp. 375-78.

58. Secretary of State for External Affairs to Dominions Secretary, Telegram 108, June 27, 1944, *DCER*, vol. 10, pp. 380-81.

59. Todd to Secretary Naval Board, "Canadian Participation and the General Strategy for the War after the Defeat of Germany (PP1/44)," Aug. 3, 1944, file "Policy and Plans Reports from 14 Jan. 1944 to 7 Sept. 1944" in NHS 1650-1 "Policy" pt. 3, DHH.

60. For example, CNMO to NSHQ, signal 1640A, Sept. 30, 1944, DHH 75/ 197 pt. 2.

61. Hodgson to Director of Plans, "The RCN in the Pacific Theatre," June 24, 1944, NSS 1655-2 pt. 1, NAC, RG 24, vol. 8150, quoted. This paper was incorporated in Miles, director of plans, "Defeat of Japan," June 28, 1944, which was approved by the Naval Staff as item 245-9 at its meeting of July 3, 1944, ibid. See also Miles to Assistant Chief of the Naval Staff, "Defeat of Japan," Sept. 1, 1944, ibid. The extent to which Canadian naval planning for the Pacific focused on London to the virtual exclusion of Washington is demonstrated by the Pacific planning file of the naval member of the Canadian Joint Staff in Washington, TS 4-18, NAC, RG 24, vol. 11, 960, which consists solely of copies of correspondence generated by the other services and by the naval staffs in Ottawa and London.

62. [British] Joint Planning Staff, "Employment of Canadian Forces after the Defeat of Germany (JP (44) 176 (Final))," July 24, 1944, CNMO file NA (PP) 104 "Japan War—Policy," NHS 1650-1 (Policy and Plans), DHH.

63. Todd to Secretary Naval Board, "Canadian Participation and the General Strategy for the War after the Defeat of Germany (PP1/44)," Aug. 3, 1944, file "Policy and Plans Reports from 14 Jan. 1944 to 7 Sept. 1944" in NHS 1650-1 (Policy), pt. 3, DHH.

64. NSHQ to CNMO, signal 1333, Aug. 28, 1944, "Personal for Head of Mission from CNS," DHH 95/197 pt. 2.

65. Nelles, "Aide Memoire for the First Sea Lord on the Employment of Canadian Naval Forces after the Defeat of Germany (PP8/44)," Aug. 31, 1944, file MS 46-1-1 "Far Eastern Policy," NHS 1650-1 (Policy and Plans), DHH.

66. King Diary and CWC Minutes, Aug. 31, 1944.

67. Macdonald Diary, Sept. 6, 1944, quoted; see also King Diary, Sept. 6, 1944.

68. Macdonald Diary, Sept. 13, 1944; see also King Diary, Sept. 13, 1944.

69. Macdonald Diary (quoted), King Diary, and CWC Minutes, Sept. 14, 1944; see also Greenhous, et. al, *The Crucible of War,* 113.

70. CNMO to NSHQ, "Personal for Minister," signal 1600, 5 [Oct. 1944], DHH 75/197, pt. 2 (quoted); see also CNMO to NSHQ, signal 1800 A, Oct. 2, 1944, File 376, Macdonald Papers, PANS.

71. Macdonald Diary, Sept. 22, 1944.

72. Macdonald Diary, Oct. 5, 1944.

73. NSHQ to CNMO, signal 1712Z, Oct. 13, 1944, file MS 46-1-1 "Far Eastern Policy," NHS 1650-1 (Policy and Plans), DHH.

74. CNMO to NSHQ, signal 1736A, Oct. 16, 1944, signal 1730A, Oct. 17, 1944, file MS 46-1-1 "Far Eastern Policy" in NHS 1650-1 (Policy), DHH; CNMO to NSHQ, signal 1744A, Oct. 16, 1944, File E/32, Nelles Papers, DHH biography files.

75. NSHQ to CNMO, signal 2009Z, Oct. 20, 1944, DHH 75/197 pt. 2; CNMO to NSHQ, signal 0920A, Oct. 26, 1944, File 736, Macdonald Papers, PANS.

76. NAPP, "Report on visit to NSHQ," Nov. 15, 1944, file MS 46-1-1, NHS 1650-1 "Policy and Plans," DHH.

77. Macdonald to Nelles, draft of letter "not sent," Jan. 2, 1945, Macdonald to C. G. MacPherson, Feb. 5, 1945, folder 736, Macdonald Papers, PANS.

78. On the conscription crisis of 1944, see J. L. Granatstein and J. M. Hitsman, *Broken Promises: A History of Conscription in Canada* (Toronto, 1977), chap. 6.

79. King Diary, Apr. 11, 13, 18, 19, 1945; J. Hawkins, *The Life and Times of Angus L.* (Windsor, NS, 1969), pp. 225-34, captures Macdonald's bitterness towards King.

80. Kealy and Russell, *Canadian Naval Aviation,* p. 36.

81. King Diary, Feb. 14, 1945.

82. RCN Press Release, circa July 25, 1945, NAC, RG 24, vol. 11, 755. I am grateful to Bill Rawling for this reference.

EIGHT

FINANCE AND "FUNCTIONALISM"

CANADA AND THE COMBINED BOARDS IN WORLD WAR II

HECTOR MacKENZIE

JUST OVER FIFTY YEARS AGO, shortly after imaginative and generous accounting had transferred items potentially worth about one billion dollars from British to Canadian account, British Prime Minister Winston Churchill met with Canadian Prime Minister William Lyon Mackenzie King and other members of Canada's Cabinet War Committee in the Château Frontenac. Churchill was in Quebec for the Octagon Conference, while Mackenzie King was acting as host for the British leader and American President Franklin Delano Roosevelt. Privately, Churchill paid tribute to the latest example of Canadian generosity.[1] While personal praise was welcome to King, as was the reflected glory of public appearances with the principal leaders of the wartime alliance, there was another significant form of recognition, which was also linked to Canada's war effort. That contribution to the common cause was the most frequently cited justification for a greater say for Canada in the higher direction of the war. This chapter deals with the interrelationship between this question of status or recognition and Canada's material and financial aid to its Allies, particularly with respect to the United Kingdom.

Most accounts have tended to focus on the intellectual rationale for Canada's appeal for enhanced participation in Allied decision making—the concept of "functionalism" that for Canadian policy-makers was defined by Hume Wrong and endorsed by Mackenzie King.[2] That notion certainly helped to justify Canada's pretensions, but it is also important to examine how perceptions of Canadian public opinion by ministers and officials in Ottawa, as well as their personal reactions, affected the decisions about Canada's involvement in the combined boards established by Roosevelt and Churchill in early 1942. For this purpose, we will also consider the additional boards announced in June 1942, with a cursory look at the organization that became the United Nations Relief and Rehabilitation Administration (UNRRA). Not only was the scale of Canada's war effort an important justification for exceptional treatment by the senior partners in the struggle, but the redefinition of financial assistance to Britain critically affected British attitudes on this question. For that reason, we will examine Canada's quest for recognition and responsibility through the prism of Anglo-Canadian economic relations. This perspective is vital to an understanding of the Canadian government's position as well as of its choice of tactics. Before we look at Canada's relationship to the combined boards, therefore, it makes sense to glance briefly at the form and scale of Canada's aid to its wartime allies.

During the "phoney war"—from September 1939 to April 1940—Canada produced and supplied familiar goods to its Allies, with food and raw materials more common than munitions or other manufactures. In the early months of the conflict, as later, a remarkable proportion of Canada's output went to its partners in the struggle, especially the United Kingdom. After the fall of France, war orders from Britain expanded exponentially and the industrial potential of Canada was realized more completely. Eventually, that production would reach its peak in the final quarter of 1943, though the flow of deliveries across the North Atlantic would continue at a level unimagined before the war.

The question of how to pay for these goods arose as a consequence of Britain's financial plight, particularly its shortage of dollars. Perhaps the greatest spur to Canadian generosity came from the extraordinary actions of a neutral—the United States—in assisting a belligerent—the United Kingdom. Lend-Lease followed soon after the British ambassador's admission that Britain was "broke" and it deferred indefinitely the awkward problem of how Britain could afford to acquire the instruments of its own salvation and ultimate victory. It provided both example and incentive for Canada, then Britain's most important ally, to adopt a more generous approach in its own dealings with the United Kingdom, which had thus far been tentative and limited.[3] After considerable discussion and debate within the Canadian government, its belated answer to Lend-Lease was the "Billion Dollar Gift" that was announced near the end of the Arcadia Conference between Churchill and Roosevelt in Washington. But the Billion Dollar Gift was a political failure as a format for aid to Britain, particularly as it became ensnared in the campaign against conscription in Quebec.[4] Two years after Lend-Lease was enacted, Canada passed the Mutual Aid Act, which mirrored the American legislation.[5] In other words, the crucial period for the elaboration of the Anglo-American machinery for the higher direction of the war was also when Canada redefined its aid to Britain. These two themes were interwoven and nowhere was this more evident than in how Canadian policy-makers reacted to the combined boards.

In the early months and years of the war, the Canadian government occasionally chafed at Britain's presumption to speak for its allies or to make commitments without information or effective consultation. For the most part, however, Mackenzie King and his colleagues displayed no interest in assembling with the wartime leaders in London or elsewhere for rituals associated with coalition warfare. King certainly had no wish to revive the imperial framework constructed in World War I, which was fundamentally at odds with his notion of the present and future of the Commonwealth. Canada also had no formal contact with the Supreme War Council established by Britain and France and it resisted efforts by the British to revive it in late 1940 as a meaningless "facade." Even so, there was some resentment when the Atlantic Charter was issued after a meeting that took place without consultation so near to Canada.[6] One unintended consequence of that encounter between Roosevelt and Churchill was to flush King out of his lair. Soon afterward, he discovered that the problems of leaving Ottawa in wartime were not insurmountable and that he was able to attend four meetings of the British War Cabinet. Within weeks, however, King had resumed his more familiar posture and it was not until after the attack on Pearl Harbor brought the United States into the war that Canadian policy-makers turned their thoughts once more to the unresolved question of how to influence Allied decisions.[7]

While the Arcadia Conference was underway, the Under-Secretary of State for External Affairs, Norman Robertson, assessed the implications of American involvement for the prime minister. With the shift for the United States in perceptions, interest, and activity from a continental or hemispheric to a global basis, Canada likely would lose both influence and attention in Washington. "As an American nation in the British Commonwealth, this country was, in the first years of the war, visible and important evidence of the war's nearness to America. Now that the United

States is itself at war with Germany, Italy and Japan, and allied with the British Commonwealth and the USSR, this phase of Canada's historical role is completed and Americans are once more viewing Canadian questions in a more modest and more nearly domestic perspective." The United States was already striving for unification and centralization of the war effort. More direct and forceful in its approach as a cobelligerent, it possessed a new awareness of its standing as a world power.[8] As the Minister-Counsellor of the Canadian Legation in Washington, Lester Pearson complained, "our cherished status is more respected in Downing Street than in Washington." To his chagrin, the Americans preferred to deal exclusively with the British.[9]

The new partnership at the helm was formalized by the announcement that followed the Arcadia Conference. In addition to establishing the Combined Chiefs of Staff, the two leaders set up the Combined Raw Materials Board, the Munitions Assignment Boards, and the Shipping Adjustment Boards.[10] From the Canadian Legation in Washington, Hume Wrong raised the question of "the nature of the Canadian representation which should be sought and the status with respect to their British and U.S. colleagues which should be claimed for Canadian representatives on any of the combined organizations." Wrong's answer was to articulate what was later defined and elaborated as the "functional principle"—"that each member of the grand alliance should have a voice in the conduct of the war proportionate to its contribution to the general war effort." Though Canada's military contribution was ranked lower, "among suppliers of war materials for the use of the United Nations, Canada ranks third and only after the United States and United Kingdom."[11]

In Canada's Cabinet War Committee, the response was less certain. When it first considered Canadian representation on the combined boards, C. D. Howe, the minister of Munitions and Supply, recommended that Canada should not seek membership of the Raw Materials Board nor participate at any lower level. In his view, "it was far better for Canada to retain her present trading position and let any initiative come from the United States." As for the Munitions Assignment Boards, the interest of Howe's department lay in production, not distribution, of war goods, so he was unconvinced of a meaningful role for Canada. But King had been more ambivalent when he had spoken with the senior British representative on the Combined Chiefs of Staff Committee in Washington: "The Prime Minister said that he had informed Sir John Dill that, while Canada realized the practical necessity of limiting representation upon combined bodies for the efficient conduct of the war, and would not seek to complicate the situation by unreasonable requests, at the same time Canada had been in the war for more than two years and Canadians would expect that their interests would not be ignored in any of these fields."

Although the Canadian government was dissatisfied with the arrangements, King conceded that "there was, at present, no useful initiative that Canada could take."[12] The formal Canadian reply to British information about the establishment of the combined boards and a proposal for consultation in London stressed Canada's association with the United States through various joint committees.[13] In the weeks and months to follow, Howe argued that Canada's position was better protected through existing arrangements and personal rapport rather than by assumption of a subordinate position in the combined boards.[14] As a net contributor to any pool of raw materials or munitions, Canada was "in a strong position" to wait for an approach from the principal allies. Initially, this stance was supported by Minister of National Defence Layton Ralston.[15]

The first real test for "functionalism" and Canada's relationship to the combined boards concerned the Munitions Assignment Boards, though the outcome was more a reflection of divisions within Ottawa than responses from London or Washington to a novel concept of representation. After a visit to Washington in early March, Howe commented that "there is nothing in the Joint Boards situation that should be disturbing to Canada's war effort. I cannot see that our position has changed materially, and I think the course we should pursue towards the Joint Boards is clear in all particulars." When matters relating to Canada were discussed, Canada should be represented.[16] From the start, the main point of contention was the form of Canada's association with the Munitions Assignments Boards.[17]

At the War Committee, Howe stressed Canada's position as a producer, whose "customers"—the United States and the United Kingdom—"could agree between themselves as to the allocation of Canadian production for their accounts." The counterargument, advanced by Ralston, was that "Canada's position as a merchant should not be allowed to interfere with her position as a belligerent." Ralston especially worried about civilian interference with military requirements. At this point, the War Committee was satisfied with the informal procedures already adopted, whereby Canadian production for British orders was pooled in London while that for American orders was assigned in Washington.[18]

Meanwhile, the Canadian Legation in Washington indicated that the American government would agree to "Canada having equal representation with the United States and the United Kingdom on the Munitions Assignment Board and related Committees." So it was decided that such an approach should be made in Washington.[19] As King recorded in his diary, "we are all of one mind that our relationship should be with the US who are quite prepared to give full representation on boards there," rather than with Britain, which was suspected of opposing any concession to Canada alone among the Dominions.[20] King personally informed the British High Commissioner in Ottawa, Malcolm MacDonald, who acknowledged "that the British Government did not recognize the importance of the Dominions, and Churchill is apt to forget their significance altogether."[21] This unfortunate coincidence of a misleading American indication of support and a presumption about British preferences contributed to a false impression that Britain effectively blocked recognition of the importance of Canada's contribution.

At a meeting in Washington, King emphatically rejected a suggestion from the Australian Minister of External Affairs, Dr. Herbert Evatt, that Canada would represent Australia and New Zealand on the Munitions Assignments Board. As King put it, Canada was not "there to protect the interests of any particular parts of the Empire." Instead, "our right to representation grew out of our being the third largest producer of war supplies."[22] When he spoke with Roosevelt the next day, King underlined the close relationship between the North American nations. This seemed to have an effect on Roosevelt, who apparently agreed with King "that Britain and the US and Canada were the big producers," who should be represented on the Munitions Assignment Board. Roosevelt promised to tell Harry Hopkins "that matters should be arranged in this way: representatives of Britain, one of the US and Canada."[23] Thus, when word came from London that the British government had decided to support the claim, Canadian membership seemed assured.[24] After a brief flurry of anxiety in Ottawa about the implications for Canada's financial position,[25] the Canadian Minister in Washington, Leighton McCarthy, formally proposed membership for Canada on the Munitions Assignment Board on May 13, 1942.[26]

Nearly one month went by with no reply. Hopkins, who would have to implement Roosevelt's commitment, was dissatisfied with Canada's proposals.[27] But it was unclear to the Department of External Affairs whether or not he wished to restrict membership to Britain and the United States.[28] Lester Pearson attributed Hopkins's doubts to reluctance "to alter in any way the organization of a Board which at present is functioning satisfactorily," as well as to a misunderstanding of the scope and implications of Canada's involvement. McCarthy tried to reassure Hopkins informally on these points.[29]

While Hopkins contemplated, an interdepartmental conflict emerged in the Canadian government between the defense and supply departments. With two strong-willed ministers, Ralston and Howe, carrying the fight to the War Committee, this dispute would ultimately thwart a satisfactory conclusion.[30] Still hopeful of Canadian membership, however, King discussed the issue with Hopkins when he returned to Washington in late June. But King's emphasis on the significance of the question to Canada had little impact on Hopkins.[31] King was starting to resent the treatment of Canada in this matter. "Mr. King had been quite upset," the American Minister in Ottawa, Pierrepont Moffat, reported, "because Harry Hopkins had uncompromisingly rejected the Canadian desire for membership on the Munitions Assignment Board." King had been confronted with familiar objections to precedents for other countries and American concerns about being outvoted: "Mr. Hopkins obviously wanted Canada to be a subcontractor. Canada wanted to be a junior partner." King suggested to Moffat that there might be a price to pay for this treatment. As he put it, this disagreement "was bound to color [Canada's] attitude on a number of war problems."[32]

When Hopkins replied formally, Canada was offered "full opportunity to present [Canadian] needs and [Canadian] views to the Munitions Assignment Board, its staff, and the Departmental Munitions Assignments Committee" rather than full membership.[33] But as this had been implicit in the announcement of the creation of the boards in January 1942, it was not an advance for Canada. More recently, according to the Department of External Affairs, public pressure had grown for recognition of Canada's role in the work of the combined boards.[34] This sentiment—as well as the impression from King that Roosevelt had agreed to Canadian membership—was conveyed in a letter to Hopkins in early July.[35] Meanwhile, Ralston and Howe continued to feud over control of production and assignment of munitions, with Howe favoring acceptance of the proposal from Hopkins.[36]

Recent experience, however, did not inspire confidence that Canada's interests would be taken into account without a seat on the board. Only on the advice of the prime minister did the War Committee stop short of a threat to withhold Canadian production.[37] There then followed considerable efforts by Canadian officials in Washington, ultimately successful, to secure a better offer. Under the revision, Canada would be a full member of the board and its committees when Canadian production was assigned. Canada's representatives would also have the power "to bid for items of United States production required by Canadian forces in the North American area." In effect, the American authorities "had conceded every point we originally made excepting the one that Canada should have a voice in the assignment of United States production bid for by countries other than herself."[38]

Unfortunately, this deal failed to mollify Howe, who argued that Canada would gain little in return for uncertainty and difficulty regarding supply and finance. Though there was arguably insufficient difference between the request and the response to justify refusal of the settlement, the resistance of the supply ministry produced a stalemate in Ottawa.[39] King would not divide his Cabinet over the issue, so the incoming letter with the revised offer was simply left unanswered.[40]

Before any further advance, or retreat, was made in the negotiations over the Munitions Assignment Board, the question had become complicated by Canada's relationship to other combined boards. After Roosevelt had announced the establishment of the Combined Production and Resources Board (CPRB) and the Combined Food Board (CFB), King promised to make a statement to the House of Commons. That commitment prompted a review of the position by the Cabinet War Committee. King observed that Roosevelt had stated that the American member of the Combined Production and Resources Board would "speak for North America," including Canada. That arrangement initially satisfied Howe, who opposed full membership for Canada on the Combined Production and Resources Board as "inappropriate" and a threat to Canada's existing bilateral arrangements. But Ilsley "queried the soundness of accepting silently a position of exclusion" from the combined boards. To do so would reduce Canada's role to that of "a mere supplier, rather than that of a partner in a great enterprise." That sentiment was echoed by Ralston, who "suggested that the Canadian public would expect Canadian representation," particularly on the Combined Food Board.[41] In the House of Commons, King referred to existing collaboration and integration of Canadian production with both Allies. Then he announced that Canada would seek a seat on the Combined Food Board.[42] In this domain, Canada's position as an exporter merited recognition that had been denied on other boards.[43] Exceptional assistance justified exceptional status.

At first, neither the Combined Food Board nor the British government was sympathetic.[44] Late in July, R. H. Brand of the British Food Mission in Washington, also a member of the Combined Food Board, and Sir Frederick Leith-Ross, the principal adviser to the British government on relief questions, visited Ottawa to discuss Canada's relationship to the combined boards. Once more, Canada was offered limited and subordinate affiliation as well as consultation, but not membership. That did not address the "largely political" problem: "Canada felt she was a great producing country. The billion dollar gift had been accepted without a murmur by the Canadian people but it was a shock to the taxpayer when he found that it represented 25% of Canada's total expenditure in the new and extremely drastic budget recently introduced. The Canadian people felt that notwithstanding their tremendous efforts they were not being asked to take any responsibility for the conduct of the war and this he [Norman Robertson] thought bad." As Robertson put it, "something would have to be done to satisfy the Canadian people that their Government had some part in the direction of the war and in responsibility for the measures taken." In this case, Canada deserved a seat at the table. When he encountered Brand, King likewise underlined the "unique position" of Canada in food and financial assistance to the United Kingdom. Despite an overwhelming parliamentary majority, King claimed that he would encounter difficulty in the House of Commons "unless it was clear that United States and United Kingdom would actually recognize the important part which Canada was playing in the war." King would "consider any solution that might be proposed." But "he had a political problem and must be helped to meet it."[45] Brand had offered only crumbs.[46]

At the War Committee, Howe led the opposition to Brand's proposals. "Experience with others of the combined organizations in Washington," Howe contended, "had shown the ineffectiveness of Canadian participation in the work of the Boards at any but the highest level." Howe reconciled this with his own approach to the other boards by alluding to his reliance on collaboration at the top rather than involvement at lower levels. Howe's position was endorsed by King, who objected to participation in a joint committee that was subordinate to the combined organization. Brand's submission was turned down.[47]

Leith-Ross fared no better with plans for postwar relief. When he discussed the Canadian contribution with the Deputy Minister of Finance W. C. Clark, he found him outspoken in his criticism of the composition of the combined boards and in his belief that distinct treatment for Canada was justifiable. "Canada might not be one of the great Powers, but her position could be distinguished from that of the other United Nations. No other of these Nations had contributed as much as Canada in the way of food, munitions and shipping. Canada was the only United Nation which did not accept Lease-Lend aid. She had been helped out in other ways but she regarded it as essential to maintain her independence of America. Her special position deserved to be recognized and otherwise there might be great difficulties in any renewal of the billion dollar gift." There would certainly be sympathy for the purposes and postwar implications of relief, "provided that Canada was brought into full partnership." But what Leith-Ross had outlined fell far short of that objective. The scheme "showed the same disregard of Canadian interests as had been shown in the organization of the Food Board and the Munitions Assignment Board." Canada, Clark contended, "would not be satisfied with being admitted by the back door while the Great Powers occupied the four-poster bed." Canada was not convinced "that the Four Powers had shown sufficient altruism or competence to guide the destinies of the world." Failure to make some concession, Clark implied, might affect Canada's contribution.[48] Certainly the significance of his allusion to the Billion Dollar Gift was not lost in London at a time when replacement of that measure was under active consideration on both sides of the Atlantic.

After Brand's visit, the Canadians were convinced "that if we press our request for membership [of the Combined Food Board], it will be rejected." This despite the fact "that our desire for effective representation on certain of the international bodies created to further the war effort and post war relief has not been caused by considerations of prestige or status." Instead, the Canadian government had "limited our requests to bodies in the work of which we are inevitably called upon to play a large part." This latest rebuff simply reinforced the growing impression, in Canada and elsewhere, "that the direction of the war (except so far as Russia is concerned) is too much of an Anglo-American monopoly."[49] These decisions had had a cumulative effect.[50]

The British High Commissioner in Ottawa was similarly perturbed at the indifference of his government to public attitudes in Canada. In his view, earlier mistakes had been compounded by the failure to consult before the Combined Food Board and Combined Production and Resources Board were announced. "If we are to recover Canada's goodwill in these matters," MacDonald warned, "I think some early concession to meet them is highly desirable."[51] There were soon ominous indications that the alienation of Canadian opinion might adversely affect financial assistance to the United Kingdom.[52] After a visit to Ottawa, Sir Frederick Phillips reported to the Treasury that the Canadian government did not favor another grant to Britain. In fact, the experience with the combined boards endangered comparable generosity. Clark's attitude "is coloured by his strong resentment, which is shared in various degrees by all Canadian officials, at exclusion of Canada from Combined Boards and now from Relief Council."[53] As well, the Governor of the Bank of Canada, Graham Towers, had complained that "it is as if Canada were regarded as a small boy to be relegated to the side lines." Without a sop to Canadian aspirations, Towers had suggested, the "contribution to the common effort would also be on a small scale."[54] Certainly, the Treasury drew the connection between finance and the combined boards, as it became the strongest advocate within Whitehall of a conciliatory approach to Canada.[55]

The first concession to Ottawa's attitude came over the question of membership of the Combined Production and Resources Board. Apparently, Sir Robert Sinclair of the Ministry of Production "had been deeply impressed with what he has seen of Canadian munitions production during a visit to the Toronto and Montreal regions."[56] As a result, he recommended that Canada should be added to the Combined Production and Resources Board. When King passed this news on to his colleagues on the Cabinet War Committee, Howe reversed his earlier opposition.[57] Perhaps more important, Howe shared this conversion with a sympathetic Donald Nelson, head of the War Production Board, during a fishing trip in July 1942. Confronted by the prospect that Howe might pursue a bilateral deal with Nelson rather than participate in a trilateral arrangement that included the British, the Ministry of Production eventually dropped its objections.[58]

Like Phillips and MacDonald, Sinclair believed that this gesture would ease political and financial relations with Canada.[59] MacDonald had detected a "hardening" of the Canadian stance in the weeks since Brand's visit, reinforced by a perception of restive public opinion that MacDonald shared. Failure to meet Ottawa's views could result in "a serious deterioration in Canadian goodwill towards the United Kingdom."[60] Even so, there was resistance from the Ministry of Food, which feared a precedent for the Combined Food Board, and the Foreign Office, which fretted that this might be "the thin end of the wedge."[61] But so convinced and convincing was the Treasury that it contemplated reconsideration of Britain's position with respect to domination of the relief organization by the Great Powers (defined as Britain, the United States, the Soviet Union, and China) and it persuaded the Foreign Office to support the addition of Canada if membership of the Policy Committee were enlarged.[62]

When Sinclair and Brand next discussed the subject with Canadian ministers and officials in September 1942, it was already understood that the Roosevelt administration would approve Canadian membership on the Combined Production and Resources Board.[63] A deal was struck with the Prime Minister, then confirmed by the War Committee. A Canadian member would be added to the CPRB "on the principal ground that this was necessary to ensure the integration of North American production with that of the United Kingdom." However, Canada would rely on informal arrangements for assignment of munitions. After Brand clarified the purposes of the Combined Food Board, the Canadian government decided to work through its committees rather than seek membership. To appease public opinion, a statement would be issued that this procedure would not alter orders from Canada or the priority for Canadian supplies.[64] Though Ralston later questioned the authority of the Combined Production and Resources Board, he eventually conceded Howe's point that membership should be accepted "without reservation or not at all."[65] So Canada became a member of the Combined Production and Resources Board, though it would be difficult to attribute the outcome to acceptance of the principle of "functionalism" by its allies.

After his own visit to Ottawa, the Secretary of State for Dominions Affairs, Clement Attlee, pleaded with the War Cabinet for more careful handling of Canadian affairs. In effect, Canada had been shunted aside while priority was given to relations with the United States and the Soviet Union. "If uneasiness on this score were to spread from Canadian official circles to the Canadian public," Attlee contended, "the results would certainly be serious and far-reaching. . . . We shall need the utmost assistance which Canada can give us not only in materials and man-power, but also financially; given a sense of partnership with us, we can count on the Canadians as on our own people, and they will, I am sure, be ready to face any and every sacrifice in the common cause. But once we let them feel that they are regarded here as playing only a minor role, the sharp edge of their enthusiasm will be blunted and their willingness to give of their utmost impaired by a barrier of mistrust."[66] However eloquent and justified Attlee's appeal for consideration and consultation, there is little evidence that it had any impact on the attitudes of other departments. In fact, as a senior official of the Treasury observed, little headway could be made against the stance taken by the Ministry of Food if the Canadian government itself would not insist on full membership of the Combined Food Board.[67] According to a disappointed Vincent Massey, Canada's high commissioner in London, Howe complained vociferously to him about the "virtual exclusion of Canada from reasonable participation in the joint war effort," but failed to convey that disquiet to his British interlocutors.[68]

In fact, as Norman Robertson frankly admitted, the Canadian position was "illogical and inconsistent." It was difficult to reconcile Canada's assertion of its interest in the Combined Production and Resources Board with its passive response to exclusion from the work of the Combined Chiefs of Staff or the reversal on munitions assignment. "In the circumstances," Robertson commented, "our relations with the other Boards have had to be worked out on an ad hoc basis, foregoing, for instance a pretty reasonable claim to be represented on one Combined Board in order to strengthen our case for full participation in another in respect of which there seemed to be stronger grounds of practical convenience for our full and formal participation." Seen in that light, according to Robertson, it was "not unreasonable" for Canada to be a member of the Combined Production and Resources Board but not the Combined Food Board or the Munitions Assignment Board.[69] Functionalism if necessary, but not necessarily functionalism.

Not surprisingly, implementation of the compromise reached in September 1942 did not resolve the question of the combined boards, nor did it remove the tension surrounding the issue. Privately, the most persistent critic was the deputy minister of Finance, who had been away when the settlement was accepted by Canadian ministers.[70] There was a considerable risk, which the Treasury appreciated, that inadequate recognition of the Canadian war effort might threaten the development of Canadian assistance in the form of Mutual Aid.[71] From Ottawa, the Treasury was advised that "the main question of our future financial relationship" could be delayed "until this whole wretched question of Canadian representation on Combined Boards, both during and after the war, is really out of the way."[72] Apparently, Clark's attitude made it difficult to sort out procedure, particularly for munitions assignments, under the nascent Mutual Aid Board.[73]

Clark was especially upset at the exclusion of Canada from the Policy Committee of UNRRA.[74] To one British visitor, Clark opined "that if the U.S. want to do all of the giving for relief, well and good, but there will be no contribution from Canada without representation." Only by virtue of the incompetence of the opposition and the ignorance of the public, Clark contended, had this failed to become a major political issue in Canada.[75] When he learned of the format adopted for the relief organization, he suggested an "answer" to Robertson: "Thank you boys, but count us out. We are still trying to run a democracy and there is some historical evidence to support the thesis that democracies cannot be taxed without representation. We have tried to lead our people in a full-out effort for the war, and we hoped that we could continue to lead them in such a way as to get their support behind the provision of relief and maintenance for battle-scarred Europe in the postwar years. We will not be able to secure their support for such a program if it, as well as the economic affairs of the world generally, are to be run as a monopoly by the Four Great Powers." Clark ruled out any "compromise" that would "set the pattern for postwar economic organisation as well as for postwar political organization." In his view, it was time to play Canada's trump cards and any government that failed to do so would be deservedly punished by the electorate.[76] A more temperate version of this stance was endorsed by the prime minister. "We cannot accept the idea," King wrote to Leighton McCarthy, "that our destinies can be entrusted to the four larger Powers and we have advanced the principle that representation on international bodies should depend on the extent of the contribution which each country would be expected to make to their work. We intend to continue to press for the acceptance of this principle and for Canadian representation on bodies in which we have a special interest." Finally King invoked the functional principle in his quest for a solution to what was now a political problem.[77]

Four months later, the prime minister explained his approach to higher direction of the war to the House of Commons. King depicted the agencies established by the United States and the United Kingdom as logical outgrowths of wartime cooperation and collaboration. In his statement, he alluded to Canadian representation on one of the six organizations, the Combined Production and Resources Board, which was meeting in Ottawa as he spoke, but he avoided any reference to UNRRA, preferring instead to generalize about postwar problems and the conferences devoted to them. In that context, he endorsed the application of the functional principle to the international institutions that had to deal with the "gigantic task of liberation, restoration and reconstruction." So far as the wartime agencies were concerned, he contented himself with the vague suggestion that "the government hopes that it will be found possible to have a broader basis given to some of these bodies."[78]

One aspect of the earlier settlement that Canada was able to modify to advantage was membership of the Combined Food Board. On the instructions of the Cabinet, Norman Robertson revived the question in discussions with Malcolm MacDonald and R. H. Brand. The Combined Food Board was conspicuously expanding the scope of its operations into realms with postwar implications. Food production in Canada was affected by a number of factors that came within the authority of the board, particularly as it considered a wider range of commodities. MacDonald was left in no doubt that the Canadians would renew their quest "for full membership on the Board." As he explained, the imposition of further restrictions on Canadian consumption, while production of food was expanded, complicated the political equation.[79] Like MacDonald, Brand hoped for a solution comparable to that on the Combined Production and Resources Board, whereby no other claimant was admitted.[80]

Back in London, however, the Ministry of Food continued to resist. At an interdepartmental meeting, its representative tried to downplay the practical significance of membership on the Combined Food Board, which was "little more than a rubber stamp on conclusions reached in Committees," where Canada was represented. But, as the Dominions Office understood, prestige, not practicality, was the crux of the matter. Some concession was necessary to secure support for the generous scheme to fund British requirements from Canada.[81] Still, there was some reluctance to reopen such a delicate issue. Canada was not the only major supplier of foodstuffs—Australia and New Zealand were likely contenders for similar recognition. Moreover, the United States was unlikely to accept a minority position on the board.[82] In the circumstances, and still hopeful of a better position in UNRRA, Canada's request was delayed but not abandoned.[83]

By 1943, however, the Ministry of Food had few allies in the British government and British representatives in Washington added their voices to the chorus calling for a retreat from what was increasingly regarded as an indefensible position. Contrary to the Ministry of Food's earlier impression, American authorities would *not* oppose exceptional treatment for Canada.[84] Without opposition from the United States, there was the unwelcome prospect that Britain alone would block the advance of a Dominion.[85] Finally, in June 1943, after a meeting in Ottawa with Brand and J. P. R. Maude of the Ministry of Food, the British government indicated that it would support the request for membership of the Combined Food Board.[86] After some delay, the carefully drafted official invitations from Roosevelt and Churchill to King were extended on October 25, 1943.[87] By the time of the Second Quebec Conference, whether or not the combined boards would continue after the war was a moot point.[88]

As for UNRRA, the result of considerable diplomatic and political efforts was even less satisfactory and the portent for postwar organizations no more favorable. Pearson, as Canada's representative, became chairman of the Supply Committee of UNRRA and, as such, a nonvoting participant in the Policy Committee. Brooke Claxton, who led the Canadian delegation to the founding conference of UNRRA in Atlantic City in November 1943, recalled afterward "a good many illustrations of the 'functional' principle. I mentioned this in opening and the phrase came into fairly general use."[89] The Supply Committee, at least, corresponded to "functional" representation, and, as his biographer notes, Pearson made a significant contribution to the work of the organization.[90] But it was not until the war was over that Canada made it on to the executive committee of UNRRA.[91] As James Eayrs has observed, the initial compromise on Canadian representation on UNRRA was "a severe reverse," not a triumph, for "the functional idea."[92]

After the fundamental decisions had been taken, but before membership on the Combined Food Board had been confirmed, King had an opportunity to appeal personally to Churchill. In August 1943, King took advantage of a joint meeting of the British War Cabinet and the Cabinet War Committee of Canada on the margins of the Quadrant Conference to underline to Churchill what he depicted as the concern of the Canadian public at the lack of formal or practical acknowledgment of Canada's war effort. As King put it, Canada "was not being accorded in the council of the United Nations, a role proportionate to her contribution. It was felt that in certain fields in which Canada was playing a major role her right to a more decisive voice might also be recognized." When decisions were taken by Britain and the United States that affected Canadian interests but "without opportunity for Canadian comment," that caused "serious difficulties for the Canadian government."[93]

For Mackenzie King, then as always, a crucial consideration was public opinion in Canada. Between elections, King prepared for elections. Though he had an overwhelming majority in the House of Commons, the Liberal leader was wary of any erosion of public support, in Canada generally and in Quebec specifically, for the war effort and for the government that he led. His first major statement on the combined boards, in June 1942, had come in the midst of a divisive debate on conscription and before the budget, which paid for the Billion Dollar Gift and associated measures, was tabled.[94] The Prime Minister's voluminous diaries are replete with references to the importance of the war effort to the political fortunes of the government and to the threat posed by the opposition parties, particularly the Co-operative Commonwealth Federation. In that context, public perceptions of the relative importance of Canada's contribution to the common cause were important to King.

When he reflected later on Canada's wartime experience, Pearson remarked on the limited success of functionalism. "This principle of representation was never realized as we hoped," Pearson observed, "though lip service was paid to its fairness." That outcome Pearson attributed not only to the determination to retain authority "in the hands of the two major Allies" but also to the failure of King to take a strong enough stand in dealing with Churchill and Roosevelt.[95] Whether King was as convinced of its validity as were his subordinates remains open to question.

As scholars, we are naturally drawn to the articulation of ideas such as functionalism to justify and to explain. Undeniably, the notion was important to Canadian policy-makers in wartime and in the elaboration of Canada's approach to the organization of the postwar world. However, we should also remember that other factors, including personalities as well as enlightened (or unenlightened) self-interest, are also important determinants of policy. As we have seen, Canada's war effort was a significant justification for recognition and status, particularly in relation to the combined boards. And the efforts of policy-makers in Ottawa to persuade their counterparts in London and Washington to admit Canada to the inner circle of decision making were advanced or retarded by the commitment of key individuals or departments, as well as by perceptions of public attitudes.[96]

NOTES

1. W. L. M. King Papers, King Diary, Sept. 11, 1944, National Archives of Canada [hereafter NAC].

2. The best explanations of the functionalist argument as it applies to the combined boards are in C. P. Stacey, *Arms, Men and Governments: The War Policies of Canada 1939-1945* (Ottawa, 1970), pp. 159-180; J. L. Granatstein, *Canada's War: The Politics of the Mackenzie King Government, 1939-1945* (Toronto, 1975), particularly chapter 8; and, J. L. Granatstein, *The Ottawa Men: The Civil Service Mandarins, 1935-1957* (Toronto, 1982), pp. 124-33. The prevalence of the conventional interpretation is reflected in brief references in surveys of Canadian foreign policy. See, for example, the accounts in J. W. Holmes, *The Shaping of Peace: Canada and the Search for World Order, 1943-1957*, vol. 1 (Toronto, 1979), pp. 72-73; K. R. Nossal, *The Politics of Canadian Foreign Policy* (Scarborough, 1985), pp. 10-11; J. Hilliker, *Canada's Department of External Affairs, The Early Years, 1909-1946*, vol. 1 (Montreal and Kingston, 1990), pp. 255-6 and T. Keating, *Canada and World Order: The Multilateralist Tradition in Canadian Foreign Policy* (Toronto, 1993), pp. 26-33. For a useful assessment of the origins, development and persistence of functionalism as a Canadian creed, see A. J. Miller, "The Functional Principle in Canada's External Relations," *International Journal*, 35, no. 2 (Spring, 1980): 309-28. As Miller points out, what Canadian policy-makers advocated and pursued was functional representation rather than functionalism, though this chapter employs the term as Wrong and others understood it.

3. See H. Mackenzie, "'Little Lend-Lease': the American Impact on Canada's Mutual Aid Program" (Paper delivered at the conference of Canadian Committee for the History of the Second World War, Waterloo, Ontario, December 1993); J. L. Granatstein, *How Britain's Weakness Forced Canada into the Arms of the United States* (Toronto, 1989), pp. 32-40. The best account of Lend-Lease remains that of W. F. Kimball, *The Most Unsordid Act: Lend-Lease, 1939-1941* (Baltimore, 1969). The development of Canadian war production and its relationship to British requirements (as well as the implications for it of Lend-Lease) are well covered in the British official histories World War II, particularly R. S. Sayers, *Financial Policy, 1939-1945* (London, 1956); M. M. Postan, *British War Production* (London, 1952) and H. D. Hall, *North American Supply* (London, 1955). On that subject, see also R. Bothwell, "'Who's Paying for Anything These Days?'—War Production in Canada, 1939-1945," in *Mobilization for Total War*, ed. N. F. Dreisziger (Waterloo, 1981), pp. 59-69.

4. See Granatstein, *Canada's War*, pp. 194-195, 222-228; H. Mackenzie, "Sinews of War: The Politics of Canadian Economic Aid to Britain, 1939-1945" (Paper delivered at the annual meeting of Canadian Historical Association, June 1983). For a contemporary assessment of the problem, see the exchange in April and May 1943 between the Minister of Finance, J. L. Ilsley and the Provincial Treasurer of Quebec J. Arthur Mathewson, National Archives of Canada, Department of Finance Records [hereafter DF], vol. 418, "Mutual Aid Legislation—Billion Dollar Gift 1943," as well as an unsigned memorandum dated April 14, 1943 in DF/vol. 404, 101-106.

5. See Mackenzie, "Little Lend-Lease."

6. See J. L. Granatstein, "The Man Who Wasn't There: Mackenzie King, Canada, and the Atlantic Charter," in *The Atlantic Charter,* eds. D. Brinkley and D. R. Facey-Crowther (New York, 1994), pp. 115-128.

7. See Granatstein, "The Man Who Wasn't There," pp. 123-25, and Stacey, *Arms, Men and Governments,* pp. 149-51.

8. Robertson, "Memorandum for the Prime Minister," Dec. 22, 1941 (enclosed with Robertson to King, Dec. 22, 1941), W. L. M. King Papers [KP], J4, volume 240, file 2411, NAC.

9. Pearson to Massey, Jan. 9, 1942, quoted in V. Massey, *What's Past is Prologue* (Toronto, 1963), pp. 350-351. See also L. B. Pearson, *Mike,* vol. 1 (Toronto, 1972), pp. 214-215.

10. Cabinet Records [hereafter CAB] 65/25 W. M. 8(42)1, Jan. 17, 1942 (with confidential annex); War Minutes [hereafter W. M] 9(42)8, Jan. 19, 1942, Public Records Office [hereafter PRO]. The formal announcement of the boards was made on January 26, 1942. There were boards or committees in both capitals—for reasons explained in the text, the Canadian approach to membership is directed at the Munitions Assignment Board in Washington rather than its counterpart in London. As Vincent Massey remarked in his memoirs, cooperation between Churchill and Roosevelt relieved King and Canada of the necessity to choose between the two. Massey, *What's Past is Prologue,* pp. 354-55.

11. Wrong to Robertson, Jan. 20, 1942, *Documents on Canadian External Relations,* vol. 9, ed. J. F. Hilliker, (Ottawa, 1980), pp. 106-9. In this context, "United Nations" refers to the wartime alliance. Though Canada was well behind the United States and the United Kingdom in war production (approximately 5 percent of the total for the three countries), it was well ahead of any other ally. Stacey, *Arms, Men and Governments,* p. 167; Granatstein, *Ottawa Men,* pp. 125-26. As Miller points out, when Wrong first put forward the functional principle it was one among several options rather than the exclusive position it would occupy by mid-1942. See: Miller, "The functional principle," p. 314.

12. Cabinet War Committee [hereafter CWC] Minutes, Feb. 4, 1942, Privy Council Office Records, NAC. In his memoirs, Pearson notes that King realized that participation in decision making at the highest level implied contributions of the highest order—so there was an additional reason for King not to press for influence on strategy. Pearson, *Mike,* vol. I, p. 171.

13. Secretary of State for External Affairs to Secretary of State for Dominion Affairs, Feb. 10, 1942, KP, J1, vol. 333, no. 39, NAC.

14. Howe to Batt, Feb. 10, 1942, Roosevelt Papers, Official Files [hereafter OF] 4752, Franklin D. Roosevelt Library [hereafter FDRL]. Pearson later recalled that Howe "had his own way of making his influence felt, in Washington, as in Ottawa. His procedure was personal and informal and his own strong position and prestige made it effective." (Pearson, *Mike,* vol. I, p. 214)

15. CWC, Minutes, Feb. 12, 1942, NAC.

16. Howe Memorandum, "Re: Joint U.S.-U.K. Boards for Allocation of Finished Munitions, Distribution of Shipping and Distribution of Raw Materials," Mar. 5, 1942, CWC, Documents, vol. viii, NAC.

17. Pearson Memorandum, "Re: Canada's Relations to UK-US Combined Boards," Mar. 11, 1942, CWC, Documents, volume viii, NAC.

18. CWC, Minutes: March 11, 1942, NAC. On the personal nature of the dispute between Howe and Ralston, see Dexter to Dafoe, Apr. 5, 1943, Grant Dexter Papers, TC3, folder 24, Queen's University Archives (Kingston, Ontario); and Dexter to Dafoe, Mar. 25, 1941, J. W. Dafoe Papers, vol. 12, NAC.

19. CWC, Minutes, Mar. 18, 1942, NAC. Subsequent references in the text to the Munitions Assignment Board (or MAB) are to the board in Washington.

20. King Diary: Mar. 18, 1942.

21. King Diary, Mar. 21, 1942.

22. King Diary, "Memorandum: Meeting of Pacific War Council, at Washington, D.C., Wednesday, April 15, 1942."

23. King Diary, Memorandum of conversation with Roosevelt, Apr. 16, 1942.

24. Canadian High Commissioner in United Kingdom [hereafter CHC(UK)] to Secretary of State for External Affairs [hereafter SSEA], Apr. 22, 1942, no. 1109, KP, J1, vol. 329, NAC; SSEA to CHC(UK), May 12, 1942, no. 936, KP JI, vol. 329, NAC; CHC(UK) to SSEA, No. 1387, May 23, 1942, KP, J1, vol. 329, NAC.

25. Howe to Heeney, Apr. 27, 1942, CWC, Documents, volume ix, NAC; CWC, Minutes, Apr. 29, 1942, May 1, 1942, and May 8, 1942, NAC.

26. McCarthy to Hull, May 13, 1942, No. 317, King Papers, J1, vol. 327. On the appointment of McCarthy, see Pearson to Robertson, Mar. 4, 194, Pearson Papers, vol. 2, NAC; King Diary, Feb. 15, 1945, Feb. 19, 1941, Feb. 21, 1941, Mar. 5, 1941; and Dexter to Dafoe, April 5, 1943, Dexter Papers, TC3, folder 24.

27. McCarthy to Robertson, June 9, 1942, WA-1258; and McCarthy to King, June 13, 1942, KP, J1, vol. 327, NAC.

28. Robertson to McCarthy, June 18, 1942, EX-1226, KP, J1, vol. 327, NAC.

29. Pearson to Robertson, June 19, 1942, WA-1390, KP, J1, vol.327, NAC.

30. CWC, Minutes, June 24, 1942, NAC; Ralston to Howe, June 24, 1942; Howe to Ralston, June 25, 1942; Ralston to Howe, June 26, 1942; Ralston to Howe, June 30, 1942, CWC, Documents, vol. x, NAC.

31. CWC, Minutes, June 26, 1942, NAC. See also the extract from King's Diary quoted in Stacey, *Arms, Men and Governments,* p. 169.

32. "Memorandum of Conversation with Mr. Norman Robertson," June 26, 1942, Hickerson Papers, Box 2, Moffat, Department of State Records, Office of European Affairs, National Archives, Washington.

33. Canadian Minister, Washington [hereafter CM(USA)] to SSEA, June 26, 1942, WA-1498, KP, J1, vol. 327, NAC; CM(USA) to SSEA, June 26, 1942, WA-1499, KP, J1, vol. 327, NAC.

34. SSEA to CM(USA), July 2, 1942, EX-1402, KP, J1, vol. 327, NAC. At this time, the Canadian government was not inclined to seek membership on the

recently announced Combined Production and Resources Board, as Hopkins had suggested, either on its own merits or as an alternative to membership of the Munitions Assignment Board.

35. CM(USA) to SSEA, July 3, 1942, WA-1593, KP, J1, vol. 327, NAC.

36. CWC, Minutes, July 1, 1942, NAC.

37. CM(USA) to SSEA (Pearson to Robertson), July 11, 1942, WA-1680, KP, J1, vol. 327, NAC; CWC, Minutes, July 22, 1942, NAC.

38. CM(USA) to SSEA (Pearson to Robertson), Aug. 5, 1942, no. 1978, KP, J1, vol. 327, NAC; Robertson, "Memorandum for the Prime Minister," Aug. 5, 1942, KP, J1, vol. 327, NAC. In fact, Canada's principal military liaison officer in Washington, Maurice Pope, had helped to draft the letter that conveyed the American offer. M. Pope, *Soldiers and Politicians* (Toronto, 1962), p. 201. See also, Stacey, *Arms, Men and Governments,* p. 169.

39. CWC, Minutes, Aug. 19 and 26, 1942. According to Sir Richard Clarke, who was involved in the Combined Production and Resources Board, a similar conflict between military and civilian authorities in Washington contributed to the delay in establishing the board. See *Anglo-American Economic Collaboration in War and Peace 1942-1949* (Oxford, 1982), p. 10.

40. CM(USA) to SSEA (Pearson to Robertson), Aug. 28, 1942, No. 2286, KP, J1, vol. 327, NAC; CWC, Minutes, Oct. 7, 1942; Pope, *Soldiers and Politicians,* p. 202. See also C. P. Stacey, *Canada and the Age of Conflict: 1921-1948 The Mackenzie King Era,* vol. 2 (Toronto, 1981), p. 330.

41. CWC, Minutes, June 11, 1942, NAC.

42. Canada, House of Commons, *Debates,* June 11, 1942. King's commitment to seek a seat on the Combined Food Board was made in response to a question from the Leader of the Opposition, R. B. Hanson, rather than in his prepared statement, and it was delivered in characteristically indirect language.

43. SSEA to CM(USA), June 18, 1942, no. 1226, KP, J1, vol.327, NAC; J. L. Granatstein, *A Man of Influence: Norman A. Robertson and Canadian Statecraft, 1929-68* (Toronto, 1981), pp. 139-40.

44. CM(USA) to SSEA, July 5, 1942, no.1613; SSEA to CM(USA), July 13, 1942, no. 1493; CM(USA) to SSEA, July 22, 1942, no. 1825, KP J1, vol. 327, NAC. Secretary of State, Dominion Affairs [hereafter SSDA] to SSEA, no. 156, July 18, 1942, KP J1, vol.334, NAC .

45. H. R. Brand Memorandum, "Combined Food Board," July 28, 1942 (extract from Diary for July 26-28, 1942), CAB 115/549, NAC.

46. H. R. Brand, "Memo handed to Mr. Norman Robertson...." July 28, 1942, CAB 115/549, NAC.

47. CWC, Minutes, July 29, 1942, NAC.

48. Leith-Ross, "Note for the High Commissioner," July 30, 1942, CAB 115/549. The task for Leith-Ross was made even more difficult by King's personal response to his demeanor as well as to his arguments. Unfortunately, the British representative recalled for King a phrase that he attributed to Asquith, "tranquil consciousness of effortless superiority." King's Diary, July 30, 1942.

49. Robertson to Massey, Aug. 4, 1942, KP J1, vol. 332, NAC.

50. Pearson to Robertson, Aug. 5, 1942, KP J1, vol. 331, NAC.

51. British High Commissioner in Canada to SSDA, Aug. 5, 1942, no. 1557, CAB 115/549.

52. Waley, Minute, Aug. 11, 1942; Draft letter to Sir Frederick Phillips, Aug. 11, 1942, Treasury Records T160/1252/F.17969/2, PRO.

53. Phillips to Treasury, Aug. 28, 1942, no. 1727, T160/1252/F.17969/2, PRO.

54. Phillips to Hopkins, Aug. 31, 1942, no. 64 Saving, T160/1252/F.17969/2, PRO. Appended to that message was a memorandum by R. G. Munro, "Canada-United Kingdom Financial Arrangements after Expiry of Billion Dollar Gift," Aug. 27, 1942. Norman Hillmer and J. L. Granatstein appropriately comment about this type of threat: "This was a bluff, of course, for public opinion simply would not have tolerated an end to Canadian generosity," *Empire to Umpire: Canada and the World to the 1990s* (Toronto, 1994), p. 176. But it was a bluff that the British could not afford to call.

55. Phillips to Hopkins, Aug. 31, 1942, T160/1252/F.17969/3, PRO.

56. UKHC(C) to SSDA, Aug. 31, 1942, no. 1737, CAB 115/549; Phillips to Hopkins, Sept. 1, 1942. T160/1252/F.17969/3, PRO.

57. CWC, Minutes, Sept. 2, 1942, NAC.

58. R. Bothwell and W. Kilbourn, *C.D. Howe, a biography* (Toronto, 1979), pp. 171-2.

59. United Kingdom Ambassador (USA) [hereafter UKA(USA)] to Secretary of State for Foreign Affairs [hereafter SSFA] (Sinclair to Lyttelton), Sept. 3, 1942, no. 4440, CAB109/11.

60. UKHC(C) to SSDA, Sept. 9, 1942, no. 1803; Dominions Office, "Position of Canada in Relation to Various Combined Organizations," Sept. 5, 1942; Garner to Moore, Sept. 9, 1942, CAB 109/11. The Dominions Office supported this view, even though it had some reservations about the precedent for other Dominions.

61. SSFA to UKA(USA), Sept. 10, 1942, no. 54912,CAB 115/549; Coulson Minute, Sept. 7, 1942, FO371/31543/U725, PRO. The Foreign Office regarded the Combined Production and Resources Board as the least important of the combined organizations.

62. Record of meeting, Sept. 14, 1942, and SSDA to UKHC(C), Sept. 15, 1942, no. 2073, CAB 109/11. Ronald, Minute, Sept. 16, 1942, FO371/31543/U798. Ronald's minute is quoted extensively in Granatstein, *Canada's War*, p. 302. Coulson, Minute, Sept. 21, 1942; Strong, Minute, Sept. 21, 1942; Cadogan, Minute, Sept. 21, 1942, FO/371/31543/U816, PRO.

63. UKA(USA) to SSFA (Sinclair to Lyttelton), Sept. 17, 1942, no. 4685, CAB 109/11.

64. CWC, Minutes, Sept. 16, 1942, NAC; UKA(USA) to SSFA (Sinclair to Lyttelton), Sept. 17, 1942, no. 4686, CAB 109/11; British Food Mission to Ministry of Food (Brand to Woolton), Sept. 22, 1942, unnumbered RATION, CAB 109/11. See R. W. James, *Wartime Economic Co-operation,* (Toronto, 1949), p. 234. So far as the Combined Food Board was concerned, the crucial factor had been the assurance that it would not meddle in postwar

matters. "Memorandum of telephone conversation with Hugh L. Keenleyside, American Under Secretary of State for European Affairs," Sept. 18, 1942, Hickerson Papers, box 2, Moffat, NA.

65. CWC, Minutes, Oct. 28, 1942, NAC. James, *Wartime Economic Co-operation,* pp. 241-242. Taylor Memorandum, "Report on Activities of Combined Production and Resources Board with particular reference to Canada . . ." Mar. 1, 1943, CWC, Documents, vol. xii, NAC.

66. Attlee Memorandum, "Relations with Canada," Oct. 8, 1942, CAB 66/29, WP(42)451; SSDA to UKHC(C), Machtig to Atlee, Sept. 23, 1942, no. 2121, CAB 109/11; UKHC(C) to SSDA, Sept. 24, 1942, No. 1902, CAB 109/11.

67. Eady, Minute, Sept. 24, 1942, T160/1252/F.17969/3 PRO. Contrary to the impression conveyed by Brand in Ottawa, the British Ministry of Food was hoping to use the Combined Food Board to secure postwar supplies. Eady understood that the Ministry of Food expected the Combined Food Board to survive the conflict. During a visit to London, Hume Wrong learned about Attlee's plea with his colleagues for understanding of Canada's position. He also ascertained that it was the Foreign Office that led the opposition to Canadian membership of the Policy Committee of the relief organization. Wrong Memorandum, "Combined Boards," Nov. 5, 1942, Wrong Papers, vol. 4, file 3, NAC.

68. Massey Diary, Sept. 30 and Oct. 6, 1942, quoted in Massey, *What's Past is Prologue,* p. 352.

69. Robertson to Ralston, Oct. 24, 1942, KP J1, vol. 332, NAC. That inconsistency had earlier befuddled Brand, ibid., Pearson to Robertson, Aug. 1, 1942, KP J1, vol. 331, NAC.

70. Waley, "Note of a Meeting at the Dominions Office on 31st October 1942," Nov. 3, 1942, T160/1252/F.17969/3, PRO.

71. Munro, Memorandum of conversation, Dec. 11, 1942; Munro, Memorandum of conversation, Dec. 15,1942; Munro, Memorandum of conversation, Dec. 16, 1942; Waley, Minute, Dec. 22, 1942; Eady, Minute, Dec. 22, 1942; Clutterbuck to Eady, Dec. 21, 1942; Eady to Clutterbuck, Dec. 23, 1942, T160/1252/F.17969/3, PRO.

72. UKHC(C) to SSDA, Nov. 11, 1942, no. 2269; Munro to Waley, Nov. 17, 1942, T160/1252/F.17969/3, PRO.

73. UKHC(C) to SSDA, no. 1, Jan. 2, 1943; Munro, Note of conversation, Jan. 29, 1943, T160/1252/F.17969/3/1, PRO.

74. Clutterbuck, Note of Meeting, Oct. 31, 1942, Dominions Office Records [hereafter DO] 35/1029/WT15/180; Keynes, Minute, Nov. 25, 1942; Waley, Minute, Nov. 26, 1942, T160/1252/F.17969/3, PRO.

75. Opie Memorandum, "Visit to Ottawa February 6-7," Feb. 11, 1943, FO371/35331/U915, PRO.

76. Clark to Robertson, Mar. 3, 1943, KP J1, vol. 338, NAC.

77. King to McCarthy, Mar. 1, 1943, KP, J1, vol. 343, NAC.

78. Canada, House of Commons, *Debates,* July 9, 1943. King mentioned the food and agriculture conference in Hot Springs, Virginia, whose final act had been

tabled in the House of Commons on June 14, 1943, as well as the likely
attention to refugees and the need for new international institutions. An edited
version of King's remarks has been published in J. L. Granatstein, *Canadian
Foreign Policy: Historical Readings* (Toronto, 1986), pp. 21-4.

79. UKHC(C) to SSDA, Mar. 17, 1943, no. 624, CAB 109/11. Also, President
Roosevelt drew attention to the importance of food in the postwar world
through the United Nations Conference on Food and Agriculture, which took
place in Hot Springs, Virginia, in April 1943.

80. Brand to Woolton, Mar. 19, 1943, RATION 7709, CAB 115/549.

81. North American Supply Committee, Informal Committee on Combined
Boards (19th Meeting): Mar. 24, 1943, CAB 109/11.

82. SSDA to UKHC(C), Mar. 27, 1943, no. 774, CAB 115/549.

83. UKHC(C) to SSDA, Apr. 1, 1943, no. 762, CAB 115/549.

84. Llewellin (Washington) to Air Ministry, May 12, 1943, SEVER 2, CAB 109/
11.

85. UKA(USA) to SSFA, May 19, 1943, no. 2342, CAB 109/11.

86. CWC, Minutes, June 18 and July 28, 1943; SSDA to UKHC(C), June 15,
1943, no. 1451; UKHC(C) to SSDA, June 15, 1943, no. 1417; UKHC(C)
to SSDA, June 15, 1943, no. 1424; SSDA to UKHC(C), June 28, 1943, no.
1549, FO371/35491/U2699, PRO. After the British government consulted
the Dominion High Commissioners in London and cabled its views to
Dominion governments, the invitation was regarded as imminent in late July
1943.

87. Winant to Churchill, Oct. 2, 1943; Cranborne to Churchill, Oct. 8, 1943;
Churchill to Winant, Oct. 12, 1943; SSDA to SSEA, Oct. 25, 1943, no. 158
(PM to PM); SSEA to SSDA, Oct. 28, 1943, no. 168, (PM to PM), Prime
Minister's Office Records [hereafter PREM] 3/487/7; SSDA to SSEA, Oct.
25, 1943, no. 159, KP, J1, vol. 338; SSEA to SSDA, Oct. 28, 1943, no. 169,
KP, J1, vol. 351; Telegram, Roosevelt to King, Oct. 25, 1943, KP, J1, vol.
349, NAC.

88. The question of continuation of the combined boards was considered by the
United States and the United Kingdom (in consultation with the rest of the
Commonwealth). See SSDA to SSEA, July 17, 1944, no. 105, KP, J1, vol.
372, NAC. The Canadian perspective on this topic is conveyed in J. F.
Hilliker, ed., *Documents on Canadian External Relations 1944-1945*, vol. 10,
part I (Ottawa, 1987), pp. 214-67. As in other instances, the abrupt
termination of the war against Japan prompted the temporary extension of
the mandate of the wartime organizations into the postwar period.

89. Claxton to Dafoe, Dec. 10, 1943, Claxton Papers, vol. 223, NAC.

90. J. English, *Shadow of Heaven: The Life of Lester Pearson, 1897-1948*, vol. 1
(Toronto, 1989), p. 283.

91. Stacey, *Canada and the Age of Conflict*, vol. II, p. 332. There is an excellent
account of Canada's campaign for representation on the executive or policy
committee of UNRRA in Granatstein, *Canada's War*, pp. 300-7.

92.   J. Eayrs, *In Defence of Canada: Peacemaking and Deterrence* (Toronto, 1972), pp. 162-3. In his biography of Robertson, Granatstein concludes that "the functional principle had essentially been tried and found wanting during the war." *Man of Influence,* p. 143.

93.   CWC, Minutes, Aug. 11, 1943. On Mackenzie King's role at the First Quebec Conference (Quadrant), see C. P. Stacey, *Mackenzie King and the Atlantic Triangle* (Toronto, 1976), pp. 56-59.

94.   The manpower question arose in the form of amendment of the National Resources Mobilization Act in the wake of the plebiscite releasing the government from its pledge against conscription for overseas service.

95.   Pearson, *Mike,* vol. I, p. 215.

96.   Ironically, the British department that was most attracted to the notion of functionalism, the Foreign Office, was most consistently opposed to its application by Canada to the case of the combined boards. For example, Gladwyn Jebb argued that adoption of the "functional principle" provided "a consistent and logically defensible foundation for the general set-up on functional lines which we advocate." Jebb, "The functional approach to International Organizations," Mar. 6, 1943, FO371/35331/U983, PRO. However, the conversion of the Foreign Office to functionalism likely had more to do with the presence in its midst of one of its principal theorists, David Mitrany, then working in the Foreign Research and Press Service, than to the advocacy of the Canadian government. Miller, "The functional principle," p. 316.

NINE

FRENCH CANADIANS IN THE CANADIAN ARMED FORCES IN 1944

SERGE BERNIER

INTRODUCTION

THIS CHAPTER ADDRESSES A TOPIC that until now has left French-speaking historians in Quebec cold: the voluntary participation of approximately 150,000 French Canadians in World War II. It is perhaps appropriate at this point in Canadian history that a brief review is presented of the reasons for this silence and for the fact that, given its population, Quebec supplied far fewer volunteers than it could have.

The first serious symposium on the subject of French-Canadian participation in World War II took place in October 1994 at the Collège militaire royal de Saint-Jean (an institution that was about to close its doors) and at the Université du Québec à Montréal. On that occasion, the veil was finally lifted on the role in that great world conflict of French-Canadian soldiers, some of whom, rather astonished as I recall, were in attendance. An overview of the situation was also provided at that time, the gist of which deserves to be repeated.

BRIEF SUMMARY

In 1939, Canadians, both francophone and anglophone, were emerging from a terrible depression. Far-removed from the situation and power-less to act, they were able to watch the European crisis develop, just as

we today follow other events. Some were attracted by the ideas of
Mussolini, Franco, and Hitler, but such people remained in the
minority. One week after the outbreak of war in September 1939,
Canada itself entered the fray. Faced with this imminent clash of Titans,
our country, with fewer than 10,000 professional soldiers in the three
armed forces, about 5 percent of them French-speaking, certainly had
no illusions about single-handedly tipping the balance in favor of what
were commonly referred to as the Allies. However, the expanded military
effort it envisaged would be based on volunteer enrollment for overseas
service. In addition, Canada would become an immense international
training center for aviators, earning our country the nickname "aero-
drome of democracy."

Following the defeat of the French and English armies on the
European continent, the war assumed a different aspect. In June 1940, the
Canadian government passed the National Resources Mobilization Act,
which decreed, among other things, the use of conscription in the defense
of our country. By then, tens of thousands of Canadians, including several
thousand francophones, were already serving as volunteers. Following
Pearl Harbor, the entry of the United States into the war, and the defeat
of two Canadian battalions at Hong Kong, the tempo of the war
accelerated. In the end, more than a million Canadians wore the uniform
between 1939 and 1945, either as conscripts in the territorial defense of
Canada (especially in the army), or as volunteers in General Service,
which meant that they could be sent overseas. Of these million Canadian
men and women, somewhat fewer than 200,000 were francophone, a
figure that included 150,000 volunteers. In total, 20 percent of Canadians
in uniform were French-speaking, while the country's francophone population was approximately 30 percent. The job of classifying these francophones according to their home province has not yet been undertaken. In
any case, even determining the magnitude of francophone participation
would be an immense task, since all the volunteer enrollment papers
would have to be sifted through (and we are talking here of hundreds of
thousands of documents), in order to find those on which French is
written on the line marked "language." And even then, it is probable that
francophones from Ontario or Alberta would have indicated "English."
The methodological work would be daunting, although it could be done
once the human and material resources were made available. Limited
studies lead us to conclude, however, that French speakers outside Quebec
were volunteering at more or less the same rate as their young English-
speaking counterparts, while the number of Quebec francophones who

enlisted was not at all commensurate with their presence in the eighteen-to-forty-five age group in Canada as a whole.

THE SHORTAGE OF
FRANCOPHONE QUEBEC VOLUNTEERS

The psychological roots—or mentalité—of a people are multifold and difficult for anyone to define with precision. I am nonetheless going start down this perilous road. During the period leading up to the war, there was a fundamental tendency among francophones, one that I feel is too often dismissed, to feel a strong attachment to the Americas. This concept of "American identity," supported by Donald Cuccioletta of the Université du Québec à Montreal,[1] is extremely interesting since it ties the situation in French-speaking Quebec, during the war years at least, to the profound changes sweeping the two Americas. Prior to Pearl Harbor, Canada, it should be remembered, was the exception rather than the rule in the Americas respecting participation in World War II. That francophones in Quebec (and probably Amerindians as well, but this remains to be determined) felt largely detached from the invasion of Poland, from this "mal d'Europe" as Jean-Jules Richard, himself a volunteer, called it in his excellent novel Neuf jours d'haine,"[2] should cause little surprise. We should not forget the strong tradition in American history of characterizing European conflicts as civil wars. Even if such arguments are not directly present in the Quebec historical record, which in any case are nearly silent on the topic of war, there is no doubt that this definition would have been well accepted by many Quebec historians. Furthermore, there were still many strong links binding Quebec francophones and their Franco-American cousins, who stayed out of the war in 1939. Quebec francophones—French-speakers outside Quebec were subjected to different social and demographic pressures in their part of the country—had no trouble resisting the appeals of the British motherland—or for that matter, of the French one.

Anglophones, however, still had close ties with the British Isles. Remember, if there had been no conscription in 1917, 50 percent of the Canadian Expeditionary Force of 1914-18 would have been volunteers born in the British Isles. This was not the case in 1939-45, when most of the English-speaking volunteers had been born in Canada; however, many of these Canadians were the sons and daughters of the preceding generation and therefore still had close links with British aunts and uncles whom they had perhaps never met, but who were nevertheless very real in their minds.

ANTI-BRITISH NATIONALISM

The notion of "American identity" lost much of its weight once the United States entered the war. This original rationale for the refusal of Quebec francophones to volunteer recruits was superseded by a host of others that, each in its own way, militated against out-and-out participation. Anti-British nationalism was one. The eclipse of the French empire by the English in the eighteenth century was not greeted with enthusiasm. Deep rifts between Canadians born here and the French were already apparent at the time of the Seven Years' War. The arrival of a new imperial power that spoke English and embraced a different faith was certainly not going to remedy the situation. There was a certain ambivalence among French Canadians during the American Revolution and, to a lesser degree, during the war of 1812-15. But untimely taxation during the 1837 rebellions, military campaigns in the West directed primarily against French-speaking Métis, the spirit of superiority so manifested by the British during the South African War, and their wish to "Paint the Map Red," to use the expression of Carmen Miller, a professor at McGill University, did nothing to incite les Canadiens (as all French-speaking inhabitants of this country were called up until the late twentieth century) to crowd aboard the British Imperial train. From the mid-eighteenth century until today, French-Canadian nationalism, obviously most pronounced in Quebec, has existed to varying degrees. Some of its activities were directed against the imperialism of Britain, who dragged Canada almost automatically into conflicts that posed no immediate threat to her existence. These anti-British nationalistic feelings, which spawned anti-Gaullist sentiments among many members of the Québecois elite after June 18, 1940, also fed support for Marshal Pétain. Canadian information on the Vichy regime was, on the one hand, filtered through censorship, and, on the other, supplied by the British-Canadian propaganda machine, two instruments extremely useful in wartime, even for democracies, but instruments that sometimes deliver results contrary to the ones desired. It also comes as no surprise that the Catholic clergy, omnipresent in the social and political life of the Quebec of that era, shared the prevailing notions just described, notions firmly held by the people; however, to blame the clergy of that period for this underenrollment, rather than recognizing them as a sometimes active and conspicuous embodiment of these Quebec social trends, would, in my opinion, be a mistake.

POLITICS

No one knew how to take advantage of this situation better than the politicians. The federal Liberals generally held the upper hand in Quebec in the period between the wars. Of course, the elections of the 1920s and 1930s were not about conscription. But, as René Durocher of the University of Montreal has pointed out,[3] any successful Liberal campaign in Quebec contained at least a direct or an indirect reference to the Conservative conscription policy of 1917; moreover, as the possibility of another war loomed larger and larger, the Liberals began making unequivocal promises, aimed mostly at French Quebec, that they would not institute conscription for overseas duty. Under these terms, Canada's entry into the war, predicated on use of a volunteer army, was handled extremely well. During the 1940 election campaign, even the Conservatives, with their powerful wing in the Canadian west, which was still very rural (and as we know, it is generally more difficult to get a farmer to enlist than a city laborer), had to more or less forgo any talk of conscription. However, following their defeat, a change in their leadership and, quite simply, a stint in the traditional role of Her Majesty's official opposition under our British parliamentary system, the Conservatives again embraced the notion of conscription. Even within the governing party, the English pro-conscription faction gained ground with each major development in the war, including the debacle of Dunkirk, the battles of Britain and the Atlantic, Pearl Harbor and the fall of Hong Kong. Finally, Mackenzie King, who was certainly no warmonger, had to agree to organize a referendum asking the people if they would release him from his promise not to resort to conscription for overseas duty. One consequence of this political act was to divide the country in half between an anglophone majority that voted "yes" and a francophone minority (as high as 80 percent in Quebec) that voted "no." A real mess, stemming from certain accommodating statements before the war, but also from the realities of French Quebec society. The referendum campaign was highly political, and therefore the subtle aspects of the issues were ignored by both sides; the results convinced the prime minister and his friends in the Cabinet of the rightness of their initial analysis: Quebec francophones did not want to be forced to fight overseas in causes that had little to do with them (and that, under the circumstances, were undoubtedly presented to them in a cursory manner). Despite the entry of the United States into the war and the threat now posed by the enemy against both of Canada's coasts, this attitude did not change.

"Not necessarily conscription, but conscription if necessary," declared Mackenzie King in April 1942. The results of the referendum left him practically no option as to which part of his statement he would abide by until the end of the war. Of course, he did agree, in November 1944, to send 16,000 conscripts overseas to reinforce units decimated in the Italian campaign, launched in July 1943, and the campaign in northwest Europe, activated in June 1944. But the vast majority of these conscripts would never see action and the government of Mackenzie King would survive the war, something that the Union government of 1917, with its conscription platform, had been unable to accomplish. It must be acknowledged, therefore, that the federal Liberals had recognized, in their approach to Quebec at least, the distinctiveness of French-Canadian society.

TREATMENT OF FRANCOPHONES IN ARMED FORCES

One final underlying factor deserves mention here. Canadian author and military analyst Jean Pariseau has comprehensively analyzed this aspect in a book that the two of us published together.[4] I shall take some time here to review some of the main arguments. For more than a century after England assumed control of New France, the country's defense was handled primarily by regular British troops. The reserves or militia certainly existed, but played a minor role that declined as the threat from the United States receded. This militia was often anti-francophone. When Canada finally took charge of its own defense in 1867, it proceeded by almost entirely ignoring its Francophone population. Canada's French-speaking inhabitants, without a strong military tradition and without a specific cadre within their own defense structure, distanced itself from the military machine in peacetime as in wartime. Equal treatment, as historian Jean-Yves Gravel has noted, might have meant equal service. Given the absence of the first element of this equation, the setbacks experienced in 1899-1903 and, more particularly in 1914-18, had to be expected. The fact that nothing was done between 1919 and 1939 to remedy the situation would have amazed any onlooker. Political blindness? Only partially. In actuality, we see here the almost complete lack of consideration given to Canada's defense by the country's political elite. After all, given that Canada had fewer than 10,000 men in total at the outbreak of war, was it really necessary, or even feasible, to create a military apparatus (recruiting, schools, units, and so on) functioning in the French language? Generally speaking, certain structural characteristics of Canada's defense forces would serve to alienate francophones, particularly the unilingual francophones found primarily in Quebec.

To conclude my discussion of this subject, I will quote what Brigadier W. H. S. Macklin had to say on this topic in 1946: "For all the talk there has been about 'conscription' these past seven years no one has ever explained to me how the Canadian army could have absorbed the proper proportion of French-speaking manpower if there had been compulsion in 1939. There was no trained cadre on which we could build and we never could overcome this in the stress of war."[5]

DESPITE EVERYTHING, VOLUNTEERS DID EXIST

Despite implicit and explicit social pressure from the Quebec francophone group to which they belonged, and the lack of a truly francophone structure within the Canadian forces (as I noted earlier only 5 percent of the professional cadre in 1939 was francophone), nearly 150,000 francophones enrolled in the three forces between 1939 and 1945, 85,000 to 90,000 of them from the province of Quebec. Certainly, not all of them went to the front, but the *régiment de Maisonneuve* (Montreal infantry) was one of the first to fill its ranks. After being decimated at Dieppe in August 1942, the Fusiliers Mont-Royal rose from the ashes to play a key role following their landing in Normandy in July 1944. That said, the absence of a structure to channel francophone efforts and a corresponding shortage of reinforcements for French-speaking infantry units in the fall of 1944 meant that thousands of francophones (more than 3,000, according to a Department of National Defence historical report) were incorporated into English-speaking combat units, which was almost the equivalent of an infantry battalion. This reinforcement crisis would only hit the army; the navy and the air force, which actually experienced surpluses, were not affected.

CONCLUSION

These Francophone volunteers, as we have seen, did not have it easy. Canadian war propaganda could glorify them as much as it liked (and it did so, as effectively in English as in French, through radio dramas, posters, and so on), but in the end, the general situation changed little: the armed forces remained very British, both in the language used and in the way they functioned. Furthermore, a large segment of Quebec's francophone elite did not participate in the war and fought against conscription. They undoubtedly had every right to support the "no" side in the referendum on the issue; but when these leaders closed their eyes to the worst sins of the Vichy regime and failed to acknowledge some of their own errors, they played a terrible trick on those who chose to fight in an excellent cause. Quebec's French-Canadian elite, which, from the period following the war until quite recently, claimed to speak on behalf of all francophones, decided to keep silent concerning Quebec veterans, undoubtedly to forget its own errors in judgement. Upon returning to their country, this generation of soldiers, men and women, saw their children enthusiastically embrace the grumbling nationalism of the 1960s, when the mere mention of the federal state was difficult to accept. They would often resolve to keep silent themselves, and the rare memorial ceremonies held on November 11 and on other occasions, were degraded to the point where they lost all their real meaning in the collective life of Quebec. To a certain extent, the people who had fought for liberty at the age of twenty made the decision, once they had reached forty, to hush up their glorious past (not shameful or, worse, nonexistent, as an ex-prime minister of Canada recently referred to it in his memoirs). This silence of the elites and, to some degree, of the veterans themselves, also had a major impact in other areas: Quebec history texts, even those written by her greatest historians, are silent on the subject of Quebec participation in the 1939-45 war. As political scientist Paul-André Comeau recently asked, is this forgetfulness a type of collective therapy or is it a traditional means of coping? There is still no clear answer, but at least, for some time now, the question has been deemed worthy of asking.

NOTES

1. D. Cuccioletta, "L'isolationisme ou le refus de l'Europe: les Canadiens français, les Américains et la Deuxième Guerre mondiale," *Bulletin d'histoire politique,* vol. 3, no.3/4 (Printemps/Été 1995): 129-36.
2. Nine days of hate.
3. R. Durocher, "Le Québec en 1939" in *A Country of Limitations: Canada and the World in 1939/*Un pays dans la gêne : le Canada et le monde en 1939, eds. N. Hillmer, R. Bothwell, et. al, (Ottawa, 1996), pp. 138-47.
4. J. Pariseau and S. Bernier, *French Canadians and Bilingualism in the Canadian Armed Forces: The Fear of a Parallel Army,* 1763-1969, vol. 1 (Ottawa, 1987), p. 468.
5. C. P. Stacey, *Arms, Men and Governments: The War Policies of Canada, 1939-1945* (Ottawa: 1970), p. 421.

CONTRIBUTORS

DONALD HOWARD AVERY is professor of History at the University of Western Ontario. His books include *Reluctant Host: Canada's Response to Immigrant Workers* (1995) and *The Science of War: Canadian Scientists and Allied Military Technology during the Second World War* (1998).

SERGE BERNIER is director of History and Heritage at National Defence Headquarters, Ottawa. He is also president of the Canadian Commission of Military History, a position he has held since 1988. In addition to being editor-in-chief for several series of books on Canadian military history, he is coauthor of *French Canadians and Bilingualism in the Canadian Armed Forces. Official Languages: National Defence's Response to the Federal Policy, 1969-1987*, vol. II (1994). Other recent publications include editing *Peacekeeping 1815 to Today* (1995), and coediting "French Canadians and the Canadian Armed forces: 1966-1994" in *The Canadian Strategic Forecast 1996: The Military in Modern Democratic Society* (1996).

JOHN ENGLISH is a former M. P. for Kitchener, Ontario, and professor of History at the University of Waterloo. He is also the director of the Waterloo Centre for Foreign Policy and Federalism and the author of *The Life of Lester Pearson* (1989).

J. L. GRANATSTEIN is a distinguished research professor of History emeritus, York University, and Rothwell Jackman resident fellow at the Canadian Institute for International Affairs. He is author of *Yankee Go Home? Canadians and Anti-Americanism* (1996).

WARREN F. KIMBALL, the Robert Treat professor of History at Rutgers University, Newark, was Pitt professor of American History at Cambridge University, 1988-89, and president of the SHAFR in 1993. He has written extensively on Roosevelt's foreign policy and Anglo-American foreign policy in the second world war. His latest book is *Forged in War: Roosevelt, Churchill, and the Second World War* (1997). He is presently working on a study of Reagan, Thatcher, and the "special relationship."

HECTOR MACKENZIE is the senior departmental historian of the department of Foreign Affairs and International Trade. He edited volumes 14 (1948) and 15 (1949) in the series *Documents on Canadian External Relations*. He has published numerous articles on Canada's international relations, particularly focusing on relations within the North Atlantic Triangle before, during, and after the Second World War.

B. J. C. MCKERCHER is a fellow of the Royal Historical Society and professor of History and chairman of the War Studies Department at the Royal Military College of Canada. He is the author of numerous works on British foreign policy and Anglo-American relations, including *Esme Howard: A Diplomatic Biography* (1989) and *Transition in Power: Britain's Loss of Global Preeminence to the United States, 1930-1945* (1998).

ROGER SARTY is senior historian at the Directorate of History and Heritage, National Defence Headquarters, Ottawa. He contributed to the official history of the Royal Canadian Air Force and is coauthor of the forthcoming official history of the Royal Canadian Navy. His recent publications include *Canada and the Battle of the Atlantic* (1998), *The Maritime Defence of Canada* (1996), and "Canada and the Great Rapproachement," in *The North Atlantic Triangle in a Changing World: Anglo-American-Canadian Relations, 1902-1956,* eds. B. J. C. McKercher and Lawrence Aronsen (1996).

DAVID B. WOOLNER received his doctorate from McGill University, has served as an assistant Professor of History at the University of Prince Edward Island, and is currently a Fellow of the FDR Library and Visiting Professor of History at Marist College. He was the principal organizer of the 1994 conference that led to the publication of this book and was named an Arthur Schlesinger fellow in 1996 by the Franklin and Eleanor Roosevelt Institute. He is presently working on a book entitled *The Frustrated Idealists: Cordell Hull, Anthony Eden and the Search for Anglo-American Cooperation, 1933-1938*, and is organizing an international conference on "FDR, the Vatican and the Roman Catholic Church in America, 1933-1945," to be held at the FDR Library in Hyde Park, New York in the fall of 1998.

INDEX